The Pedagogy of Standardized Testing

The Pedagogy of Standardized Testing

The Radical Impacts of Educational Standardization in the US and Canada

Arlo Kempf

palgrave
macmillan

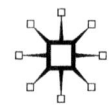

THE PEDAGOGY OF STANDARDIZED TESTING
Copyright © Arlo Kempf 2016

All rights reserved. No reproduction, copy or transmission of this publication may be made without written permission. No portion of this publication may be reproduced, copied or transmitted save with written permission. In accordance with the provisions of the Copyright, Designs and Patents Act 1988, or under the terms of any licence permitting limited copying issued by the Copyright Licensing Agency, Saffron House, 6-10 Kirby Street, London EC1N 8TS.

Any person who does any unauthorized act in relation to this publication may be liable to criminal prosecution and civil claims for damages.

First published 2016 by
PALGRAVE MACMILLAN

The author has asserted their right to be identified as the author of this work in accordance with the Copyright, Designs and Patents Act 1988.

Palgrave Macmillan in the UK is an imprint of Macmillan Publishers Limited, registered in England, company number 785998, of Houndmills, Basingstoke, Hampshire, RG21 6XS.

Palgrave Macmillan in the US is a division of Nature America, Inc., One New York Plaza, Suite 4500, New York, NY 10004-1562.

Palgrave Macmillan is the global academic imprint of the above companies and has companies and representatives throughout the world.

Hardback ISBN: 978–1–137–48664–6
E-PUB ISBN: 978–1–137–48666–0
E-PDF ISBN: 978–1–137–48665–3
DOI: 10.1057/9781137486653

Distribution in the UK, Europe and the rest of the world is by Palgrave Macmillan®, a division of Macmillan Publishers Limited, registered in England, company number 785998, of Houndmills, Basingstoke, Hampshire RG21 6XS.

Library of Congress Cataloging-in-Publication Data

Names: Kempf, Arlo, author.
Title: The pedagogy of standardized testing : the radical impacts of educational standardization in the US and Canada / Arlo Kempf.
Description: New York, NY : Palgrave Macmillan, [2015] | Includes bibliographical references and index.
Identifiers: LCCN 2015021047 | ISBN 9781137486646 (hardcover : alk. paper)
Subjects: LCSH: Educational tests and measurements—United States. | Educational tests and measurements—Canada. | Education—Standards—United States. | Education—Standards—Canada.
Classification: LCC LB3051 .K33 2015 | DDC 371.26—dc23 LC record available at http://lccn.loc.gov/2015021047

A catalogue record for the book is available from the British Library.

For Meghan McKee, the finest teacher.

Contents

List of Illustrations	ix
Acknowledgments	xi
List of Abbreviations	xiii
Introduction	1
1 The School as Factory Farm: All Testing All the Time	13
2 The History, Logic, and Push for Standardized Testing	29
3 Testing at the Tipping Point: HSST as a Governing Education Principle In and Out of the Classroom	51
4 Revising the Pedagogical Form: Test-Oriented Teaching and Learning	71
5 Not What I Signed up for: The Changing Meaning of Being a Teacher	99
6 A Lack of Accountability: Teacher Perspectives on Equity, Accuracy, and Standardized Testing	129
7 Implications: Synthesis of Findings, Resistance, and Alternatives	161
Appendix: A Note on the Survey	193
Notes	195
Bibliography	217
Index	233

Illustrations

Figures

1.1	PISA's categorization of national assessment and evaluation use	21
3.1	Student standardized test results posted in a Los Angeles elementary classroom	58

Tables

1.1	Test preparation time, Illinois teachers	17
4.1	Standardized testing and the narrowing of curriculum, Illinois and Ontario teachers	80
4.2	Degree to which standardized tests are used to improve teacher practice, Illinois and Toronto teachers	84
4.3	Standardized testing and its impact on assessment and instruction, Illinois and Ontario teachers	85
4.4	Standardized testing and meeting students' academic needs, Illinois and Ontario teachers	89
4.5	Standardized testing and student learning, Illinois and Ontario teachers	94
5.1	The use of standardized test results to evaluate teachers, Illinois and Ontario teachers	104
5.2	What standardized tests tell the public about schools, Illinois and Ontario teachers	107
5.3	Standardized testing as a reflection of teachers' ability, Illinois and Ontario teachers	108
5.4	Impact of standardized testing on the profession, Illinois and Ontario teachers	114
5.5	Standardized testing, professional judgment, and teacher learning, Illinois and Ontario teachers	119

6.1 Standardized tests as a reflection of student academic ability, Illinois and Ontario teachers   132
6.2 Standardized tests controlling for race and income bias, Illinois and Ontario teachers   137

Acknowledgments

From start to finish, this work has relied on the support of a number of individuals in Canada and the United States, without whom there would have been no study and no book. First and foremost, I wish to thank the teachers who shared their time, vision, and expertise through interviews, surveys, letters, and e-mails. Your voices have guided the journey that is this project, and I am forever grateful. A special thanks to those in Los Angeles who introduced me to colleagues, parents, administrators, and other school community members.

A million thanks to Peter McLaren, my postdoctoral supervisor in the Graduate School of Education and Information Studies, University of California, Los Angeles. Your openness, guidance, support, and time were invaluable to this work: above and beyond all the way. This work was originally supported by a Banting-Postdoctoral Fellowship, so I am grateful as well to the Social Sciences and Humanities Council of Canada. Thanks to Ana Laura Pauchulo for her help with the original grant application. Thanks to Sarah Nathan and Mara Berkoff at Palgrave for making this book a reality and for your support along the way. Sincere thanks to the anonymous reviewers who offered early and important feedback on this work, and thank you to those who have offered their insights on portions of this work presented at academic meetings in the United States and Canada. Also, my thanks to France Winddance Twine and George Sefa Dei for supporting the development of this project early on.

My sincere and deep appreciation goes to Peter Sawchuk and Nina Bascia for their time and attention throughout this project, and for their substantive feedback on early drafts of this work. I am indebted to David Lyell at United Teachers Los Angeles, Joanne Myers at Elementary Teachers' Federation of Ontario, and Felicia Samuel at Elementary Teachers of Toronto for their advocacy in getting out the survey and their guidance with its development. Special thanks to Carol

Caref at the Chicago Teachers Union, Maureen Davis at L'Association des enseignantes et des enseignants franco-ontariens, and Lindy Amato at the Ontario Teachers' Federation for making the survey happen—you were more than generous with your time and attention, and I am ever appreciative. Thank you so very much to Carl Theriault and Elisa Schwarz for your work translating the survey. To those who helped to field test the survey, thank you for your time and patience. Thanks to Andy Hargreaves for looking at an early draft of the survey, and to Todd Light and Tim Benson for your introductions and insights. Thank you to Milosh Raykov and Doug Hart for your guidance on all things quantitative.

A big shout out to Ruth Powers Silverberg, Arnold Dodge, Barbara Madeloni, Isabel Nuñez, Julie Gorlewski, Daiyu Suzuki, and Bill Ayers. Although too few and far between, our group conversations feed my soul. Thank you to Joel Westheimer for his support of this project. My sincere gratitude to Eddie Ordubegian, Siobhan Hanna, Tara Samuel, Matt Flugger, and Angie McLaren for opening your homes to me, sometimes on short notice and for your boundless generosity. Thanks to Sarah, Robin, Tim, and Carolyn for generously sharing your cabin—my second favorite place to write. Thank you to my students for pushing me forward every day, and for allowing me to learn with you.

Thank you to my friends who have heard this book in endless bits and pieces over the past few years, and to my family for your support and patience. Thanks to Randall Kempf for your encouragement from south of the border, and to Darlene McKee for your endless support of our family. To my special ones, Lola and Cy, thank you for sharing your reflections on the EQAO, and thank you for being my most important teachers. Finally, Meghan—for your patience and generosity over the course of the past couple of years, "thank you" does not begin to express my gratitude. Your insight, support, and serenity of spirit have made this book possible. I hope you'll consider reading it.

Abbreviations

Academic Performance Index (API)
American Legislative Exchange Council (ALEC)
Annual Yearly Progress (AYP)
California Standards Test (CST)
Common Core State Standards Initiative (CCSSI)
Council of Ministers of Education, Canada (CMEC)
Culturally Relevant and Responsive Pedagogy (CRRP)
Culturally Relevant and Responsive Teaching (CRRT)
Differentiated Instruction (DI)
Education, Quality and Accountability Office of Ontario (EQAO)
Elementary and Secondary Education Act (ESEA)
Elementary Teachers' Federation of Ontario (ETFO)
English as a Second Language (ESL)
Global Educational Reform Movement (GERM)
High-Stakes Standardized Testing (HSST)
Human Capital Theory of Education (HCTE)
Independent Education Plan (IEP)
Law School Admission Test (LSAT)
Measures of Academic Progress (MAP)
Medical College Application Test (MCAT)
National Assessment of Educational Progress (NAEP)
National Defense Education Act (NDEA)
Organization for Economic Cooperation and Development (OECD)
Pan-Canadian Assessment Program (PCAP)
Physical Health Education (PHE)
Professional Development (PD)
Program for International Student Assessment (PISA)
Program Improvement (PI)
Progress in International Reading Literacy Study (PIRLS)
Race to the Top (RTTT)

Racketeering Influenced Corrupt Organizations (RICO)
School Achievement Indicators Program (SAIP)
Standardized Testing (ST)
Test-Oriented Teaching and Learning (TOTL)
Trends in International Mathematics and Science Study (TIMSS)
United States Department of Education (DOE)
Value-Added Measures (VAM)
Zone of Proximal Development (ZPD)

Introduction

Standardized Testing and the Changing Form of US and Canadian Education

Few activities are more riddled with metaphor than education. Learning is a gift, a search, a path, an adventure, a blossoming, and a light bulb turning on. To teach is to conduct, to garden, to act as tour guide and custodian of the future, and, of course, to love. Students training to be teachers are often asked to identify metaphors that represent their philosophy of education. Some examples from students in a recent Masters course I teach include teaching as farming, dancing, storytelling, rain, metamorphosis, and reproduction. While there are many who may find it hard not to roll their eyes at the sometimes cutesy and oversimplified representations of education, these metaphors, indeed the most stereotypical of them all (learning as a journey, teaching as inspiration) reflect specific understandings of education that are embodied in twentieth- and twenty-first-century schools.

New educators know much more about teaching and learning than their professional forebearers. For the most part, the past 50 years have seen students gain access to not only better information (more accurate and holistic content in our schools) but better teaching as well (more inclusive, student-centered, and pedagogically sound practice), thanks in large part to education research and increasingly comprehensive teacher training. It has been a century since the revolutionary work of philosopher John Dewey argued that schools should reflect the social, democratic, and interactive potential and nature of teaching and learning; and nearly a half century since Brazilian popular educator and theorist Paulo Freire warned against the banking model in education (wherein the teacher is the only knower in the room), suggesting instead that authentic education emerges from conversation rather than monologue, and that learning occurs most powerfully when linked to the daily experiences and struggles of students. Although student teachers may not always know it, they have Dewey and Freire (and others) to thank for the daily and unrelenting call to reflect on their teaching and learning, as well as for the constant demand to consider their own identity in relation to their work as future teachers. Psychologists such as Lev Vygotsky, Jean Piaget, and others provided us with constructivist theories of learning, arguing that knowledge and indeed meaning are produced through the interaction of experiences and ideas. Technology has increased teachers' access to teaching and learning resources, and has opened up new possibilities for collaboration among students, teachers, administrators, and communities.

The works of Dewey, Freire, Vygotsky, Piaget, and other radicals-cum-mainstream-education-mainstays have indeed given us the sometimes-cheesy metaphors and idioms that dominate twenty-first-century school corridors and staffrooms in the United States and Canada. That we might take for granted that education is a journey—an act of joy, a dialogue—speaks to how far we have come, how embedded these ideas are, and how much teaching and learning have come to be defined through these concepts. The ubiquity of these metaphors speaks to a widespread acceptance of something that is increasingly at risk of slipping away. Educational standardization offers another vision of education, one perhaps not yet articulated in trickle-down metaphors, in which students and teachers are represented by related and competing numbers and scores, inputs and outputs, revenues and expenses.

Teaching and schooling are being fundamentally transformed in the United States, and to a lesser but nonetheless significant degree in Canada. The nature and experience of public education (for parents, students, and teachers) is changing radically and at a pace not seen since school desegregation by virtue of *Brown v. Board of Education* in 1954.[1] While many factors contribute to educational change, the key driver of current education reform is a radical new blanket call for standardization and data-driven accountability—with standardized testing as the vanguard initiative across K-12 education, within teacher professional development, and in the evaluation of teachers and schools.

This book is based primarily on results of the Teachers and Testing Study, a three-year project on teachers and teaching in the United States and Canada. The study looks at the effects of standardized testing on teaching and learning, based on interviews with over 100 teachers in urban schools in Los Angeles and Toronto, as well as a survey of thousands of teachers in Illinois, Ontario, California, and New York. On the one hand, the results point to teaching as an art, a love, a passion, and a profession. On the other hand, the interviews and survey results paint a picture of institutional siege; of teachers doing more with less; of teachers teaching to the test; and of teachers' lives and work having changed profoundly as they fight to serve their students against wave after wave of downloaded initiatives, pressure to raise scores, professional instability, and scapegoating. Indeed, if the current program of educational standardization continues, a similar study conducted 25 years from now in the United States will be little more than an autopsy of a system that was, with researchers confronting a teacher-proof education system with students-cum-widgets navigating high-stakes assessments; a corporate education dystopia best described by Paulo Freire's notion of necrophilia, in which there is no dialogue and where, guided by profit-driven ideological tools, children are constructed as both consumer and commodity.[2]

While there is no single opt-out movement, tens of thousands of families have found a variety of ways to opt their children out of standardized testing. Indeed, some suggest that parents' decisions are increasingly framed as whether or not to opt in to, rather than out of, testing.[3] This comes in response to not only the increased use of standardized testing but also the increasingly high-stakes nature of these tests. In various Canadian contexts, a slow resistance to standardized testing is growing among parents and teachers—arguably in direct proportion to how much high-stakes testing is used. Canadian provinces and territories use far fewer standardized tests than most US jurisdictions, and have no national standards such as the US Common Core State Standards Initiative (CCSI). In some cases, opting out means individual parents keeping their children home for the testing period, while in others, parents have organized boycotts against standardized tests (and even the field-testing of standardized tests). Opt-out parents are diverse, particularly in the United States, and include libertarians, liberals, and hard core progressives.

Although parents' motivations are diverse, as detailed in Chapter 7, one primary reason folks are opting out is the negative experience of their children with standardized tests. Many test invigilators wear disposable rubber gloves when handing out and collecting standardized tests in the classroom. This on-the-job bit of learning arose due to the frequency of children vomiting before, during, and after (and on) standardized tests—a precaution that has been codified in at least one testing manual.[4] The anxiety that accompanies testing can be severe for students, and obviously more so for some than others. Although students who suffer from anxiety (especially test anxiety) may fare particularly poorly in this regard, the stress of high-stakes tests is not reserved for nervous children. Countless opt-out parents have made their decision based on their children's academic disengagement and frustration with and around the culture of high-stakes standardized testing (HSST). Opting out is not simply a rejection of test taking but also of the increasingly central place of testing within life in schools: within pedagogy, within local and federal curricula, and within the hierarchy of what is considered important in and out of the classroom.

Teachers understand the impact of HSST on the classroom better than most. Specifically, many feel pressure to gear their teaching toward improved test results, rather than toward learning and/or toward other forms of student work and alternate methods of assessment. Teacher time and attention are increasingly taken away from a variety of important tasks in order to teach to and for standardized tests (including attention to student diversity in the classroom, student well-being, and the use of rich and varied texts and approaches that may not apply to a standardized test). This is impacting the profession itself, and brings to mind Marshall McLuhan's suggestion that "the more data banks record about us, the less we exist."[5] A career generally understood as a calling, an art, and something done "for the love of it" is increasingly a routinized, stressful, and constrained activity, with teachers pigeon-holed into a classroom-focus on improved test scores. Following the lead of many families, teachers are increasingly resisting standardization (of their work, their students, and their schools) by refusing to administer tests, by organizing against standardized testing and curriculum, and by supporting opt-out families and movements. Perhaps the best-known case came in January, 2013, in Seattle, Washington, when teachers at Garfield High School refused to administer the Measures of Academic Progress (MAP) standardized test. Garfield teachers were supported by their 600 students and the test was eventually deemed optional at the secondary level in Seattle. The Garfield example is just one among many across the United States. In Canada, the Elementary Teachers' Federation of Ontario (ETFO) has been highly active in promoting academic alternatives to standardized testing, as well as in promoting activist organizing and responses to standardized testing.

Despite the widespread controversy surrounding testing, the voices of teachers are often absent from the conversation when it comes to large-scale assessment. With this absence we lose a central perspective on the daily effects of testing in and out of the classroom. With that in mind, this book centers on the voice of teachers in an attempt to better understand the impacts of high-stakes standardized testing in Canadian and

US education with a specific focus on the effects of HSST on teacher practice; on teachers' work; and on the consequences for our most vulnerable students, schools, and communities. It would be disingenuous to suggest the discussion undertaken here is apolitical. To be quite clear, I begin and end with the premise that high-stakes standardized testing is mostly very bad, most of the time. The HSST movement is one that in my view serves a neoliberal agenda in education. In the United States, the standardization movement has courted corporate input at every step of the way, with private interests playing a key role in education policy. Achieve, for example, is an education reform organization that has been instrumental in the development and dissemination of the CCSI. Its board members include former and current presidents and vice presidents of Chase Manhattan Bank, Prudential, Intel, IBM, and other corporations. Another big player in the drive for Common Core is the Business Roundtable group whose members include leaders from big oil, big pharma, agribusiness, finance, tech, the gambling industry, and other sectors. As Ruth Powers Silverberg and I have noted elsewhere, "Business Roundtable produces policy papers on a variety of issues but appears to devote special attention to labor relations and education (fighting unions and promoting standardized testing, respectively)."[6] Another example of invited corporate interference is the American Legislative Exchange Council (ALEC), a contentious organization that "brings together business and political leaders for their mutual benefit, produces an annual education report card ranking states based on their education policies including standards, choice, and charters."[7] Educational standardization is thus not simply bad education policy; it is politics at play in our classrooms as an expression of a specific corporate vision of teaching and learning.

I came across the politics of standardized testing somewhat by accident. In 2011, I was fortunate to be awarded a Banting Post-Doctoral Fellowship at the University of California, Los Angeles, based on my proposed research on race and racism in teaching and teachers' work in the United States in Canada. I had designed a comparative study of the way race was addressed (or not addressed) in urban schools in the United States and Canada. I began my research talking to teachers in South Los Angeles. It was quickly evident that teachers in these schools were, for the most part, critical folks, committed to transformative teaching and learning in their schools and school communities (some of the most economically and racially marginalized urban neighborhoods in the United States). Teachers had excellent ideas for critical work around race and racism, but every one of them reported feeling increasingly unable to put their ideas into place, or for that matter, to engage in other critical forms of teaching and learning. As I detail in Chapters 4, 5, and 6, their time and attention were instead focused on teaching to, for, and around standardized tests. In many cases, seemingly core subjects such as history, physical health education, and social studies were cast aside in order to prepare for the literacy-, math-, and science-focused standardized tests—leaving little or no time for critical teaching around race and racism. As a Canadian, I had stumbled onto the worst-kept secret in US education: the radical impacts of standardized testing on teaching and learning. To my surprise, early interviews with teachers in Toronto, Ontario, were different from my conversations with their US peers only by degree. While Canadian teachers were not impacted as much by testing, they were responsible for administering relatively fewer tests, and school cultural was reported as relatively less test focused.

So, what was originally designed as a comparative study of teachers' work and multicultural education quickly shifted focus when, in conversation with teachers, all roads led back to the negative impacts of standardized testing. Further, teachers in both countries felt their labor, their classrooms, and indeed the education system as a whole were changing radically as a result. In two very distinct urban schooling contexts, teachers reported a changing landscape of school culture, and a move toward test-focused teaching, learning, professional development, and school–community relationships. The notion of HSST thus emerges from, and in part describes, this culture shift in education. Referring not to one test or another (even though many individual tests might be make-or-break for students), HSST refers instead to standardized testing as a governing principle in education, the high-stakes referring to the impact of specific standardized tests as well as to the overall shift that is taking place in classrooms, schools, and the educational experience of children as a result of test-oriented teaching and learning (TOTL).

The voices that guide the coming chapters come from one-on-one interviews, focus group discussions, and written comments offered in survey responses by teachers from Ontario, Illinois, California, and New York. Additionally, this book draws on quantitative results from a survey of teachers in Illinois and Ontario. The analysis here is also informed by five years of paying attention to the issue of standardized testing in K-12 education: from reading everything I could on the subject, to reading and teaching on standardized testing at my university, to presenting preliminary portions of this work at academic conferences, to speaking with teachers and academics about the issue at every opportunity, to listening closely and critically to the parents and children known to me personally when they spoke about their experiences with standardized testing, to speaking and listening at parent councils and PTA meetings in Los Angeles and Toronto, and to reading daily Google alerts on standardized testing for the past four years as a survey of popular media and reporting.

By drawing on the Teachers and Testing Study as well as other large-scale research, this book seeks to understand how HSST functions. The comparative analysis herein seeks to deepen contemporary understandings of HSST as a multinational phenomenon, with qualitatively similar effects on two distinct systems. Beyond the well-worn questions of work intensification, and a general distaste for treating students (and teachers) as numbers, the daily and holistic impact of HSST on teachers and their classrooms is yet to be researched in significant detail. Taking up this challenge, this book seeks to offer a rich and accessible analysis of these phenomena, interpreted through the looking glass of schools, learning, and teachers' professional lives.

Overview

The book begins with an introduction to standardized testing, its use, and some common arguments for and against it. Chapter 1, The School as Factory Farm: All Testing All the Time, details the current use of HSST in Canada and the United States, with a look at frequency, duration, financial cost, and types of tests used. Many teachers in the United States are spending 10 to 30 percent of class time preparing students for, and/or administering, standardized tests. This chapter also traces the increase in the use of HSST over the past 15 years in the United States and Canada, and situates these practices internationally in comparison to the use of standardized testing globally. Using data from national and international studies on student achievement, the chapter dives in to some of the connections between standardized testing, equity, student achievement, and public satisfaction with education. The chapter argues that increased standardized testing does not positively correlate with significant improvements in student achievement generally, nor does it correlate positively with the closing of gender, class, or race gaps in education.

Chapter 2, The History, Logic, and Push for Standardized Testing, sketches the century-long historical trajectory of standardized testing in the United States and Canada, including recent policy initiatives such as Race to the Top, Common Core, and No Child Left Behind. For over a century, standardized testing has fit neatly within the logic of schools as a site of production, with students as products (and more recently with schools as consumers of for-profit educational products and services). On the basis of education policy historiography, we find that standardized tests rely on a specific set of behaviorist/economic presumptions about student learning and achievement, which now, as a century ago, fail to recognize the inherently social nature and purposes of teaching and learning. While the past three decades have seen the integration of more social constructivist perspectives across and within teacher education, standardized testing and its behaviorist/economic underpinnings have become the key metric guiding organizational life for students, teachers, parents, and schools in the United States.

Guided by the Teachers and Testing Study, as well as by relevant secondary studies, Chapter 3, Testing at the Tipping Point: HSST as a Governing Education Principle In and Out of the Classroom, details the distinction between high-stakes and low-stakes standardized testing. Typically less frequent, low-stakes standardized tests are used to improve particular strengths and weaknesses of a program or curriculum and may or may not be linked to grades or the formal evaluation of individual students. HSST, as articulated here, however, refers not simply to tests or testing regimes that evaluate students and that make or break chances for advancement, but also more broadly, to the emergence of a new governing principle for understanding student, teacher, and school achievement based on standardized testing—a radical and unprecedented transformation in the United States and Canada. In the context of the emergence of this HSST dynamic, the very meaning of student ability and school performance, and with it public as well as professional perceptions of them, are radically transformed.

Chapter 4, Revising the Pedagogical Form: Test-Oriented Teaching and Learning, applies the basic criticisms and conceptual HSST framework developed in Chapter 3 to detail the interactive ways in which the manic pursuit of higher test scores is affecting the classroom and teacher practice. Beginning with a detailed look at the time challenges posed by increased standardized testing and its significance (institutionally and beyond), teachers report a radical transformation of both the depth and breadth of the curriculum, fundamentally new levels of pressure on students, and new relations between teachers and school administration. Among other things, we see evidence for how standardized testing profoundly impacts teachers' capacity to teach effectively as entire sets of pedagogical practices, theories, and tools come to be jettisoned.

It follows that as classrooms and pedagogy change, so too do the teaching occupation and the functional meaning of being a teacher. Chapter Five, Not What I Signed up for: The Changing Meaning of Being a Teacher, presents evidence of significant changes in teachers' capacity to use professional judgment, authority and latitude. Looking beyond the classroom, this chapter investigates teacher occupational satisfaction, autonomy, and fulfilment as these relate to standardized testing. Chapter Five describes the changing public perceptions of teachers in relation to the emergence of HSST, as well as teacher understandings of this shift. Teachers are increasingly alienated from the moral rewards of teaching and they note that the decline of the profession correlates to the under-servicing of students. The chapter also takes up teachers' concerns about the developmentally inappropriate use of testing with young children, as well as teacher calls for a more robust professional accountability that serves students and improves teaching. The impacts of HSST vary by virtue of context, with for the most part, low standardized test scores associated with high pressure for teachers and students, and high standardized test scores associated with low pressure for teachers and students.

US and Canadian classrooms are increasingly diverse as far as race, culture, ability, and language. Additionally, the percentage of low-income students has increased in recent years. Chapter 6, A Lack of Accountability: Teacher Perspectives on Equity, Accuracy and Standardized Testing, focuses on the impact of high-stakes testing for these equity-seeking student populations. While educational standardization has failed to close the educational achievement gaps across lines of race, language, dis/ability, gender and social class, this chapter presents findings from the Teachers and Testing study illustrating the ways in which HSST interferes and at times even prevents teachers from doing the very work needed to support students facing the greatest challenges. These professional practices include inclusive curriculum development and delivery, differentiated instruction, extracurricular activities, bilingual resource use, universal design for learning, and project-based learning led by inquiry and exploration. Questions of cultural bias as well as widespread student test-anxiety raise concerns around the limitations of standardized testing (ST) as far as understanding student and teacher ability. This chapter also looks closely at the ways in which HSST makes the introduction of critical approaches incredibly difficult for many teachers (approaches such as critical pedagogy, anti-racism, feminism, etc); HSST is a tacit assault on multicultural education in urban schools. This chapter also takes up questions of workplace equity for teachers, noting the differential impact of HSST on teachers based on where and whom they teach, in many cases punishing teachers for working with marginalized students and communities. This chapter frames the ways in which teachers in high-pressure teaching situations feel pushed to boost students' scores using a variety of methods—some ethical and some not, the latter including various subtle forms of cheating.

Chapter 7, Implications: Synthesis of Findings, Resistance, and Alternatives, begins with a summary of key findings and implications from Chapters 3, 4, 5, and 6. It then turns to an examination of the ways in which teachers are pushing back against HSST, and a discussion of alternatives to HSST in the United States and Canada, emerging from the voices of teachers in both contexts. This chapter details teacher strategies ranging from the use of critical pedagogy to problematize the test with students (including analyses of cultural bias), to advocacy for test sabotage. This resistance (intentional and unintentional) is then contextualized within regional and national movements of students, parents, and administrators who are working against HSST (movements that include radical activists, suburban soccer moms and dads, and even former Assistant Secretary of Education Diane Ravitch). Informed by additional research and teacher visions of accountability, the chapter sets forth a series of alternatives both for assessment policy and for teacher practice in the United States and Canada, based on a vision of assessment articulated by teachers in both contexts. It concludes by offering specific comments on the future of the Common Core in the United States, and on the Education, Quality and Accountability Office of Ontario (EQAO) in Ontario.

* * *

I have been fortunate to do a lot of writing and teaching within antiracist education studies, and among the many offerings of that field is the demand that authors and speakers who wish to be heard are required to let their readers and listeners know just who they are and where they are coming from. With that in mind, it may be worth mentioning that I have never taken a standardized test in a school setting. I have never been traumatized by the specter I spend the next seven chapters taking apart in this work. Further, my daughter wrote her third and sixth grade, week-long, standardized tests without incident in Ontario; she survived with neither physical nor psychological scars. In the ninth grade, she chose to opt out of that year's one-day standardized test (with her parents' support) and it was neither complicated nor uncomfortable at any point along the way. Years ago, as a high school teacher in Toronto, over seven years, I never administered a single standardized test. At the postsecondary level, I teach upper year undergraduate, graduate, and teacher education courses and, as a result, have never even had to give (or grade) a formal examination of any kind—nothing for which sitting in rows has been required. As I first wrote this introduction, however, my partner and I were in the midst of plotting our son's path forward as he approached the grade three standardized test run by Ontario's testing body, EQAO. The EQAO tests are known by many children as young as six, as Evil Questions Asked of Ontarians (or Attacking Ontarians). Although that year's test would eventually be cancelled as part of a teacher job action, eight years after my daughter wrote the same test, my son was coming up in a very different educational world. My daughter did not know what it was until the morning of the first day of testing (this was closer to a true snapshot as far as her experience), while my son has known since the start of second grade (almost two years before he was set to write his first standardized test).

Teachers and friends had directed my son to websites, which are fun versions of the drill and kill skills needed to succeed on the test. His teacher was a woman whom I consider a friend, and for whom I have tremendous professional respect and personal gratitude. She, personally, shepherded my son through a number of significant learning hurdles—a task beyond the grasp of his educator parents. Further, I was fairly confident the test would not stress out my son very much; however, he did at one point mention being worried about "the multiple choice portion." Living in Toronto, I know only a few parents who have chosen to opt out their children (indeed, from time I spent as a postdoctoral fellow and visiting scholar at UCLA I know more of these folks in California than in Canada). Doing this work in LA I was able to speak critically about testing and opting out without raising too many eyebrows, a skill I have yet to figure out in Toronto. Although I may have far more education credibility and more cultural capital around schooling than most people, I still struggle in casual conversation to raise my voice about testing in Canada (the same way I still sometimes struggle to be the one to speak out about a sexist joke). A big hetero white guy with two children—I live and breathe testing issues, education conversations, and analyses of teaching, but I am at times apprehensive when talking to Toronto neighbors about pulling my kid for the test.

So, my entry point for this conversation—for the standardized testing issue—is at once personal, academic, and activist. Asking questions about the classroom and teacher practice has led me here, led me to understand that a massive change has taken place in the United States and that nothing short of radical resistance and ground-up re-visioning of education is needed to chart a better path forward for students. A slower path, in roughly the same direction, is on offer in Canada if Canadians are not careful, mindful, and critical of education standardization. The push for standardized testing is a misguided response to a phantom menace, a crisis of accountability that never was. This manufactured catastrophe has acted as midwife to a ghost in the machine, an unpleasant dark passenger that has found its way into our classrooms and indeed the conscious and subconscious life of schools. As far as I can tell, it's time to push back.

CHAPTER 1

The School as Factory Farm: All Testing All the Time

In 2004, leading testing expert Robert L. Brennan[1] explained: "I failed to recognize that a testing revolution was underway in this country that was based on the nearly unchallenged belief (with almost no supporting evidence) that high-stakes testing can and will lead to improved education."[2] Despite such cautions from mainstream assessment and measurement scholars, the current frequency and use of standardized testing is unprecedented in US history. In Canada, despite significant variation across its provinces and territories, norm-referenced standardized testing (ST) has scarcely been as widely used as it is today. To be clear, testing is not the only important development underway in education. Despite a push against social foundations in education[3] in some teacher preparation programs, teacher training is generally more comprehensive than it used to be. New teachers are better versed in supporting diverse students, they have access to a greater variety of instruction and assessment techniques and they have a deeper applied understanding of education research and technology than many of their predecessors. However, while testing is not the only driver of change, it is the most significant. Standardized testing is best understood as a technology, the nature and effects of which can be read a number of ways.

Understanding technology and its impact is a central question for education. Feenberg's *Critical Theory of Technology* suggests three interpretations, or methodologies, for understanding technology and its impacts. The first is an instrumental interpretation that views technology as impartial; ST understood in this way is a neutral tool for assessment—universally rational and objective in character. The second is a substantive interpretation that views technology as value laden, and as necessarily reflective of particular biases. Understood through this lens ST comes with particular cultural and/or ideological assumptions and impacts. The third methodology is a critical approach, in which technology is ambivalent and contested, with the politics of its development being equally as significant as its use and application. This equivocality can inform our understanding of ST. Feenberg suggests that the "ambivalence of technology is distinguished from neutrality by the role it attributes to social values in the design, and not merely the use, of technical systems. On this view, technology is not a destiny but a scene of struggle."[4] As a frame that recognizes technology as political, mediated, contested, resisted, and negotiated, this third (critical) interpretation of technology is useful for understanding ST and education.

We see technology as a site of struggle in daily attempts to accommodate standardized testing by jurisdictions, schools, teachers, students, and parents. More broadly, calls for standardization in education (embedded in the rhetoric of accountability) are emblematic of an ideological belief about the very nature and purpose of teaching and learning. Similarly, arguments against ST also rely on specific ideas, ideologies, and biases. The title of Howard Zinn's 2002 autobiography *You Can't be Neutral on a Moving Train* is informative for any and all contemporary discussion of ST—testing is inherently political and these three conceptions (instrumental, substantive, and critical) give us a backdrop against which to proceed. On a moving train, even those sitting still are moving down the track. All policy, all technology, and all curricula move in a particular direction and represent a certain political and/or ideological approach. While recognizing that standardized tests are simply a thing—a tool—an object, ST emerges from and for specific ideas, purposes, and goals.

Before going any further down this track, however, the remainder of this chapter provides an introduction to standardized testing, its use, and some common arguments for and against it. The following section details the current use of high-stakes standardized testing (HSST) in the United States and Canada, looking at how often students are writing these tests, the classroom time devoted to ST, and the financial costs associated with these tests. The next section situates these practices internationally, in comparison to the use of ST globally. The chapter then explores some of the correlations between ST, equity, student achievement, and public satisfaction with education.

Testing by the Numbers: Frequency, Duration, and Cost

In the United States and Canada, many different standardized tests are administered to measure the learning, understanding, and ability of children. Some are diagnostic, meaning they are geared to measure students' knowledge and ability in preparation for teaching and learning in a certain area or areas. Diagnostic assessment (including ST) is often used near the beginning of the school year, or the beginning of a unit of study. The results of diagnostic assessments are often not reported to students but are used instead by the teacher to gauge where to start, what to focus on, and what he might be able to skip over if his students are already proficient in a given area. These may not rightly be called high-stakes standardized tests as they are often true random snapshots of learning and/or knowkedge, generally administered without much fuss or preparation; they do not determine whether students advance or not; and the results are less likely to impact school funding, school reputation, or teacher salary. With that in mind, we can leave these out of the discussion going forward and look instead at ST that is not diagnostic, and that which is used across entire districts, states, and/or provinces.

Quantity of Standardized Testing

In the United States, the number of tests varies by district and by state. Although some states administer standardized tests in the first and second grades, many begin in kindergarten and continue through the twelfth grade. In addition to state- and district-mandated testing, the Common Core State Standards Initiative (CCSSI) sets out guidelines for curriculum, delivery, and assessment (including standardized tests) in states that have adopted the Common Core (46 as of November 2014). Common Core may ultimately replace some local standardized tests, but for the time being, CCSSI has added to an already heavy ST load. A 2014 study by the American Center for Progress focusing on 14 districts in 7 states found that students are writing up to 20 standardized tests per year, with an average of ten per year in grades three through eight (this does not include optional university entrance assessments such as SATs, the Medical College Application Test [MCAT], and the Law School Admission Test [LSAT]).[5] These figures are in line with additional research conducted by the American Federation of Teachers.[6]

Chicago teachers surveyed for the Teachers and Testing Study administer an average of 11 standardized tests per year, while *Education Week* suggests that in many urban schooling districts, students are writing an average of 113 standardized tests between pre-k and twelfth grade.[7] Although there are few United States jurisdictions in which students write fewer than five per year, the research mentioned above indicates there are many in which students write up to 20 or more on a yearly basis. In Canada, we see similar variation but much less testing on the whole. Canadian provinces and territories use different tests and different numbers of tests. There is no federal testing standard or mandate, although the Government of Canada and local bands share responsibility for education on Aboriginal reserves. Similar to the United States, the use of testing in some Canadian areas is in flux. Alberta, for example, is rolling out a new computer-based ST system to be administered in grades three, six, and nine to replace its 30-year-old Provincial Achievement Test. Ontario is also moving to an online ST platform for its grades three, six, nine, and ten standardized tests. Canadian students write between three and five standardized tests from grades three to twelve, averaging fewer than one per year.[8] Tests in both contexts can range in length from a few hours, to multiple days. Test delivery can vary as well, even within a given jurisdiction. For example, in Ontario, Canada, third- and sixth-grade students write a province-wide standardized examination focusing on mathematics, reading, and writing. The test is six hours in length, and schools have the freedom to determine when and for how long students will write over a two-week period (usually in late May and/or early June).

Time Allocated to Test Preparation and Associated Activities

The frequency of testing, like the length of a particular test, does not tell the whole story of a test's impact on a given student, group of students, classroom, teachers' work, school, or district. As a share of total classroom time, hours spent writing are generally fewer than hours spent preparing for standardized tests. While often touted as providing "snapshots" of student progress, demonstrating what students "already know," teachers in the United States and Canada regularly devote significant class and homework time to test preparation.[9] The Ontario grades three, six, and ten teachers I interviewed spent an average of one month preparing for year-end standardized tests administered by the Education, Quality and Accountability Office (EQAO).

In the United States, more testing means more time on test preparation and administration, as illustrated by Table 1.1, which breaks down survey responses from the Chicago teachers surveyed for the Teachers and Testing Study.[10]

Table 1.1 Test preparation time, Illinois teachers

Over the course of a normal school year, what percentage of instructional time do you devote to preparing students for standardized tests?

% of Classroom Time	% of Respondents
0–10	32.3
11–30	29.9
31–60	20.4
61–80	13.7
81–10	3.7

The Chicago results may be relatively low as far as how much time many teachers are spending on testing and ST-related activities when compared to other US jurisdictions. A 2014 *New York Times* article about parents resisting the onslaught of increased testing describes the situation in Florida where "many schools this year will dedicate on average 60 to 80 days out of the 180-day school year to standardized testing. In a few districts, tests were scheduled to be given every day to at least some students."[11] Florida tests more than most other states, and broader studies tend to support the Chicago results rather than the statistics from Florida. For example, Former Assistant Secretary of Education Diane Ravitch suggests that in late 2013, many districts were allocating "20 percent of the school year" to test preparation.[12] This is typically two full months out of the school year, and comes in response, she suggests, to an education culture in which "schools lived or died depending on their test scores." The American Federation of Teachers study mentioned above found that each year approximately one month of instructional time is used in test taking, administrative activities, and test preparation.[13]

Financial Costs of Standardized Testing

Testing is not only significant as far as classroom time; but comes with significant financial costs as well. A report by the Washington-based Brown Center on Education Policy, at the Brookings Institution, suggests that ST costs the United States $1.7 billion annually on state- and No Child Left Behind (NCLB)-mandated standardized tests.[14] Although research suggests more effective use of existing funds may be adequate to cover the cost of Common Core assessments,[15] the total costs of Common Core are unknown at this point and are subject to change in the coming years. Figures for federal policy can exclude district level tests, and do not consider the opportunity cost of significant classroom time devoted to testing, which might be used to attend to other issues that end up costing schools and districts even more money (e.g., afterschool tutoring programs, which often come as extra costs to school budgets). Of the US $1.7 billion, most goes to contracts with private testing companies, six of which account for 89 percent of this spending.[16] The highly controversial firm Pearson Education accounts for 39 percent of this spending, with McGraw-Hill Education at 14 percent and Data Recognition Corporation at 13 percent.[17] Although testing is obviously very big business, the report provides some relative terms for understanding the money spent on testing. For example, money from all statewide standardized tests would amount, alternately, to a one percent raise for teachers across the country, or to a reduction of the student-to-teacher class size ratio of just 0.1 percent.[18]

The Brookings report also notes that this is a relatively low cost for large-scale testing but nonetheless suggests strategies for further reducing the cost of testing (including investing in larger quantity economies of scale—presuming the inevitability of a central role for private corporations in public education). With the US Department of Education annual budget sitting at $67.3 billion, $1.7 may not seem like a very big number, and maybe it is not in relative terms. Perhaps we are not spending enough. The Brookings report, as well as a 2010 report from the Brown Center, suggest the average per student costs for testing is $27,[19] a figure supported by a 2010 report from the Stanford Center for Opportunity Policy in Education.[20] This may indeed be too cheap for something that eats up 10 to 30 percent of class time in our schools. Understood this way, our alarm at how much the United States spends on ST should perhaps be matched by a considered alarm at how little we spend on something so important to education. Although tests are expensive, they are in many cases among the cheapest possible versions available of a particular technology. Perhaps testing should not be a bargain, particularly given that arguments for its affordability have nothing to do with teaching and learning.

Although the cost of ST varies significantly across Canada's ten provinces and three territories, it is generally higher than in the United States. For example, British Columbia spends approximately $20 per student,[21] Alberta spends approximately $30,[22] Nova Scotia spends approximately $70 per student,[23] and Ontario's testing body, the EQAO, lists the cost of testing per student per year at $17.[24] Canadian students, however, write far fewer tests overall. For example, Ontario students write standardized tests in grades three, six, nine, and ten. When calculated to reflect only students in those grades (rather than all of the province's 2,031,195 students) the province spends almost $60 per student per test. Given the high cost in Ontario (which has almost 40 percent of the nation's population) and the dramatic variation between the territories, a national average for Canada is thus of little use.

In summary, it is safe to say that on the low end in the United States, ten percent of class time is used for activities related to ST, with a number of jurisdictions devoting upward of 20 percent. It is challenging to think of other activities that play an equally central role in daily life in schools; and remember this is not teaching content but rather test preparation. Indeed, a student who devoted a day per week (20 percent) to football would be a student athlete, while another who every Friday had attended specialized music instruction would be considered a musician. In this light, the common specialization of twenty-first-century students is test taking. While school, teacher, student, and parent time and attention are increasingly focused on ST, the financial cost of the standardization revolution is significant and on the rise, although if tests are worth their salt, their cost should not guide their use. As explored further in Chapters 3, 4, and 5, the effects of ST in US and Canadian classrooms are hardly limited to time and money.

Standardized Testing in International Perspective

In broad strokes, the United States not only uses more standardized tests, but also uses standardized tests more than most national and subnational (such as provincial and territorial) jurisdictions. On the one hand, US children write more standardized tests more often than most students around the world. On the other, these tests are not just used to find out more about students but also to evaluate teachers, schools, districts, and states under the rubric of data-driven accountability (for students, for parents, for taxpayers, etc.). With the United States at the high-end of the spectrum as far as testing, Canada places roughly in the middle as far as the number of standardized tests used, and the use of the test results.

On the low end, Finland uses only one standardized test, at the end of the secondary panel. Sixteen-year-old students in England write a series of high-stakes examinations (approximately 15–20), which determines their path forward in high school and in subsequent potential opportunities to continue to college or university. Japan has entrance exams for some high schools, and at the postsecondary level individual institutions often have their own entrance examinations.[25] The use of testing in Turkey is similar to that in Japan, with access to top high schools and universities dependent upon entrance examinations.[26] South Korea, a country whose students once wrote middle school entrance examinations, now uses high school and college entrance examinations. According to one study, the high school and university an individual attends is more important than work experience or other considerations, making these examinations very important.[27] The high stakes of testing are not lost on South Korean youth. According to the Center for International Education Benchmarking, research on South Korea suggests: "three-quarters of middle and high school students consider running away from home or committing suicide because of the pressure to perform at high levels in school."[28] In Singapore, students are tested on physical fitness as well as academics, and schools are publicly ranked according to the overall standardized test results from the secondary level. While there is a move in Singapore to reduce testing pressure, it remains very important for students to do well on the country's national examinations, as they affect postsecondary opportunity.[29] While a country-by-country discussion of testing would be a book unto itself, data from the Program for International Student Assessment (a test given every three years to 15-year-olds) run by the Organization for Economic Co-operation and Development (OECD) offers an overview of the role of testing in countries around the world.

The Program for International Student Assessment's (PISA) 2012 study offers educational measures of 65 countries around the world, and provides by far the closest thing we have to a global perspective on the areas it covers. One measure relevant for understanding testing in comparative perspective is PISA's look at the use of examinations at the lower and upper secondary levels. According to the OECD, lower secondary generally refers to schooling for students aged 10 to 16. It begins between "the ages of 10 and 13 and ends between the ages of 13 and 16. It is compulsory across OECD and partner countries. It marks the end of compulsory education in a number of countries."[30] Upper secondary is typically two to three years, with students generally entering at 15 or 16 years of age. While PISA 2012 does not offer data on ST at the elementary level (what the OECD calls the preprimary and primary levels) findings on the use of ST for older students are important. PISA differentiates between assessments and examinations. Assessments "take stock of students' performance in order to make decisions on future instruction or to summarise performance for information purposes" and "do not have direct tangible consequences for students."[31]

By contrast, examinations "determine students' progression to higher levels of education (e.g. the transition from lower to upper secondary school), selection into different curricular programmes (e.g. into vocational or academic programmes), or selection into university programmes."[32] While all 65 countries have some assessment and/or evaluation at the lower and/or upper secondary levels, there remains significant variation, and the PISA results group countries in four categories as described below:

> A first group of countries and economies tends to have assessments at the lower secondary level and national examinations at the upper secondary level, with few tertiary fields of study requiring a special examination for admission. A second group of countries and economies tends to have national examinations at both the upper and secondary levels. A third group of countries and economies tends to rely on not only national examinations, but also on other types of examinations or on other types of examinations only. The fourth group of countries and economies tends to have no examinations at the lower or upper secondary level, but a large number of tertiary fields of study require examinations.[33]

Figure 1.1 identifies the countries in each group.[34]

	Group One
Assessment in lower secondary, national exams in upper secondary, few fields requiring tertiary exams	Australia, Croatia, Czech Republic, England (UK), Finland, Hong Kong-China, Hungary, Israel, Luxembourg, Scotland (UK), Singapore, Slovak Republic, Tunisia
	Group Two
Only national examinations in lower and upper secondary	Albania, Bulgaria, Denmark, Estonia, France, Germany, Indonesia, Ireland, Italy, Jordan, Latvia, Lithuania, Malaysia, the Netherlands, Poland, Portugal, Romania, Russian Federation, Shanghai-China, Chinese Taipei, Thailand, Viet Nam
	Group Three
National or other non-national examinations in lower or upper secondary	Belgium (Fr. Comm.), Liechtenstein, Montenegro, Norway, Qatar, United Arab Emirates, United States
	Group Four
No national or other examinations, most fields requiring tertiary exams	Austria, Belgium (Fl. Comm.), Brazil, Chile, Colombia, Greece, Iceland, Japan, Korea, Macao-China, Mexico, Peru, Spain, Sweden, Turkey, Uruguay

Figure 1.1 PISA's categorization of national assessment and evaluation use.[35]

As Figure 1.1 illustrates, the United States is among a small number of countries that uses national/state and additional examinations at both the lower and upper secondary levels. While there are fewer high-stakes entrance exams for high school and postsecondary opportunities than many other jurisdictions, the intensity of testing beginning as early as pre-K is unprecedented and is unlike anywhere else in the world. Canada follows suit but to a far lesser degree, with few high-stakes examinations as far as educational access but with a significant presence of province- and territory-wide standardized tests for relatively young students.

Standardized Testing, Accuracy, Equity, and Public Satisfaction with Education

Among the typical arguments for standardized testing (ST) in the United States and Canada are that ST offers an objective measure of students' achievement, ability, and knowledge in a given area or areas; that these objective measures provide a level playing field that supports traditionally marginalized students (mitigating the educational impacts of racism, sexism, homophobia, ableism, classism, and other forms of discrimination, prejudice, and stereotyping); and that ST provides accountability to the public in the form of a return on taxpayer investment. While the next chapters return to these arguments, it is worth taking them up briefly here before moving on.

Objectivity

The most obvious barrier to objectivity is inaccuracy, and pervasive incidents of cheating raise serious questions about the validity of the ways in which testing results are used in some cases (a quick internet search reveals hundreds of examples in just the past decade). Cheating, however, is not the biggest issue as far as objectivity and ST (Chapters 6 and 7 return to the topic of cheating in greater detail). In order for standardized tests to be objective they of course have to be clear (what they aim and claim to measure must be what they actually measure); they must be accurate (based on classroom and in-school learning, and without any interference or cheating); and they must be relatively value-free, ensuring that social identity (culture, class, gender, and other markers) do not advantage or disadvantage any students in preparing for and taking the test, nor any teacher in preparing students for it. To the question of clarity, and whether or not they measure what they claim to measure, well-known critic of ST Alfie Kohn argues that "[n]orm-referenced tests were never intended to measure the quality of learning or teaching" and suggests "the main objective of these tests is to rank, not to rate; to spread out the scores, not to gauge the quality of a given student or school."[36] Norm-referenced ST in schools compares one student's performance to that of all others taking the same test. This is different from evaluating what a student has learned or what a student knows. Just as we do not know a child's height when a doctor says she falls within a particular height percentile, norm-referenced tests only tell us how well students have done on that test (on that given day, or days).

A host of critics have suggested that ST frequently fails to meet sufficient standards of both reliability and validity.[37] It is unclear how reliable information from standardized tests is with regard to individual children. A group of researchers from Chicago, borrowing from Thorndike, provide an excellent definition of the difference between reliability and validity using the metaphor of two broken scales. One gives you a different weight each time you step on it (unreliable) and the other is always ten pounds over—it is reliable but invalid.[38] James Popham suggests that validity is the most important component of any evaluation.[39] This is a standard, however, that testing has failed to meet in eyes of many education researchers of all stripes for the last quarter century. As I take up in subsequent chapters, the issue is not simply one of whether or not we use norm-referenced tests but rather what these tests mean for students and teachers, what we use them for, and how they impact education. The solution to bad high-stakes tests is not good high-stakes tests.

The Myth of a Level Playing Field

It is difficult for a test to measure only that which has been taught at school. Similarly, when considering students' knowledge, ability, understandings, strengths, challenges, and behaviors it is impossible to completely separate school and non-school influences. Much ST inevitably evaluates students on what they have learned in and out of school. For example, the student who spends her Sundays in an expensive science-based museum camp will come to school on Monday with a leg up over her peer who perhaps spent his Sunday in bible study. Each will have been learning but one is learning ideas, language, and analytical processes that are validated and recognized as legitimate in-school knowledge. As far as testing, the issue here is not which weekend learning is better but instead that one student is coming to school with a tool for success, a tool to which most students have no access, and our use of standardized tests will equate this advantage with intelligence.

So, not only does ST fail to account for economic, cultural, and other differences within the student population, but it can also introduce a space in which knowledge from outside the classroom is a marker of student advantage for some and disadvantage for others. The latter is not necessarily a problem in every case but it becomes one when test results are used to judge schools, districts, and increasingly teachers for things over which they may have limited or no control. Kohn suggests that while standardized tests tell us little about individual teachers and students, "they offer a remarkably precise method for gauging the size of the houses near the school where the test was administered."[40] His suggestion of course is that wealth and poverty, like racial advantage and disadvantage, play a role in testing results. The findings from this study (presented in Chapter 6) powerfully bear this out.

It is tempting to suggest that ST might play a positive role as far as identifying what students most need (based on school and nonschool learning), identifying which populations are underserved in schools, and informing teachers and principals about potential areas of strength across all student populations. Armed with these data, teachers might then identify best practices that could then be applied in these trouble spots and thereby address social disadvantage. While this is certainly part of the rhetoric, it is far from the reality. If all standardized tests were simply diagnostic (or what PISA calls assessments) this might be the case, but they are not. Standardized tests are used to measure achievement (rather than just to help teachers plan a path forward) and to assess the quality of schools and teachers. Schools are branded positively or negatively by virtue of their test scores, a trend increasingly common in many Canadian jurisdictions and a long-standing feature of US schooling. As Kohn's comment portends, high test scores often correlate to more money in the school community. On the flip side, perhaps predictably, low test scores correlate to higher rates of poverty. The large houses Kohn refers to can sponsor and create a variety of school supports that are impossible in high-poverty areas. Further, many NCLB as well as numerous state-level policies keep underperforming schools under constant threat of closure, privatization, or re-staffing (a reality not lost on teachers and many students). Kohn is only one among dozens of scholars who have identified the ways issues of race and class inequality are indeed exacerbated rather than mitigated through ST.[41]

In the United States, Race to the Top (RTTT) picked up where NCLB left off and its intense use of ST (along with other standardization measures) has failed to close the race and class achievement gap. The Trends in International Mathematics and Science Study (TIMSS), released in 2011, reported wide differences between the reading and math performance of eighth grade white, African American, and Latino students.[42] Additionally, there was no change in the gap between performance of 17-year-old African American and white students on the National Assessment of Educational Progress in both reading and math since 2004.[43] Using graduation rates as a measure of school success, there was a 20 percent decline among students in high-poverty schools, while rates for students in low-poverty schools remained the same.[44] ST in its current form has failed to level the playing field. Chapter 6 further takes up these questions of educational inequality.

Accountability

The driving rhetorical force in the push for standardized testing is the idea of accountability. It is a seductive discourse. Who would dare disagree that teachers should be held to high standards, that students should be well educated and cared for, that money from taxpayers (otherwise known as citizens, or even sometimes as people) should be carefully spent, that public servants who do their job poorly should be forced to improve or lose their job, or that we should have clear tools for understanding how well our education systems are working? I happen to agree with each of these claims. These common sense arguments make up simple and seductive justifications for standardization. The problem, and herein lies the big grift, is that there is no proof ST (or standardization of education more generally) accomplishes any of these objectives. So, what does it do? Standardization opens the door for more teacher-proof teaching (regimented curriculum, assessment, delivery, and reporting); it delegitimizes teaching activities that may not show up on test scores; and it opens the door for certain students to be seen as dangerous risks to the reputations of teachers, principals, and schools. As detailed in Chapter 6, understanding student and teacher ability through testing can lead teachers to favor teaching only in high scoring populations, and indeed push them away from serving marginalized students. The standardized education context can professionally disadvantage teachers and administrators who work with student populations with low test results. Considering the relationship between social identity and test results (wealth and poverty as well as race advantage and disadvantage) a culture of so-called accountability may produce teachers averse to teaching low-income and racially minoritized students.

After over a decade of increased ST and increased educational standardization generally in the United States and much of Canada, we are no closer ensuring the sort of accountability suggested by the questions posed above. For example, where are we on protecting taxpayer money; holding teachers to account; and creating smarter, happier, and more successful students? As far as the gains we have seen in education—such as better support of students with diverse learning needs, more inclusive curriculum, and increased teacher access and application of research into teaching and learning—standardization has largely hindered rather than promoted these improvements. There is a painful gap, then, between blanket calls for accountability and educational improvement. In the meantime, standardization has helped to turn education into big business. In the United States, the testing companies increasingly write the unaffordable books in which the only correct answers are found, while an exploding charter movement pulls tax dollars away from public schools.[45] Whereas there is no doubt that education in the United States faces many problems, there is no proof that standardization will fix any of them. Rather, we seem to be doubling down on a proven failure. We ask standardized tests to measure teachers, schools, and districts—a job they were never designed to do—and insist on more tests when we don't like the results. Who, then, is held to account? Who answers? And *cui bono*?

Although the United States is far further down the road than its northern neighbor, Canada's use of testing is more American than Finnish. At present, Canada is not experiencing a ST crisis equal to that in the United States. Yet, as discussed in Chapters 3, 4, and 5, the rhetoric of accountability is alive and well in many Canadian jurisdictions. Similarly, after more than a decade of testing (and intensification of testing pressures for many Canadian teachers) Canada is no closer to solving the accountability issues ST purports to address (in Ontario, for example, public confidence in education has not risen significantly in the decade since province-wide ST results have been available).[46]

From a wider international perspective, Finnish schooling proponent and renowned educationalist Pasi Sahlberg suggests we are now witnessing a "Global Educational Reform Movement" (GERM) and argues systems that have experienced increased standardization (specifically a move toward test-based accountability, standardization, school choice, and human capital model thinking) have seen a corollary decline in academic performance.[47] Citing 12 years of OECD/PISA data from 2000 to 2012, Sahlberg traces the decline in mathematics learning outcomes in the United States, England, Canada, Australia, New Zealand, the Netherlands, and Sweden—all jurisdictions, which have embraced the GERM approach, to albeit different degrees.[48] In the United States in particular, over 25 percent of students fail to meet OECD/PISA's baseline for math proficiency, and nationally the United States ranks 27th among OECD countries.[49] While standardization does not correlate with academic improvement, OECD/PISA data on social and economic equality tell us that improvements in social and economic equality correlate with improved performance on OECD/PISA evaluations,[50] a conclusion supported as well by the work of Wilkinson and Pickett.[51] The United States, which has the same levels of inequality today as it did in the 1790s,[52] also lags in its educational performance. Canada, with greater social and economic equality, scores higher than the United States on the PISA/OECD measures.

Summary and Implications

Andy Hargreaves argues that "accountability is what remains when responsibility has been subtracted."[53] It has become clear through interviews with over a hundred educators, and a survey of thousands in the United States and Canada that the overwhelming drive, hope, and desire among them is to be given the opportunity to take responsibility; to be given the tools needed to serve their students and their conscience; and to be given the freedom and support to act as professionals charged as custodians of the future. The push for accountability (when understood as test-based liability; as standardization; as school choice; and as a vision of students and teachers as little more than price points) deprofessionalizes teachers' work; anchors competition at the core operation of our education system; and alienates students and parents from the constructive, experiential, and social elements of learning. Internationally, the United States is a radical ST outlier, testing more and more often than anywhere else. Although the United States uses fewer make-or-break examinations than some other places, the culture of intense testing (beginning as early as Pre-K) sets it apart from many other education cultures—constituting a new version of a HSST environment.

Canada, although an education leader that scores very high on most international measures and that traditionally engages broad support and satisfaction with public education, is cautiously dabbling with an HSST path (much more slowly, and with far less corporate guidance and involvement). To be clear, Canadian education systems are models the world over, however, as subsequent chapters illustrate, ST is increasingly significant in the daily school life of students and teachers. So-called top schools are often closed for admission to folks living outside the local catchment area as housing prices skyrocket therein. In Toronto, real estate agents often list and compare test scores of in-district schools.

Children are stressed, and test preparation for province-wide standardized tests happens, in various forms for much of the year, with a slow arc toward competition coming into ever clearer relief. Although there is no research to suggest that all kids suffer all of the time from ST, there is no evidence to suggest we should be testing all kids all of the time. Although most Canadian standardized tests do not count toward a student's grade, we see an explosion of commercial and government-provided test preparation resources targeting standardized test takers and their parents. Ontario teachers report that many students lose sleep, experience anxiety, and often find themselves in tears around Ontario's standardized tests (known collectively and individually as EQAO). On test days (with tests that are supposed to be just a snapshot) schools feel and look much different than on all other days. As detailed in the chapters to come, test days are a sort of backwards day: "wear your lucky hat indoors," "have a snack," "chew gum," "have some lemon water." This is the beginning of a Canadian HSST environment, and to what end? Over a decade of testing has done nothing to bring up Canadian scores in mathematics as measured by the OECD/PISA assessments. Despite a host of methodological issues (accuracy, reliability, validity) and other concerns (including a virtual academic consensus that ST is inappropriate for younger children), standardized tests serve increasingly as a popular go to for understanding teacher and student ability in the United States and Canada.

Most teachers assess students very frequently, and the vast majority of that assessment would make no sense expressed as a number (or as a state-provincially-territorially-referenced percentile). Often lost in the HSST classroom is the context, the fecundity, and the unique challenges, strengths, and opportunities that are taken into consideration in the course of rich and useful assessment and evaluation. Over a half century has passed since Marshall McLuhan suggested: "we become what we behold...we shape our tools and afterwards our tools shape us."[54] It is obvious that people have created ST, but it is far more challenging to accept that it will one day create us (or what's more, that in some cases it already has). If our tools frequently remake us, then it seems we must frequently remake our tools. We do well to return then, to the idea of ST as a technology (as a tool) that is value-laden (neither rational nor neutral) and that is characterized by ambivalence and contestation. Chapter 2 investigates the historical trajectory and logic of ST, fleshing out the contestations and politics that have both underpinned and underwritten educational standardization for a century.

CHAPTER 2

The History, Logic, and Push for Standardized Testing

Karl Marx suggested that people "make their own history, but they do not make it just as they please..., but under circumstances directly encountered, given and transmitted from the past."[1] With this in mind, history is not merely impacted by a perpetual push and pull but rather it is forged by it; through struggle, through controversy, and through dispute (over ideas, over survival, over competitive advantage, etc). To understand our own time, the early twenty-first century, is to recognize that we are simultaneously producers of history on the one hand, and that we are produced by history on the other. Among the most important communal human systems is government, which, for a variety of reasons, often tends to reflect the values of only a small minority. In the United States and Canada, governments at various levels are responsible for systems that organize much of our social and cultural existence: these range from schools, to transportation, to international and military relations (determining which wars and humanitarian efforts we do or do not engage in), to our access to health care. In addition to systems that are actually run by the state, governments regulate access to food, beverages, and drugs; commercial transactions; travel; and in most places, our sexual behavior.

Today's laws, cultural norms, and systems all emerge from a politics and a history—they exist for a series of specific reasons and schooling is no exception. Many of the first schools in the United States and Canada were tacit prisons for abducted Indigenous children. Called residential schools in Canada and mission schools in the United States, these places aimed, as Canadian prime minister Stephen Harper has said, "to kill the Indian" in order to "save the child" through a program of forced religious conversion and cultural assimilation.[2] The evangelical ethos of schooling was not limited to the quasi-prison model of the mission or residential school, however, as public schooling in the United States and Canada has had until recently, specific religious undertones (sometimes with overtly religious curriculum). Religion was not the only contested feature of early schooling. Many of the first public schools in the United States and Canada were burned to the ground, the school teachers assaulted. The culprits were angry parents (many of them farmers who needed their children to help on the farm) and their children (many of whom may have had their own reasons). Some early schools in the United States and Canada operated on a schedule that gave students spring and fall breaks to help with planting and harvesting at home. At its inception, public mass education was unpopular among many parents and students.

Although we now tend to speak about universal access to school, the flip side of that coin, and one that was certainly foregrounded in the push for national public schooling, was a universal obligation to ensure one's children were in school. While today's truant officer may enjoy more support from parents than her predecessors, she is engaged in the very same struggle. Contemporary popular understandings of schooling insist, of course, that being in school is good and that being out of school is bad. The limits of this common sense are visible in school attendance age requirements—ages under which kids are not allowed to not be in school. Sold as the great equalizer, sitting at the center of civil rights struggles for decades, the promise of public schooling for many is still more chore than gift—a legal obligation and privilege that many cannot wait to shed.

Politics and tensions are inherent in our schooling systems. Although Chapter 7 looks specifically at the tensions (contestation, resistance, and struggle) surrounding high-stakes standardized testing (HSST), the remainder of this chapter looks at the politics, history, and logic of standardized testing—the most controversial issue in education today. To contextualize our current climate of testing in which students write mandatory tests containing references to Mug™ root beer and Lego® products, and in which teachers' worth is often measured by student test scores, this chapter first sketches the history of standardized testing in North America, including a look at recent policy initiatives such as Race to the Top (RTTT), Common Core State Standards Initiative (CCSSI), and No Child Left Behind (NCLB). The next section looks at the thinking and rationale that underpin standardized testing (ST) in four categories: efficiency and fairness, sorting and social hierarchy, the human capital model in education, and education as a market place. Standardized tests rely on a specific set of presumptions about student learning and achievement that now, as a century ago, fail to recognize the inherently social and experiential nature and purposes of teaching and learning. While the past three decades have seen the use of more social constructivist perspectives across and within teacher education programming in North America, ST (which is a move away from social and experiential teaching and learning) has become the primary tool with which to understand the success of our students, teachers, administrators, and schools.

A Brief History of Standardized Testing in US and Canadian Schooling

ST relies on the premise that we need to compare people to one another in order to rank them for one or more purposes. Generally, standardized tests are norm-referenced, which means individual test takers' scores are compared with that of a standard test taker. Standard test takers are hypothetical. Rather than reflecting the average score (or results) of all test takers, the imaginary standard score is determined using a norming process, in which testing bodies and test developers employ various statistical methods to determine norms for use in interpreting test results. Understanding people's abilities and knowledge using standardized tests is a practice that education has imported from the medical, business, and employments worlds, with the oldest known use found in China during the fifth century as part of the Imperial examination system. Özturgut explains tests began, "during the Sui Dynasty in 605 B.C., and consisted of military strategy, civil law, revenue and taxation, agriculture, geography, and the philosophical works of Confucius and his disciples."[3] Different tests were used to determine aptitude for various levels of government posts, with specific knowledge required for specific jobs.[4] The use of standardized examination(s) for employment is, centuries later, a worldwide phenomenon encompassing everything from physical tasks such as timed stair climbs for fire fighters carrying heavy loads, to language examinations for the diplomatic core. These tasks are often norm-referenced because the timed stair climb for the firefighter is not a race but a measure against a standard. Similarly, the prospective diplomat is not measured on whether or not she speaks a certain language better than her peers but instead on whether or not she meets a particular standard of language proficiency.

The use of ST with children is more recent and its use in schools more recent still. French psychologist Alfred Binet is credited for developing the first of many intelligence tests that would eventually fall under the umbrella term of intelligence quotient, or IQ, testing. Universal education in France prompted the formal scientific study of childhood development and intelligence, and in particular, prompted the push to study children thought to have learning disabilities. Binet was asked to develop a system to identify students needing special assistance.[5] Based on research with children who had been deemed average by their teachers, Binet and his junior colleague Theodore Simon established an age-based standard of intellectual comparison called mental age, and contrasted this with a child's chronological age. Binet (1904) describes the testing scale as:

> [C]omposed of a series of tests of increasing difficulty, starting from the lowest intellectual level that can be observed, and ending with that of average normal intelligence. Each group in the series corresponds to a different mental level.[6]

A decade later, the Binet-Simon test would morph into the Stanford-Binet test, and the following formula was developed for assigning a comparative number to children: 100 multiplied by mental age, divided by chronological age to determine a child's intelligence quotient or IQ. Despite issues of accuracy (particularly when used with older children and adults), as well as fundamental problems with cultural relativity in determining and assessing average intelligence, the IQ test (in various forms) has been in use in various contexts for over a century.

Until the mid-nineteenth century, in-class testing of students primarily took the form of oral examinations. Universal access to education and a massive growth in the US population (and of its educationally enfranchised working-class population in particular) prompted greater standardization between classrooms, schools, and jurisdictions. According to one US Congress report, written tests were introduced to ensure fairness among larger numbers of students and to address the assessment challenges of an exploding student population.[7] From 1820 to 1860, the US population grew tremendously, with urban areas experiencing unprecedented growth.[8] The use of ST immediately led to resistance and controversy based on the perception by teachers and school administrators that the tests were unfair.[9] To be clear, although many students in the same school, and in some cases region, would write the same test, norm-referencing was rare in this period, and the comparative function of the tests was limited to other students taking the same tests (rather than a calculated norm or standard).

In the late nineteenth century, the use of written testing expanded to measure not only student ability within schooling contexts but also aptitude for postsecondary study and success. The move to written testing was part of broader change in pedagogy, one driven by technological change and characterized, Kaestle suggests, by "the withering of oral traditions and the increase in writing. No more was writing confined to copybooks and slates. Now there were notebooks, essays, improved pens and pencils, blackboards and written assignments."[10] This sea change of standardization, and the widespread resistance to it, continues over a century later with the push for online standardized tests.

In 1908, Cliff Stone created what is credited as the first standardized achievement test in the United States, and many more were soon to follow. While Stone's test looked at arithmetic, subsequent tests would analyze handwriting, grammar, spelling, language (Latin), drawing, reading, and vocabulary.[11] Standardized assessment moved from a focus on intelligence to a focus on achievement. Under the dual guise of objectivity and efficiency, by the 1920s, standardized achievement testing relied primarily on multiple choice, a technology adapted from the military for children. By the end of World War I, testing was also used by the US military to assess the aptitude of potential officers. The use and significance of ST grew between the 1930s and 1960s, and as Kaestle notes, by 1954 the *Fourth Mental Measurements Yearbook*[12] "described 4,417 tests, of which about one-fourth were intelligence tests."[13] At the same time, tests for university admission were created during this period; many of which are in use today, including Scholastic Aptitude Tests (SATs), which aim to assess both aptitude and intelligence.

In 1958, US president Eisenhower authorized the National Defense Education Act (NDEA) as part of a soft Cold War competition with Soviet technological achievements generally, and the launch of the *Sputnik* satellite in particular. The NDEA authorized state funds to raise test scores and improve educational performance and achievement through testing. The linking of local performance to federal money is significant here, and would be entrenched further with introduction in 1965, by President Lyndon Johnson, of the Elementary and Secondary Education Act (ESEA), and Title One School Funding. The ESEA was part of the broader policy push informally titled the War on Poverty; related measures included creation of the Economic Opportunity Act, as well as the Office of Economic Opportunity. During this period the idea of accountability began to play a directive role in education policy at a federal level for the first time. ST results would provide Congress with evidence of whether federal money was being well spent at the state level. Indeed, among the first amendments to the ESEA was a requirement, proposed by Robert Kennedy, that standardized test results be used to hold states and schools accountable by tying test scores to federal funding.

The 1960s also gave rise to the push for national standards, realized fully only now with Common Core, as a way of assessing US students as a whole. Unlike Common Core, however, the 1960s vision was not one of measuring individual students or schools but instead of having a national picture (one perhaps that might be juxtaposed with that in the USSR). U.S. Commissioner of Education from 1962 to 1965, Francis Keppel was instrumental in advancing a program of national testing. Supported by a Carnegie grant, Keppel's work would lead to the creation of the National Assessment of Educational Progress (NAEP). First conducted in 1969, the norm-referenced test is still administered today, and, indeed, it has forged partnerships with other wide-scale testing initiatives. Designed and administered privately, NAEP is the standard national measure for educational achievement in the United States.

In this context, the 1970s and 1980s saw the development of standardized tests and testing at the state level, beginning in Michigan, which corresponded with further concurrent expansion of the testing industry. The ESEA had inconsistent effects nationally, suffering from underfunding and ineffective implementation. Even the Title One provision, mentioned earlier, required rewriting in 1994, to better support students at risk. Kaestle writes, it took "decades before evaluations of the program began to have consequences for individual schools or districts."[14] Despite limited efficacy, the ESEA laid the groundwork for the current relationship between Washington and individual states. The vanguard policy of the current standardization movement was the No Child Left Behind Act of 2001, which was US President George W. Bush's reauthorization of ESEA, ushering in the current era of standardization. With President Obama as midwife, NCLB would give birth to the Race to the Top Initiative (RTTT) in 2009, which more tightly tied federal monies to standardized test results, set performance standards for teachers and principals using a point system, and eased restrictions as well as increased support for charter schools. Common Core appears to be, in teacher parlance, the culminating activity of the standardization movement: a virtual standardization of curriculum and assessment at a national level, developed through consultation with education experts of all stripes, including testing companies such as

Pearson Education. The role of big business in federal education policy in the development and roll out of Common Core is unprecedented.

The use of ST in Canada follows a unique but related trajectory to that in the United States, although without the acceleration represented by NCLB, RTTT, and CCSSI. Students first wrote standardized tests in the mid-nineteenth century, mostly as either entrance or exit examinations. Similar to the United States, ST emerged as the ranks of students in public education systems swelled. Although not as ethnically diverse as the United States, universal schooling in the mid-nineteenth century saw low-income children enter the system at unprecedented rates.[15] ST in Canada came alongside a more hands-on role for the provinces in education, a move away from local school and school board autonomy. As mentioned in Chapter 1, Canada's education landscape is rigidly divided by province (ten in total) and territory (three in total), each of which is responsible for education within that jurisdiction. There is no through line of ST in Canada but, instead, a series of local histories. Generally, however, the use of ST in education increased from the mid-nineteenth century until the early twentieth century. The work of Klinger and colleagues outlines the back-and-forth use of large-scale assessment in the early and mid-twentieth century wherein teacher- and principal-generated large-scale assessments were used in different proportions in different jurisdictions to determine and measure student success.[16]

While many Canadian jurisdictions relied on subject-specific examinations to complete high school, these tests could, for the most part, be determined by a teacher or team of teachers and were not province-wide or norm-referenced. From the 1930s to the 1960s, accreditation systems replaced (or some cases complimented) formal exit examinations and although standardized provincial exit examinations persisted (and are still used today in some places) they were no longer used to determine college or university admission, but instead to measure basic competencies. In the 1960s, Alberta was the first province to adopt cross-curricular and widespread ST, using norm-referenced measures not only to certify readiness for graduation but also to assess literacy and numeracy (students were first tested in grades three, six, and nine). Other provinces tended to rely more heavily on teacher-driven assessment in schools. In Ontario, Canada's largest province by population, the Ministry of Education emphasized skill building for teachers around assessment and evaluation at the classroom level. Indeed, as recently as 1994, the province's influential Royal Commission on Learning argued for the importance of teacher assessment, however, it suggested there needed to be standards for that assessment.[17]

As part of a larger push for accountability with taxpayer dollars on the one hand, and the call to for schools to get back to basics on the other, education in Canada increased its focus on content-driven (rather than student-driven) teaching and learning in the 1980s and 1990s. As indicated in Chapter 1, each of Canada's 13 provinces and territories uses some form of standardized assessment, and these tests were for the most part developed and implemented (or at least significantly redesigned from the ground up) after the mid-1990s. Even in Alberta, where ST got off to an early start, the ST regime is undergoing a top-to-bottom overhaul.

Further distinguishing the US context from that in Canada is the relationship between the federal and state/provincial/territorial governments. Absent in Canada are both the persistent tension between local and federal control (beginning in the United States with ESEA and its various incarnations and effects) and the recent move to federal standards for curriculum and funding (Common Core). Where US federal involvement in ST has intertwined the national with the local, in Canada the national testing picture has operated parallel to provincial and territorial testing regimes, albeit with impact on the direction of policy at the provincial and territorial levels. In Canada, work at the national level is conducted primarily by the Council of Ministers of Education, Canada (CMEC).

Founded in 1967, the CMEC is a pan-Canadian intergovernmental body run, as the name suggests, by the Ministers of Education from all 13 jurisdictions. In addition to monies from individual provinces and territories, it is funded by Human Resources and Skills Development Canada, a federal body concerned, among other things, with the relationship between education and the workforce. The CMEC is as close as Canada comes to a federal body on issues of education, and its work (from assessment, to policy recommendations, to reports on licensing directives for teachers) is widely instructive but not prescriptive for education policy at the provincial/territorial and school board levels. The CMEC is best known for its national testing program, developed in 1989 (after nearly decade-long economic crisis) under pressure to better equip Canadian students for a changing economy and workforce.

From 1993 to 2004, the CMEC conducted the School Achievement Indicators Program (SAIP). Reinvented as the Pan-Canadian Assessment Program (PCAP) in 2007, the standardized test measures the performance of 13- and 16-year-olds. Additionally, the CMEC "is involved in the design, implementation, and analysis of both pan-Canadian and international assessment programs" in addition to "other large-scale studies to examine the educational environments and whether or not they are meeting expectations for students' performance at strategic points in their education."[18] These additional tests include: The Programme for International Student Assessment (PISA), the Programme for the International Assessment of Adult Competencies (PIAAC), the International Computer and Information Literacy Study (ICILS), the Teacher Education and Development Study in Mathematics (TEDS-M), the Progress in International Reading Literacy Study (PIRLS), and the Trends in International Mathematics and Science Study (TIMSS). Indeed, CMEC administers PISA in Canada, and the organization as a whole provides Canada's major contribution to the comparative international measurement of student achievement. Data from these tests, as well as from provincial and territorial standardized tests, are used by CMEC to make policy recommendations, and to understand the strengths and weaknesses of Canadian education systems. CMEC's national testing program is based on a random sample of students, with little or no direct impact on classroom instruction or school culture. Despite the rather benign nature of the testing, CMEC writes Canada's national report card, and it does so almost exclusively on the basis of standardized, norm-referenced testing. As discussed in previous as well as subsequent sections, this is too little information with which to understand a system and/or collection of systems. To understand the overreliance on standardized measurement in both the United States and Canada, the rest of this chapter focuses on the thinking and the politics that have created and driven the current overuse of standardized tests.

The Logic and Push for Standardized Testing in the United States and Canada

Standardized tests in the United States and Canada were first used as part of larger attempts to reform education systems seen by reformers as being in decline.[19] The aim of ST has always been to improve upon the status quo, and it was often introduced as part of a broad platform for educational change, which, according to William Reese, included: "more centralized authority, the setting of academic standards by elected officials or administrators, better age-graded classes taught by women, and more uniform textbooks and curricula."[20] Although a variety of demographic, political, economic, and cultural factors have impacted the uncomfortable march forward of ST across both national contexts, the most significant drivers of educational standardization can be described in four general categories: first, the demand for efficiency and fairness in the face of changing student demographics and expanding educational bureaucratization; second, sorting and social hierarchy in the context of eugenics, IQ testing, and aptitude assessment; third, the human capital model of schooling that focuses on job readiness on the one hand and accountability for public monies on the other; and fourth, a hypercapitalist vision of public education as a market place.

The Medium Is the Message: Efficiency, Bureaucracy, and Fairness

Standardized tests are, in theory, easier to grade than nonstandardized assessment activities. Even before mechanized grading in the early 1900s, standardized tests offered a relatively quick solution to the problem of assessing and generating marks for large numbers of pupils. The growth of ST corresponded, in the late nineteenth and early twentieth centuries, with universal schooling and increasingly swollen school roll calls in many towns and cities, making the one-room, multigrade school house increasingly untenable, particularly in urban areas. Between 1820 and 1860, an average of 125,000 people immigrated to the United States each year.[21] The task of schooling was growing. Amidst the push for automation shepherded by the Industrial Revolution on the one hand, and by the application of statistical data to understand the world on the other, the standards-based lens for understanding schooling fit nicely with a concomitant vision of schooling as factory production (Charles Parker called the nineteenth century the "age of examination").[22] Students were divided into grades and into levels within grades. Among some school leaders, there appeared an obvious analogy between "educational tests and thermometers and gauges in industry."[23] ST was part of a revision and restructuring of schooling, and as Ken Robinson (2009) reminds us, the current system for grouping children by date of manufacture is a practice bequeathed to us from this industrial era—echoing a vision of schools as sites of mass production.[24]

Although we commonly recognize that many schools follow an industrial model of production, we seldom recognize that from the start, this model itself was contested, controversial, and that it found its way into education only through a push-and-pull process of reform and resistance. The increased size of the schooling population drove the bureaucratization of public schooling. ST was part of the accompanying reform. A 1992 US Congress Report suggests, "from their inception standardized tests were perceived as instruments of reform: it was taken as an article of faith that test-based information could inject the needed adrenalin into a rapidly bureaucratizing school system."[25] Research suggests bureaucratization was driven as well, by the change in the administration of schooling, as well as the feminization of the teaching workforce.[26]

Newly created school boards, and eventually departments of education, would come to wrest school governance and direct control from local organizations. Often led by prominent businessmen, these new levels of bureaucracy provided a natural entry point for industrial models of production to gain traction within public education. Standardization became the hallmark of mass education in the United States and Canada, representing on the one hand a shift from education reserved for the elite (called equality of access) and on the other, a tool for ensuring against wide variation between different classrooms, schools, and eventually districts (called equality of treatment). As far as the latter is concerned, the question of equality of treatment arose in response to claims by educators and education officials that great gaps existed between schools and teachers. Further, some of the first advocates for ST were specifically concerned with ensuring fair treatment for economically and ethnically diverse students, raising questions about the relationship between sorting technologies (such as standardized tests) and justifications for social hierarchy.[27]

This conversation continues, with many of the same ideas in play, well into the twenty-first century. In 2014, Linda Darling-Hammond and Beverly Falk argued with reference to Common Core that "educators are seeking ways to support an increasingly diverse student population to meet these more demanding expectations."[28] Common Core architects are thus grappling with many of the same issues as those facing policy makers a century ago.

When You're Holding a Hammer, Everything Looks Like a Nail: Sorting and Social Hierarchy

Claims of testing as an enemy of inequality are not unfamiliar in the twenty-first century. Although ST today comes in response to a crisis of inadequate resources (broadly conceived) as far as serving large, growing, and diverse populations, many children were left behind under NCLB; further, these children are disproportionately African American, Latino/a, and from low-income backgrounds.[29] The bubble test, perhaps the epitome of the standardized test in which test-takers fill in select answer bubbles subsequently graded by a machine, is now widely maligned even by researchers who defend some degree of educational standardization (including Linda Darling-Hammond, who has led an education working group for US president Obama, and who has supported various elements of the Common Core).[30] We can link these phenomena in the nineteenth century to those of our current era, in which the central promise of NCLB was fairness for twenty-first-century US children, the most diverse student body in the nation's history. The current policy response is thus a sort a weighty echo of a past reflex.

While it is unclear to what degree standardization delivered on its promise of fairness in the nineteenth and early twentieth centuries, from its inception, even early ST faced critics who claimed that far from being a great equalizer, standardized tests unfairly advantaged some and disadvantaged others.[31] Despite the perhaps well-intentioned hopes that standardized tests would level the education playing field, "mental measurement," and intelligence testing in particular, would give rise to discussions of "the role of heredity in determining intellectual ability and the effects of education. Some theorists used the results of intelligence and aptitude tests to support claims of natural hierarchy and of racial and ethnic superiority."[32] In his seminal work on testing, *Unequal by Design,* Wayne Au suggests: "standardized testing, at its very root in intelligence testing and the eugenics movement, provided the technology to sort groups of people along race and class socioeconomic hierarchies."[33] Perhaps most famously illustrated by the use of pacifist Albert Einstein's work to develop a nuclear weapon, the original purpose of a given tool or technology often may have little impact on its subsequent use or application. On the use of standardized intelligence assessment, its first and most well-known author discussed in Chapter 1, Alfred Binet, offered the following caveat in 1905, which we do well to consider as far as the contemporary use of HSST:

> We have nothing to do either with [the child's] past history or with his future; consequently we shall neglect his etiology, and we shall make no attempt to distinguish between acquired and congenital idiocy; for a stronger reason we shall set aside all consideration of pathological anatomy which might explain his intellectual deficiency. So much for his past. As to that which concerns his future, we shall exercise the same abstinence; we do not attempt to establish or prepare a prognosis and we leave unanswered the question of whether this retardation is curable, or even improvable.[34]

Sorting through the outdated language, the reader finds Binet establishing numerous significant limitations to the intended use of his results.

First, the test tells us little about the child's ability or condition in the past or the future. Second, the results tell us nothing about why a child achieved her particular score. Third, the results cannot separate the social from the biological. Fourth, the results do not indicate whether the child's condition, as indicated by the test results, can or will ever be changed. Over a century later (with billions of dollars spent on testing), these same problems plague questions of validity and the use of ST results.

These caveats represent not simply the limitations of Binet's particular test but also the limitations of norm-referenced testing used to understand children's ability, intelligence, and learning. Although Binet's century-old measure is a different animal than many of today's standardized tests, his warnings remain salient today. Such concerns, however, are largely overlooked within current US and Canadian testing regimes. While many standardized tests are billed as snapshots of learning they are often used as a comparative measure of a student's overall learning during a given period (summative evaluations). In many cases, the results of ST affect advancement or remediation for students; are used to measure teacher, school, and district quality; and (particularly in the United States) are increasingly used as the primary measure for understanding student ability, intelligence, and learning. Expecting ST results to guide us in all this is akin to expecting a fish to walk on land (just before demanding it sprout wings and fly away)—it simply does not have the capacity to perform these tasks. A norm-referenced standardized test can only measure a student's performance on a given test on a given day in a given location in comparison to that of a hypothetical standard—nothing more. While ST may thus provide diagnostic value (low-stakes and often nongraded assessment of children at the start of a year, term, or unit) there is widespread misuse of ST results in the United States and to a lesser degree Canada; with the primary issue being the expectation that tests work as a definitive sorting tool for children, teachers, schools, districts, and jurisdictions—a task for which they were not originally designed and one which they do not have the capacity to accurately perform.

Even if we believe objective grading is possible when students choose rather than create their answers, there remains an inability of norm-referenced ST to accommodate for context (we know students often do better on tests if they write them where they learned the information on which they are being tested), for student diversity (a variety of learning abilities and disabilities), for cultural knowledge and relevance (we see persistent race gaps in testing), and learning styles (the use of the written form alone advantages some students and disadvantages others).

A century of the industrial-era drive to sort and rank has not led to the creation of objective means for doing so, yet standardization has never been more central to public education than it is today. Perhaps more importantly, with the justified marginalization of eugenics, of racial anthropometry (the comparative measure of physical characteristics by race), and of other racist disciplines from mainstream science, no further rationale has emerged for sorting and social hierarchy that is actually grounded in what we know about the ways teaching and learning occur.

The Purpose and Price of Schooling: Job Readiness and Accountability

While sorting and hierarchy have been of limited value to our children, these phenomena have been central to the argument that schooling is preparation for work and that students can accrue capital via education; capital that can be exchanged for remuneration through employment after graduation. Along with the phenomena of bureaucracy and sorting discussed earlier, ST has also been driven by the human capital theory of education (HCTE). With a focus on the relationship between schooling economy, HCTE reduces the concept of schooling to an investment in economic stability, prosperity, and competitiveness. On the government side of things, education is an expenditure that will yield productive workers necessary for a prosperous future (other buzzwords commonly inserted here include: innovation, progress, competitiveness, a global economy, technological change, etc). From the student side, the purpose of education is to prepare, train, or become job ready (education today for the jobs of tomorrow!). Indeed, this may be the most commonly held belief about the purpose of schooling, a view that, according to some scholars, is more common among the working class (which includes the majority of the population) than it is among the wealthy.[35]

In this view, education beyond a marketable skillset becomes a luxury item, an idea confirmed by the high costs of postsecondary education and the historic wage and wealth disparities in Canada and the United States. We see this idea hidden in the popular defense of liberal arts education that suggests technology and other cutting-edge sectors require creative people who can think outside of the box. In this frame, thinking outside of the box is valued for its ability to create new boxes. No longer ends-in-themselves, divergent thinking and creativity become the means necessary for innovation and competitiveness. People, however, in their decisions with regard to their society and their children have always disrupted the HCTE paradigm.

While the link between learning and work is no doubt significant, few would argue with a straight face that all learning serves only economic ends. We do not celebrate a baby's first steps because she'll walk right into a job one day on those very legs; and most extracurricular activities are not job-oriented (think of dance, piano, swimming, Tajweed, and other religious studies). Within school, students have citizenship education and music, and until recently, US and Canadian schools provided religious education (Ontario still has public Catholic schooling). This is all to say nothing of the life-long learning so many of us commit to (indeed spend money on rather than earn money from) under the banner of hobbies. All of these belie a belief that learning is and should be reduced to economic behavior.

Enter the notion of accountability, however, and the argument runs something like this: public money should benefit the public, and each and every dollar should be accounted for. Schools should teach the things students need to know to get a job on the one hand, and to keep our economy strong (modern, competitive, dynamic, twenty-first-century-ready, better than somewhere else, etc) on the other. This argument is commonly paired with fears of other countries displacing American economic dominance—most recently China (previously India, Japan, and the USSR). As mentioned, it was the idea of global competition that drove the push for national educational standardization in the United States following the launch of the *Sputnik* satellite by the USSR in 1957. The synergistic drive for centralized bureaucracy alongside the push for human capital theory–oriented approaches in education has only intensified within neoliberal economic globalization.

The push to remain globally competitive (a notion open to so many possible interpretations as to be nearly rhetorical) is now familiar to us all. Standardized tests are a quick and dirty measure of our competitive rankings—particularly in mathematics and sciences. PISA has yet to rank countries by creative potential. Although experts in both North America and Europe investigated new methods for measuring intelligence, ability, and aptitude, the practice has always had more traction in North America than in Europe. Margaret Dagenais suggests that while the introduction of ST at times followed a similar trajectory in the United States and Canada as far as its relationship to fears of economic stagnation, the United States emphasized a competitive element largely absent in the Canadian context, where the push was instead for citizenship education and student readiness for a changing economy.[36]

Human capital theory suggests that a person's wages, accomplishments, and success will be directly related to her or his skills, training, and knowledge. It is controversial in and out of education, and it has become an area of study unto itself within the fields of industrial relations and economics. While a full accounting of HCTE is beyond the scope of this work, its role in promoting a one-dimensional view of the purpose and thus direction of education should not be underestimated. Along with bureaucratization, sorting, and ranking, and the increased impact of private business in public education (discussed later), HCTE is an increasingly important driver of educational standardization. This was powerfully evidenced in the push to demonstrate Canadian and US global competitiveness through near-knee-jerk policy reactions to declining math scores on the OECD's PISA 2013 tests, when jurisdictions in both countries immediately implemented changes to both curriculum and teacher training. While new competition on global measures has replaced that of the Cold War (the OECD rather than the USSR) the impacts on the classroom are much the same.

Human capital thinking is also evident within even critical conversations about ST. The link between creativity and productivity has (alongside a larger critique of ST) fueled a call for better, rather than fewer, tests and standardized performance assessments. The idea here is that good tests should replace bad tests, wide-ranging tests should replace tests that are too narrow, and that tests that fail to measure creativity should be replaced by those that do. On the one hand, this thinking relies on the premise that standardized tests and performance assessments are necessary, inevitable, and capable of fully measuring students' and teachers' knowledge and ability. On the other hand, this approach sees expanded educational standardization as the only way to achieve holistic understandings of what is happening in our schools, and indeed of provoking and promoting creativity. This overlooks, unfortunately, the displacement of these very things by ST, a theme explored further in the coming chapters. With the deification of technology's most prominent authors such as Bill Gates and Steve Jobs, creativity is now worth something on the open market of educational exchange; indeed, it may even be worth testing. This represents an ironic full-circle journey. The coming of ST was part of the very education reform that made plays, recitations, poetry bees, and other student performances impossible.

The Classroom as Untapped Market and the Business of Standardized Testing

A perhaps predictable extension of the idea that education is little more than market preparation, is the notion of education itself as a potential market. The political battle over Common Core fleshes out this connection. Among the major proponents of Common Core is the United States Chamber of Commerce Foundation (USCCF), which funded a giant lobbying effort to sway mostly Republican lawmakers to support Common Core. The USCCF is a business lobbying nonprofit affiliate of the U.S. Chamber of Commerce "dedicated to strengthening America's long-term competitiveness and educating the public on how the Free Enterprise system improves society and the economy."[37] Standardization (and Common Core in particular) is a critical nexus between business and education.

For well over a century, the standardization movement in education has had a shadow that has followed it wherever it has gone. Depending on the time of day, the shadow even takes the lead sometimes. Kaestle (2013) suggests that as districts established grade levels:

> [T]extbook publishers provided grade-level texts. Soon tests were available for grade-to-grade promotion and then manuals and test-prep books to match. Teachers still made the decisions, but tests were becoming part of the system in many school districts.

In the United States in particular, increased standardization has intensified the role of private companies in public education. Standardized measurement constitutes the key private to public access point, both currently and historically within education. While the relationship between textbook companies and other educational service providers is an old one, the twenty-first century has seen unprecedented intermingling of corporations, lobbyists, and private sector interests with the policy and direction of public education.

Pearson Education now boasts a 39 percent market share of the multibillion dollar testing industry. In the premarketing of its Common Core products, Pearson's website boasts that its "close association with key authors and architects of the Common Core State Standards ensures that the spirit and pedagogical approach of the initiative is embodied in our professional development."[38] In addition to creating, selling, and grading examinations and other standardized measures for teachers and students, Pearson publishes Common Core textbooks, as well as Common Core staff development and training resources and services. Indeed, Pearson has had a seat at the Common Core policy table from its inception. Comedian John Oliver correctly suggests that a child entering school could, in theory, take Pearson tests from kindergarten to the eighth grade (studying for them using Pearson guides and text books and taught by teachers certified by the Pearson test). Concurrent assessments for learning disabilities might also use Pearson tests. The comedian suggests that if the hypothetical student dropped out and took her General Education Diploma test, this too would be a Pearson test.[39] In January of 2014, the Pearson Education website reported on a summit convened by the Obamas, US Education Secretary Arne Duncan, and Pearson executives to discuss educational futures in the United States—the commodity trading terminology seems appropriate.[40] In addition to spending millions of dollars lobbying elected officials, Pearson makes financial contributions directly to key political campaign races.[41] Finally, Pearson has opened the door for test content as commodity with mentions of Mug™ root beer, IBM™, Lego®, FIFA®, and Mindstorms™ in its tests.[42]

Pearson is the largest but not the only company to make billions on ST. CTB/McGraw-Hill is Pearson's main competitor, with revenues of more than $2 billion, while Education Testing Services (a subsidiary of Riverside Publishing and its parent company Houghton Mifflin Harcourt) likely finishes a close third. The business impact on policy, however, is not limited to testing companies and publishers. As mentioned in Chapter 1, Achieve, the Business Roundtable, and the American Legislative Exchange Council (ALEC) have been instrumental in the development and dissemination of the US Common Core State Standards Initiative. *The Washington Post* suggests that Common Core itself would have been impossible without the money and influence provided by the Bill and Melinda Gates Foundation, which "didn't just bankroll the development of what became known as the Common Core State Standards," but that with "more than $200 million...also built political support across the country, persuading state governments to make systemic and costly changes." Microsoft then quickly partnered with Pearson, "to load Pearson's Common Core classroom materials on Microsoft's tablet, the Surface. That product allows Microsoft to compete for school district spending with Apple, whose iPad is the dominant tablet in classrooms."[43]

Big Edu (like Big Pharma and Big Tobacco) may be an accurate way to frame the partnership between business and government with its perpetually revolving door of lobbyists-cum-policy makers-cum-millionaires-cum-billionaires. Remarkably, this massive transfer of public money into private hands has been ushered in under the banner of accountability for tax payer dollars on the one hand, and global competitiveness on the other. In an ironic twist, those in the business of education policy and the development and sale of education products that promote accountability are perhaps the least accountable education stakeholders. The transfer of public money to private charter schools illustrates this powerfully: a 2015 report from the Center for Media and Democracy suggests that the US government has spent more than three billion dollars on the charter school industry over the past 20 years, with nearly no oversight, regulation, or accountability. The report calls for a moratorium on charter funding and argues there is no adequate database detailing how these monies have been spent, or exactly just what that spending has achieved.[44] A Center for Popular Democracy Report found "fraud, waste, and abuse cases totaling over $100 million in losses to taxpayers" in just 15 US charter markets.[45] Adding insult to industry, the children of central players in the push for educational standardization (including Education Secretary Arne Duncan, President Obama, and NCLB architect and Pearson lobbyist Sandy Kress) have all attended test-exempt institutions where progressive pedagogies rule the day and teachers are free from teaching to the standardized test.[46]

Missing in Action: Teaching and Learning

As the preceding sections illustrate, the push for standardization is varied and has a complex historical trajectory. Although distinct, the various driving forces discussed here are powerfully linked and share at least one dangerously important commonality: the near-total absence of any consideration of how learning happens. Standardization has been driven by industrial, management, and market logics but absent here is the educational psychology that tells us that learning happens constructively; this is to say through interaction with others, the world around us, and with the help of teachers who know and consider the individual strengths and challenges of every student. There is a functionalism that runs through the drive for standardization, understood clearly through the human capital approach discussed earlier. Functionalism here refers to learning with only specific ends in mind; it is an approach that encourages creativity only as far as it serves a specific goal (most commonly in twenty-first-century education this goal is innovation). Missing here is exploration, learning through doing, and the idea of critical consciousness-raising through the related processes of teaching and learning.

As described in greater detail in the coming chapters, the standardization of education often reduces learning and the conditions of learning to behaviorist relationships focused on test results and thus test preparation. Understood this way, students develop test-taking habits (and teachers develop test-preparation habits) in response to the external stimuli of testing pressure, a pressure that creates the operant conditions for teaching and learning to the test as the means and the ends of student learning. Part and parcel of behaviorism in education is the notion of the tabula rasa or blank slate as the starting point for children in school. Teachers are then charged with filling in the children's blank slate. This idea was famously critiqued by Brazilian popular educator Paulo Freire, who called this the banking model of education and suggests problem-posing, or dialogue-based learning, in its place.[47] In classical Greece, for the very few who received formal education, knowledge was assessed through rhetorical methods, including what would later become known as the Socratic method of strategic dialogue: elaborate probing, questions and answer, and heuristic contemplation.

Test-oriented teaching and learning (TOTL) is not a reflection of, to use education-speak, best practice. Any teacher candidate in an education psychology course can tell you that effective teaching and learning rely on the interaction of the individual with others, with the world around the individual, and on curiosity and exploration. Indeed, the most effective learning is fuelled by intrinsic motivation (curiosity driven) rather than extrinsic motivation (driven by external rewards and punishments). This is hardly controversial stuff but in many test-focused classrooms, these simple premises are nowhere to be found. Rich, engaged, and student-led pedagogy is harder than test-driven teaching (which we might say is increasingly teacher-proof), but it is far more rewarding for teachers and students alike. In the larger perspective, with regard to NCLB, Darling-Hammond reminds us that "the United States has not shown comparable gains on international assessments of student learning since the law passed in 2001."[48] Quite simply, there is no acceptable justification for the current use of testing.

For centralized education bureaucracies, standardization may be the most efficient approach to dealing with large numbers of diverse children, relying on economies of scale, and expecting little from teachers beyond teaching to the test. And, classrooms driven by curiosity have rarely made anyone much money in the public schooling context. Regardless of how compelling these motivations for test-driven schooling might be, we should bear in mind that standardization is largely immune to research on teaching and learning with children, and is guided by organizational, structure-based, and management concerns rather than considerations of the complexities of teaching and learning.

Conclusion

The history of standardization within K-12 education in the United States and Canada is, in many ways, one of the consolidation of powers by the state, and has proceeded as a contested push-and-pull process. In the United States in particular, increased standardization has correlated with the increased influence and impact of the private sector in public schooling. It has become common sense that public education is right, is an equalizer, and that kids should be in school. Further we are asked to believe that what happens in schools is on the one hand good, and on the other beyond the understanding and thus purview of most people. This common sense is the child of conflict, however, as people have resisted a great deal along the way. We may not consider the modern-day truant officer as a state enforcer fighting public resistance to state control, but children are still legally compelled to go to school, and the upper end of the mandatory schooling age tends to go up rather than down. Skipping, dropping out, and disengagement are sometimes forms of resistance; evidence of this common sense not being so common. After well over a century of public schooling, tensions persist.

To be justified in legally requiring people to spend their childhoods in schools, government policy must at a minimum be guided by both the best interests of our children on the one hand, and by the best education research on the other. This has not always been the case as the current use ST and ST results demonstrates. ST has been a site of contestation since its inception, and it has evolved as a result of a combination of factors. The four general categories outlined here (efficiency and fairness, sorting and social hierarchy, the human capital model, and education as a market place) are in no way discrete sets of phenomena but instead intersect and interlock in various ways. On the whole, the forces driving standardization have left out much of what research tells us about child and adolescent development, as well as much of what we know about the ways in which humans learn best. Further, the voices and expertise of teachers have been routinely excluded in the development of standardized assessment policy. In the meantime, education is big business. From Pearson Education's record profits to the private tutoring companies eligible to receive NCLB funds for students attending low-performing schools, standardization has overseen a massive transfer of public money into private hands.

The history, logic, and push for ST sketched in this chapter provide by no means a full accounting of the march of educational standardization but rather an introduction that sets the stage for a deeper exploration in subsequent chapters of the impact of ST on our children, our teachers, our classrooms, and our schools. Chapter 3 turns to the changing role of standardized tests in our classrooms, schools, and teachers' professional lives, with a focus on the ways ST has in many contexts become high stakes at the student, teacher, administrator, school, district, subnational, and national levels.

CHAPTER 3

Testing at the Tipping Point: HSST as a Governing Education Principle In and Out of the Classroom

At a recent academic conference a senior Canadian scholar who has worked closely with Ontario's standardized testing body (the Education Quality and Accountability Office, EQAO) argued there were no high-stakes tests in Canada. While he was wrong (there are a few such tests, including the pass/fail literacy test in Ontario, which is a graduation requirement) it is easy to see what he meant. As discussed in the previous chapters, Canadian and US schools rarely use tests to decide whether or not a student can graduate, and when they do, there is often a great deal of support to help students reach the finish line. Increasingly, US colleges and universities are looking beyond standardized tests such as the SATs to assess applicants more holistically. The SAT Optional Movement has emerged, in part, as a result of persistent critiques from scholars citing persistent socioeconomic gaps in SAT results, suggesting a bias in favor of middle- and upper-middle-class white test takers.[1] In Canada, colleges and universities evaluate the grades and relevant experiences of applicants to many undergraduate programs, and pass/fail examinations at the end of high school are largely a thing of the past. While there is specialized testing for hopeful medical and law school students—the Medical College Application Test (MCAT) and Law School Admission Test (LSAT), respectively—these are required specifically for specialized professional degrees. A variety of standardized tests are used to measure everything from language proficiency, to swimming ability, to driving skills, to ongoing job readiness; but these tests are largely voluntary and are taken at the request of the taker, in order to achieve specific certification or employment goals. This, perhaps, is what the EQAO scholar was talking about.

How, then, can we talk about the United States and Canada as high-stakes testing environments? First of all, we are talking about very distinct national contexts. Testing has reached a fever pitch in the United States not seen in Canada. Further, at the subnational level (from jurisdiction to jurisdiction within each country), there are varying degrees of testing intensity. Tania, a first grade teacher in Los Angeles, told me in tears, that she was excited for the year-end test to be finished, so she could get "at least a few weeks of real teaching in before the year was over." Sandra, a third grade teacher in Toronto, suggested that teachers had not "been thrown into a boiling pot of high-stakes testing water" but instead that the "temperature seems to be changing all around us" and that "sometimes [teachers] find [themselves] teaching to the test without even realizing it." For some of the Canadian context, standardized testing (ST) results are increasingly important but are not yet an overwhelming quotidian pressure in most schools or for most teachers. The inverse holds true in the United States with, for many teachers, a daily concentration on teaching to and for the test, interrupted (certain times of the year, certain units, certain conversations, etc.) by opportunities to approach teaching and learning as exploration, as dialogue, and as potentially student-led endeavors. Although the temperature of the water varies from country to country and from region to region, things tend, with a few exceptions, to be getting warmer all over as evidenced and driven by a variety of factors. It is thus from this larger picture, not one particular make-or-break test, that the idea of high stakes comes in as far as the US and Canadian education contexts.

This chapter focuses on the ways ST is increasingly a governing, and thus high-stakes, factor in education, impacting life and learning in and out of the classroom. The chapter begins with a look at what Ruth Powers Silverberg and Arnold Dodge refer to as the "interactive processes" of normalization, simplification, and conflation as far as the way ST has become an accepted and required measure of what is happening in our education systems.[2] The chapter then takes up the way these processes play out in the related but distinct domains of students, teachers, administrators, boards, subnational jurisdictions, and national jurisdictions.

The Architecture of High Stakes

Student test scores are at the core of the accountability mandate in education, be it under the auspices of proving taxpayer money is well spent or of ensuring international competitiveness and labor-market readiness. The standardized test provides the easiest metric for understanding educational success and failure in comparative perspective. While education has always been contentious—has always had people inside and out fighting to change it in one way or another—the standardization movement begun in the late twentieth century has driven education reform that is unprecedented in its scope, depth, and pace. To wit, never have things changed so much, so quickly, particularly in the United States. Education researchers Arnold Dodge and Ruth Powers Silverberg suggest high-stakes testing produces, "conditions in which all that is taught and learned is dictated by reductive assessments, both inhibiting the goals of public education and nurturing corporate interests, rendering improvement of schooling for all children unlikely."[3] This sea change has relied upon the production and maintenance of specific ways of thinking. Dodge and Powers Silverberg narrow this down to three specific phenomena: normalization, simplification, and conflation.

Normalization

In broad strokes, normalization refers to society becoming accustomed to ST as a common occurrence in education, and as an integral and reliable measure for the teaching and learning that happens in schools. The norm is tacitly acceptable and is value laden, making that which breaches the norm unacceptable. The use of norm-referenced standardized tests creates definitive expectations as well: students meeting and exceeding state/provincial standards require no remediation—as if their learning is on pause until everyone else catches up—while those whose results are subpar are brought up to the prescribed norm. The focus on test scores normalizes specific curricular focuses as well, including a focus on language and mathematics (and sometimes science) to the exclusion of other subjects.[4] In the United States, this narrow metric is increasingly used to assess teachers, schools, and districts.

Simplification

Testing results provide easy answers to complex questions. The discourse of simplification in education provides shortcuts for understanding what is good and bad, what is right and wrong, and what is working and what is not. Dodge and Powers Silverberg observe: "We look to the numbers, the percentages, and the rankings to answer our most mysterious and ineffable dilemmas...Simple answers become even more powerful if they are readily available," which, they suggest, lead to quick and misguided "short cuts" in our thinking and understanding.[5] Simplification also relies on seemingly palpable or self-evident normative truths (things that, obviously, should be true). These might include assertions that there is nothing wrong with students learning the basics, or questions about ensuring literacy-for-all as an untouchable, near holy goal. These are ideas with which it is nearly impossible to disagree. However, when bandied about without a close look at how these goals are best achieved (or how they are or are not being achieved currently) or without considering the cost of focusing on one thing over another, they dangerously serve a discourse of simplification that silences an informed conversation, invoking instead a seductive knee jerk engagement with education.

The simplification discourse relies, as well, upon a total disregard for context. What works in one instance will not necessarily work in another; this applies to individual students and groups of students, to individual teachers and groups of teachers, and to individual schools as well as groups of schools. Informed by the premise of simplification, individual occurrences—of either success or failure—are applied as rules for other contexts, with little concern for the countless contextual barriers that impact teaching and learning, including social, cultural, economic, language-based, and geographic realities.

Conflation

Conflation refers to an assumed validity. This third element identified by Dodge and Powers Silverberg relies on normalization and simplification. Embedded in the notion of accountability, test scores provide a measure with which to legitimize or delegitimize schools, teachers, students, and sometimes even communities. Informed by what seems normal and by what appears easiest to recognize, it is understandable that public perceptions of schooling are often dominated by the belief that standardized test results are measures of student achievement, learning, and success/failure. The most obvious expression of this is found in the linking of test scores with individual school success (and in some cases, school viability) that has impacts everywhere, from school choice movements to real estate prices. Conflation relies on the premise (for which there is insufficient evidence) that standardized tests measure students objectively, and that norm-referenced measures and their results are being used in a valid way, measuring what they were designed to measure. From considerations of the persistent concerns about test results and social inequality, to the hundreds of cheating scandals we have seen across the United States, to the outright disregard for context, the presumed validity of standardized tests is unfounded.

Even for those of us who do not support widespread ST, it is very difficult not to ascribe meaning to the results of ST, particularly when we see test scores rise. Dodge and Powers Silverberg argue that the positive responses from all involved when test scores increase, provide clear evidence of this conflation. They argue: "implicit in [interpreting student] reading score improvement is that students have improved in reading when in fact what they have done is improved in taking a reading test."[6] They go on to suggest, "there is no evidence to support that a reading test measures the construct of reading" and they ask us to consider instead: "Will our students enjoy reading more, want to expand their reading horizons, use reading as a tool to understand other disciplines?"[7] Simplification and conflation are disturbed by the complex, hard-to-measure, and impossible-to-measure features of literacy learning. This brings us back to the discourse of normalization and the widespread expectation of total measurability all of the time. In our current test-driven education context, the unknowable has become the unacceptable. Those who challenge this paradigm, particularly teachers, are often marginalized and can face significant professional risk for speaking out. Ironically, teachers' professional skills and knowledge hold the key for useful and rich assessment of the most nuanced elements of teaching and learning.

In Ontario, students must successfully complete a tenth grade literacy test in order to graduate. An academic who works for the Ontario testing body EQAO once asked me, "Do you really object to making sure every graduate is able to read?" Justifying the test when it was introduced, Ontario Minister of Education, Janet Ecker, proclaimed in 2001, "It is important that students in Ontario have strong reading and writing skills."[8] A bold statement indeed; and no one wants a generation of illiterate high school graduates. This implies of course that there was a crisis in literacy up to this point. It also neglects the fact that Ontario high school students complete a minimum of four full English or French courses, each of which provides three formal reports on student ability and progress. Additionally, Ontario students take social science, history, geography, and other language-intense and language-dependent courses throughout their four years of high school. There are several existing, curriculum-based opportunities for ensuring students are literate, for fostering strong reading and writing skills, and for measuring this learning with low-stakes assessments.

Thus, the powerful rhetoric of simple ideas can cloud our understanding of these issues, and the three-part frame developed by Dodge and Powers Silverberg provides a useful backdrop against which to understand the notion of high-stakes testing as a governing principle in and out of the classroom. Guided by this frame, the following sections focus on the general impacts of ST in the related but distinct domains of students; teachers; schools and school boards; and regional, national, and international levels.

High Stakes for Students

Among the most immediate impacts of educational standardization for students is the increased classroom time spent on test preparation and test taking, alongside a curriculum which itself is increasingly test-focused. The narrowed curricular focus is also meaningful for many students whose favorite parts of school might include physical education, history, social studies, and other less-tested content areas which are frequently pushed aside by test-oriented teaching and learning (TOTL). Many students enjoy and gravitate toward the areas in which they have success. Narrower content under TOTL can mean reduced opportunities for individual student success. The same holds true for teaching and learning strategies. When testing drives instruction, it also inevitably drives instructional methods, so in addition to time spent on some things in place of others, pedagogy itself is narrowed. Rote learning and what many call drill and kill replace project-based exploratory approaches, to the detriment of students who benefit from varied teaching and learning strategies.

Midway through this study, I was sitting in a high school staffroom drinking coffee with eight English teachers on a cold spring day in Toronto. That morning, nearly 150,000 tenth graders across Ontario were scheduled to write the provincial literacy test. A spring snow storm had rolled in, which would eventually cost the government thousands to reschedule for students who couldn't make it because of inclement weather. Tom, a 20-year veteran teacher was wearing a two-way radio in order to communicate with the other test coordinators. It chirped on his lapel and a crackled voice reported: "Ryan's father is in front of the main doors." After pulling on his hat, coat, and boots, Tom ran to the car parked in front of the school to pick up the package. Ryan, a struggling student who had failed the literacy test once before, had forgotten his lucky hat. Although talking is frowned upon during the test, he had flagged an invigilator and reported the forgotten hat. Teachers quickly rallied to get in touch with the father, and in under an hour, Ryan had his lucky hat. At this large outer urban high school, hats are forbidden most days as they render closed-circuit surveillance less effective when they obscure the faces of students.

A few weeks later, in much nicer weather, I was sitting in an elementary classroom in South Los Angeles, speaking at length with a new teacher about ST and her student community when she was called to the office to meet a delivery person. She asked if I'd mind giving her a hand with a few boxes. The boxes were light—full of nut-free chocolate wafers donated by a local bodega whose owner's children attended the school. These were for students to eat on test days—stored in plain sight to build excitement. I was there two weeks later when the juice was delivered (those cases were heavier). Some teachers eschewed the juice and snacks, instead providing lemon water and chewing gum in order to promote mental acuity, a practice found in Ontario as well. A high school teacher in North Hollywood made coffee for his students but provided no snacks. Be it a lucky hat that on any other day would be confiscated, or eating and chewing gum in class, which might normally land a child in detention, testing days are exceptional for students.

Teachers don't usually act like this. In the operation of a school, testing days are standalone occasions when everything else comes to a halt, a reality not lost on students. Snacks and chewing gum are indeed at the positive end of the spectrum here but the classifications that emerge are of course no picnic for anyone. Although norm-referenced tests are designed to rank, not rate, they are often used to do both. Individual students are often accountable for their low results on standardized tests, particularly in the United States, and high-scoring students are often made invisible by virtue of their successes (they no longer need to be worried about). As far as comparative ranking via ST results, students are ground zero of a large-scale competition. Figure 3.1 shows student test results posted in a Los Angeles elementary classroom.

While the teacher in this classroom did his best to encourage students to work toward individual goals (asking C students to hit a C+ and B+ students to shoot for an A-) the children nonetheless were ranked and rated publicly, and ranked from lowest to highest. The message is clear: students are being compared to one another and are competing against one another. Most teachers do not post scores publicly; however, in many cases, this is not required for students to feel the pressure of ST. Beyond the comparisons and implicit competition with classmates, other classes, other schools, and even districts, the act of writing tests

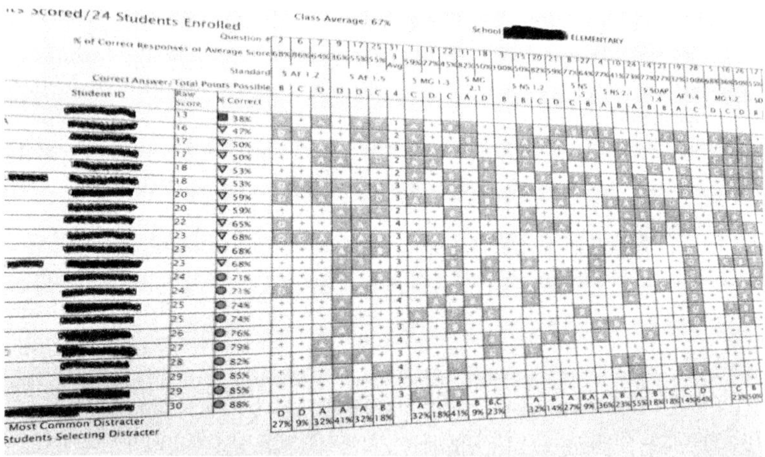

58 • The Pedagogy of Standardized Testing

Figure 3.1 Student standardized test results posted in a Los Angeles elementary classroom.

has become the single most important thing a child does as a student in many US schools. While learning and development in areas that have largely eluded ST such as citizenship education, cooperation, and leadership are important, students rise and fall on the tests they take. The lower performing the school, the higher the stakes for the kids charged with turning things around. At its most impactful, schooling defines for students their worth and place in society in relation to their peers.

Of course, these are not the only impacts of schooling in the lives of many kids. Students can come to self-define according to a host of false paradigms delivered year after year by school: it teaches them whether or not they are smart (or school smart), whether or not they are math people, language people, social people, whether or not they march to the beat of their own drum or someone else's, and whether or not they are university-caliber individuals. In the age of standardization, schools increasingly figure kids out—they understand and communicate the answers to these questions—through the questions and answers of standardized tests. Indeed, many students do not get the supports they need (be it learning accommodations or modifications[9]) until test time rolls in. Whether we think this is good (at least they are getting help) or bad (why do we have to wait this long?), it is powerful evidence of the high-stakes nature of standardized tests. One Chicago teacher explains, "In Chicago, third grade students who do not pass the [Illinois Standard Achievement Test] do not pass 3rd grade, it's summer school or retention." One Toronto teacher suggests this pressure impacts parents' decisions as well, commenting: "Many parents send their children to school even if they are sick, because of the test scheduled."

One very common phenomenon in many so-called low-performing schools is to build community around the overall school test results. For students, testing pressure is not confined to the classroom. For many schools in California, the Academic Performance Index (API) and/or the Annual Yearly Progress (AYP) scores are at the center of school life. From school songs based on raising the score, to daily recitations of a school-wide promise to improve results, children at many schools have a hard time missing the significance of testing. As discussed further in Chapter 6, higher-performing schools often do not center school life around the test to the same degree as schools where test scores are lower. Intensive test preparation is often the mark of a struggling school, and for many teachers, an indicator of a place where work is harder and less rewarding than that at schools that engage in relatively little test preparation. This holds true for teachers and students alike. Privileged communities and their schools can experience lower amounts of pressure and less need to formally teach to the test. Rigorous TOTL can thus be a mark of disadvantage. Testing, and TOTL specifically, thus hit low-income and racially minoritized communities harder and more deeply than more advantaged contexts. Advantaged parents may thus fail to recognize the broader impacts of testing. Nadra, a 14th-year teacher in a fairly well-off school in Los Angeles, explains:

> [I]t's sad to say but if they aren't testing gifted here, and this is a chill school, they won't get into the magnet middle and high schools in the surrounding areas and will be forced to go to the schools with lower test scores where they do test prep 24-seven.

Test preparation is a negative consequence here, a move from an advantaged educational context, to a disadvantaged educational context. Indeed, among the teachers with whom I spoke, there was a consistent correlation between high results and low pressure, as well as the inverse of low results and high pressure.

High Stakes for Teachers

Teachers are in the unique position of knowing what their students are missing when testing dominates schools and classrooms. Many veteran teachers who can remember teaching before the age of standardization are clear on the differences between now and then; however, even new teachers are often conscious of the gaps between what they learn in university teacher training programs and the daily expectations of the twenty-first-century classroom teacher. While the chasm between theory and practice predates the standardization movement, this gap has rarely been so wide or so clearly defined by one issue. Mandatory attention to testing often flies in the face of good teaching; of using diverse planning, instructional, and assessment strategies. There may be kindergarten teachers out there who feel their students are well-served by norm-referenced, bubble-test, multiple-choice examinations, but I have not met one. Whether or not teachers have read the research suggesting it is developmentally inappropriate for children under nine to write standardized examinations, most recognize the tests' limited utility for understanding and assessing their students, and know that pressure to bring up test scores can take time away from other activities that are important for children's learning and overall development.

With the time crunch comes a narrowed curricular focus. This overall contraction of time and content is not a simple replacement of the old ways with the new. Instead, teachers are asked to do more (often with less) and add test preparation to an already packed agenda. As discussed in Chapter 7, teachers who manage to teach critical consciousness, to use exploration and student knowledge in their classrooms, and whose pedagogy is based in dialogue rather than rote memorization, are often only able to achieve these goals after their class test scores are attended to. These teachers (often single, without childcare responsibilities, and relatively young) frequently work 70- and 80-hour weeks—an impossible standard to sustain over the course of a career. Teachers lucky enough to have the time, knowledge, ability, and an enabling teaching environment are thus often left with a choice: be superhuman or underserve their students.

As a teacher educator, former teacher, and parent, I am among the first to demand great things of our teachers. High expectations of teachers necessarily precede high expectations of students. However, just as our expectations of students need to be clear and reasonable, so too must those we have of our teachers. There is a dangerous rhetoric within many fields of education (including assessment, equity and inclusion, curriculum studies, and others) to define good teaching through a laundry list of demands with no consideration for how teachers will accomplish the myriad tasks required to serve their students. Although professional development and training cannot be overlooked as central to supporting successful teacher practice, the gap is not always one of knowledge, but rather frequently one of time and space to do the work needed to serve all students. A recent mental health initiative in Canada illustrates this dynamic. Recognizing a widespread crisis in youth mental health and wellness, one provincial Ministry of Education mandated online training and launched a series of mental health–focused professional development sessions for teachers in which participants were taught about the signs of particular mental health issues facing students. While it was good information, much of it was contained in documents that the teachers had already received. The issue for many teachers was not an inability to identify the signs of anxiety or depression; nor was it one of not knowing what to do to support students exhibiting these signs. Instead, teachers struggled (and continue to struggle) with inadequate time and resources to provide the planning, instructional, and assessment modifications required to support students in crisis. Beyond the classroom, teachers have trouble helping students get the help they need in the face of inadequate availability of guidance counsellors, school psychologists, social workers, and other (largely itinerant) support personnel at schools.

Standardization is by no means the root of all education dysfunction, but it powerfully compounds and intensifies issues in already struggling systems, adding to an already heavy burden for teachers. While it is easy to suggest that a good teacher can meet (and even raise) standards while simultaneously attending to his work as unofficial social justice advocate, psychologist, nutritional expert, education technology specialist, assessment specialist, etc., this is both unrealistic and unreasonable. In the face of this trade-off, many teachers are understandably pragmatic, choosing test preparation over other concerns, a choice not of their making, and not taken lightly for most. Indeed, being recognized for high test scores is hardly a career goal for many teachers. One Chicago teacher describes part of the rewards system for teachers at his school:

> The assessment is on my mind the entire year because that is the focus of all of our staff development. The focus is analyzing test data. Therefore my curriculum and instruction are contaminated with assessments. We are recognized and rewarded with t-shirts not just at a staff meeting, but at a school assembly with students present. How humiliating is that!

As standardized test scores are increasingly used to assess teacher competency (and even teacher value), a disincentive emerges to teaching students whose scores may sully one's professional reputation and, in many US states and local jurisdictions, even reduce pay and limit professional advancement opportunities (a proposition supported by only a small number in Canada).[10] One Chicago teacher explains:

> In the past, I've spent very little time on test prep and was adamantly against teaching to the test. However, beginning next school year, test results will be tied into teacher evaluations, so I may have to reevaluate how I feel.

Testing is increasingly a nexus in which the pressure facing teachers joins that facing students. Another Chicago teacher explains:

> Too much time must be devoted to test prep—I have tried it both ways and my students do not perform as well when I eliminate test prep. Their test results are used to screen them for selective enrollment high schools so the scores are important to the students. The test results are used in my evaluation so good results are also important to me.

On a broader scale, this gives some teachers a powerful reason to stay away from low-performing schools, and as a result, from schools that disproportionately serve low-income and racially minoritized students. At its darkest, the pressure of standardization has given us cheating scandals across the United States. These scandals, however, are merely the visible tip of the high-stakes iceberg, a phenomenon taken up further in Chapter 6.

This focus on testing is happening, for teachers, against the backdrop of their professional knowledge and expertise, which, for many, tells them this is not the right direction for education generally, or for the students they teach each day. As professional development is increasingly focused on interpreting and improving test results, teachers are directed away from the important professional learning required to stay current and engaged as a career teacher. Such non-test-oriented learning for teachers might be guided by interest; however, it may also be guided by teacher and administrator identifications of weak spots for which teachers need further professional development. That teacher voices are nearly absent from the conversation further marginalizes teachers as professionals (nearly all professional teacher organizations in the United States and Canada have come out against the current regime of ST). Indeed, the EQAO scholar mentioned earlier warned me about the limits of this study, cautioning that I could not trust teachers when it came to understanding what was happening in the classroom.

Even when salary and advancement are not linked to test scores, many teachers nonetheless face pressure.[11] In Los Angeles and New York City, test scores are linked to teachers' full names and are routinely published in the popular press. As detailed in Chapter 5, teachers in the United States report an increasingly strained relationship with parents as the home–school relationship is increasingly focused on testing preparation and results. In his important work on the impact of ST on education, James Popham traces the negative correlation between public support for teachers and increased ST;[12] findings that are further fleshed out by this study in Chapter 5.

High Stakes for Schools and School Boards

The preceding sections have introduced the high-stakes impacts of standardization on the schooling lives of students and teachers, respectively. This section turns to schools, boards, and education jurisdictions. The notion of high stakes does not rise and fall on one test, but rather emerges through the atmospherics of daily life in schools (as is the case with students and teachers). Schools and school boards face very high stakes when it comes to educational standardization. At its most extreme in the United States, the underlying pressure exerted by standardization (the elephant in the corridor) is the fight of public schools and boards for the right to exist as funded public entities that provide equitable education guided by respected, well-educated, and well-paid professionals. This struggle proceeds on two fronts.

First, within our YouTube tutorial-rich universe, it is easy to think of teaching and learning as activities reducible to instructional videos—it is easy to confuse our ability to pause, jump back, jump ahead, restart, and even take a test at the end, with a conversation. This is the Khan Academy model in which education consumers choose what they want to learn, when, and at what pace. There are tremendous opportunities here, and we are just beginning to understand the potential of this approach. Two interesting examples are the flipped classroom approach and the explosion of massive open online courses (MOOCs) offered by universities, often at no charge, to students around the world (enrollment in a 2011 MOOC at Stanford exceeded 160,000). While education will no doubt continue to be powerfully impacted by technology, instructional-video-culture runs the risk of convincing many that education is a simple consumer-driven deposit of knowledge into an empty vessel. Implicit here is the idea that teaching itself may be an outdated activity and schools and boards represent an outdated, increasingly irrelevant and expensive behemoth. As venture capitalists set their sights on education, edupreneurs are busily imagining schemes that may one day do for schooling what Uber did for transportation and Airbnb did for accommodations. While the behemoth argument is tough to reasonably counter, missing of course are the complexities of teaching and learning (the social pieces, the mentorship, the professional knowledge, and judgment). Although schooling certainly needs to be more adaptive, there is a much greater difference between a how-to video and a learning-rich classroom, than there is between an Uber ride and a trip in a taxi.

The second and related way in which public schools and boards fight for their lives is through the constant threat of privatization and quasi-privatization. The proliferation of charter schools in the United States is, in many instances, radically undermining the viability of their public school counterparts. Charter schools are subject to fewer regulations than regular schools, and can run as for-profit businesses. While there may be some important lessons to be learned from the myriad approaches we see in charter schools across the United States, research suggests charters may not get the best out of our teachers.[13] Teachers at charters are for the most part insecure workers. Just seven percent of charter schools are unionized and charters have relatively low retention rates; on average, almost 20 percent lower than those for public schools.[14] In the United States, many public schools thus compete with private and quasi-private firms for the government's education business (and confidence). This threat is far from rhetorical. In 2014, Netflix CEO Reed Hastings called for the elimination of elected school boards,[15] while post–Katrina New Orleans created the country's first all-charter school district in 2014/2015.[16] In the some US jurisdictions, schools can be closed due to persistent low test results on standardized tests, even in cases where there is widespread improvement on test scores. In California and many other states, so-called parent-trigger policies have been passed, which, with a simple majority of parent signatures collected, can allow for low-performing schools to be retooled with all staff replaced, to be closed and reopened after what amounts to an auctioning of the school, to be privatized outright, or to be closed entirely. This is a key entry point for charter schools, as the local school board cannot always afford to reestablish the school it has just lost. Although these are extreme scenarios, many schools whose test scores remain low live in the constant shadow of imminent seizure, closure, and/or privatization.

Nearly half of US schools are deemed Title One, which refers to federal government funds available to schools in which at least 40 percent of students come from low-income families.[17] According to the US Department of Education (DOE), Title One funding "is designed to help students served by the program to achieve proficiency on challenging State academic achievement standards" and they can be withheld if schools do not meet these criteria.[18] These state standards are most commonly measured on standardized tests, meaning that most US schools rely on test results to maintain funding essential to supporting low-income students.

Testing thus sorts schools as well as students and teachers. At the 2014 American Education Research Association (the world's largest education association and conference), Mark Gleason (director of the Philadelphia School Partnership, which is leading the charter movement in that city) suggested that "losers" (schools with low state standard performance) be "dumped" in favor of charter options.[19]

This is only one example of the countless comparative measurements performed to rate schools using standardized measures. Schools, and by extension boards and jurisdictions, are marked as good or bad—are valued or devalued—according to the test, leaving school leaders to struggle for both their professional lives and the lives of their schools. One Toronto teacher explains the way these pressures impact administration and ultimately student well-being:

> In Ontario, when a student does not write the EQAO, and he or she does not have an official exemption, a mark of zero is entered and it brings the overall score down. My principal has made kids write who should not be writing—they have been crying, shaking, or are new students without special education or ESL [English as a Second Language] designations and the test is a monster for them to write—they could easily get an exemption with more time but they haven't. He'll say, "just write in something, whatever you can, fill in the space" all to avoid the zero mark.

Importantly, this behavior comes in the Ontario context, where test results do not impact school funding or teacher tenure. These are the conditions that, of course, impact all education stakeholders: conditions that on the one hand implicitly demand a narrowed curriculum and classroom time spent increasingly on test preparation, and on the other hand lead to the test-score–oriented school songs, mascots, and recitations mentioned earlier. This creates environments in which the central point of connection and coalescence is the pursuit of higher test scores. For school leaders, as the example above illustrates, this can color interaction with students, teachers, and even parents (getting them on board). These are unenviable tasks as many teachers and students may actively and passively resist standardization in multiple ways. Further, at least one study suggests, "parents of public school students in states with more extensive and stringent student assessment systems express lower trust in government and more negative views of their children's schools," suggesting the job of school leaders is that much more challenging and the impact of ST that much more profound.[20]

High Stakes at the Regional, National, and International Levels

The high-stakes pressure of testing is, predictably, not confined to students, teachers, schools, and boards. In the United States, complex regulation of education makes for stakeholders at the federal, state, and municipal levels, while in Canada, each province and territory is a distinct education jurisdiction (on some international ratings, Canada is a collection of subnational regions). While policy makers and education leaders at the municipal, state, and provincial/territorial levels are often the architects and promoters of standardization, these ideas can be contested and complicated in these spaces as well. It is through the complex web of governors, special advisors, chancellors, superintendents, commissioners, trustees, state boards, state departments, supervisory officers, and other education leaders (some elected and some appointed) that education policy and practice are directed. For the most part, these are intensely political positions, with many folks bringing specific ideological concerns and positions to the table. These spaces can also provide entry points for corporate influence on educational standardization; from policy makers with connections to testing companies, to lobbyists working directly for education companies, to direct campaign contributions at the municipal and state levels, as described in the previous chapter.

Test scores, widespread and comparative, have been important tools for politics and politicians. Scores can powerfully support the rhetoric of accountability and they can appear to both illustrate and solve problems. The incumbent politician proudly declares that literacy rates have improved ten percent under her stewardship, while the outraged challenger points out that 30 percent of children still cannot pass a basic proficiency test. Parties promising change rely on education reform to articulate and define policy, and ST results are among the most convenient and communicable metric. We see Dodge and Powers Silverberg's frame of normalization, simplification, and conflation playing out in public discourse on education—an arena in which politicians angle for position using sound-bite–sized pieces of information geared for maximum efficiency and minimum unpacking. Successful politicians often rely on the simplest messages, and when it comes to education, accuracy be damned, testing results are about as simple as it gets. Education bureaucrats are left with the task of implementing reform (often with the guidance and assistance of corporate partners) until the next big thing comes along.

The seeming immunity of state, provincial, and municipal education leaders to the widespread opposition to standardization testing by teachers and teacher associations (detailed further in Chapter 7) illustrates a depth of commitment to standardization. Holding fast in the face of academic and professional evidence (both anecdotal and empirical), many jurisdictions have pushed ahead, while some in Canada, for example, have pulled back. For those who forge ahead, and in the United States, the Common Core State Standards Initiative (CCSSI) may make it very hard not to, friction with teachers and teacher associations only intensifies. Additionally, despite the political value of testing, widespread parent pushback is occurring. The path to standardization is thus fraught with costs and contradictions, yet it is the only way forward for many education leaders. Put another way, there are potential political points to be scored for anti-testing politicians yet we see a widespread resolve to push ahead. This speaks to just how significant, how high-stakes, this issue is, and it extends beyond the state level.

The central role of the US federal government adds another dimension to educational standardization. Beginning in earnest in the late 1950s, as described in Chapter Two, Washington has played an increasingly central role in education systems across the United States. While Title One funding is instrumental in the standardization of nearly half of all US schools, No Child Left Behind, Race to the Top, and most recently Common Core have cemented the influence of the federal government in almost every US public school classroom. This is not a libertarian critique but instead an illustration of the latest and most powerful structure for promoting standardization. Common Core steers pedagogy, content, and assessment, as well as directs teacher training, certification, and remuneration. The driving force for much of Common Core is ST. While the ideological and corporate push and pull which happens federally runs parallel to that at the state and municipal levels, the national reach of federal funding incentivizes standardization at the state level. So, although these subnational jurisdictions direct policy they also (like teachers, schools, and boards) are guided by policy and politics from above. These policy and politics in turn, are often guided by international comparative ST.

Standardization has become a high-stakes game on a global scale. While change in education is famously slow, few things get policy makers swinging into action faster than worsening test scores on the Programme for International Student Assessment (PISA) test. This international comparative measure run by the Organization for Economic Cooperation and Development (OECD) is the global benchmark for national (and with cases such as Canada and China, subnational) education performance. When math results from the United States dropped in 2009, panic set in from the Secretary of Education right up to US president Obama. In his response to the scores, Duncan argued:

> President Obama has repeatedly warned that the nation that "out-educates us today will out-compete us tomorrow." And the PISA results, to be brutally honest, show that a host of developed nations are out-educating us... And the jewel of China's education system, Shanghai, debuted this year as the highest scoring participant globally.[21]

We see here, the idea of competition at the core of human capital theory in education, as well as the idea of winners (jewels) and by necessity losers. Secretary Duncan went on to mention the high-performer nations, suggesting "Finland, Korea, and Canada are consistent high-performers."[22] Ironically, Canada had in fact slipped in math that year, and school leaders and the popular press were busy with their own panic north of the border—a process that would repeat itself after the release of the 2012 PISA results when Canada slipped out of the top ten in math scores internationally.[23] Canada, today, remains a panicked top performer. Although PISA is considered by many to be a progressive test measuring twenty-first-century skills,[24] it is also the primary example of high stakes for subnational and national stakeholders. In addition to garnering prestige, PISA results can also be linked to Word Bank education project funding.[25]

Conclusion and Implications

That our current epoch is one of high-stakes standardization is evident in the multiple elements (large and small) that make up education systems at the national, regional, board, school, teacher, student, and in some cases, parent levels. Taken as a whole, the sum is greater than the parts. The significance of these myriad factors, when taken together, is that ST has become a high-stakes endeavor, even in the absence in some cases, of specific tests which make or break a student's or teacher's career. The preceding sections sketch the emergence of a new governing principle for understanding student, teacher, and school achievement based on ST—a radical and unprecedented transformation in North America.

The interconnection between the spheres described earlier is also important. The realities of one group overlap and intersect with those of another, with multiple groups mutually informing each other. When the 2012 PISA results were released in Ontario, they were read in conjunction with province-wide ST results in mathematics of grades three and six students. The Ontario Ministry of Education rolled out new training for teachers; my university introduced a diagnostic mathematics test upon entry into our teacher education program for all elementary panel students; and for the popular press, the education sky was indeed falling (one headline in Ontario's paper of record read "Math: Number One Problem for Ontario School Boards").[26] Here, the global meets the provincial, to impact teachers and ultimately students. This is an instance as well of testing driving instruction, rather than the reverse. These norm-referenced measures give a comparison (rank) but not an overall picture of what students know or have learned in relation to what is taught.

Before moving on, it bears repeating that US and Canadian contexts are vastly different when it comes to high stakes and standardization. While jurisdictions such as Ontario appear, for now, committed to enhanced and more far-reaching use of ST (and of the results of ST) this is still a far cry from the situation in many US contexts. Other parts of Canada are far less committed than Ontario, and the notion of high stakes does not apply in quite the same way. In rough terms, Canadian education has pockets of high-stakes testing within an otherwise largely low-stakes landscape; while in the United States, low-stakes environments are the exception with an otherwise high-stakes education terrain.

This work now turns to the voices of teachers from the Teachers and Testing Study, as well as to other relevant research to unpack the effects of standardization on our education systems. Guided by US and Canadian teachers, the coming chapters look more deeply at the issues raised here. Chapter 4 looks closely at classroom trends and the TOTL identified earlier, while Chapter 5 looks at the changing nature of teachers work. Chapter 6 focuses on questions of accuracy and ST, as well as the equity impacts of standardization for students and teachers.

CHAPTER 4

Revising the Pedagogical Form: Test-Oriented Teaching and Learning

Introduction

I walked into Eddy's[1] classroom at just after 7 a.m. on a Monday morning. I thanked him for seeing me before class; for taking the time out of a busy day, week, and month to talk about his professional life and practice. We spent the next few moments standing on chairs, opening one large white-framed window after another, until we had let in enough cool morning air that I had to put my jacket back on. "By midmorning, it'll be very warm in here, and other than lunch, my guys won't be going anywhere today." When I asked why, he told me, "all testing all the time; math and science until the end of the week, that's it." We had dinner that evening, the temperature had dropped again, and I asked if he had spent the day inside as he suspected. He had, and would do the same for the remainder of the week.

In broad strokes, Chapter 3 explored the landscape of high-stakes standardized testing (HSST) at the student, teacher, school, district, subnational (state and provincial), and national levels. This chapter details daily life in the high-stakes classroom and, in particular, the way teachers' classroom practices are impacted intentionally and unintentionally as they grapple with high-stakes testing. This chapter explores the shifting relations between teachers, students, the objects of learning, and the often reactive pedagogical consequences of HHST as one of the central focuses of teaching and learning. In general, administering a greater number of standardized tests tends to correspond to greater pedagogical response from teachers, including adjustments and adaptations of various kinds. Teacher practice is also impacted by past, present, and future school test scores; by the role of testing at their schools in general; and by the challenges and opportunities experienced by students inthe classroom.

Concerns that assessment drives instruction (rather than the reverse) have long been raised by educators and parents under the banner of quips such as "tests not worth teaching to" or "you get what you test," and it is no secret that teaching to and for the test happens often, when standardized tests are involved. Too often absent from this conversation is an analysis of what this looks and feels like for teachers from day to day. Pedagogy is a process of assertion and contestation, of trial and error, a dialogue facilitated by reflection and hard work. It is also, as the teachers we hear from here indicate, a profoundly adaptable and iterative process of doing and redoing, thinking and rethinking, and of being unexpectedly disappointed and thrilled in perhaps equal measure.

This chapter takes a look at pedagogical revision—this adaptation—under the weight of standardized testing—with a focus on four phenomena. First, it looks at the chronological crunch presented by high-stakes standardized testing (ST) in a profession whose most precious commodity has long been time. Teachers struggle to meet instructional demands (implicit and explicit) of the test, while attending to the untested areas of the formal (physical and health education, social studies, art) and informal (mental health, inclusion) aspects of the curriculum. Second, this chapter takes up the contraction of the curriculum, both the breadth and depth of what is taught, in the face of the often narrow focus and format of standardized tests. Third, teaching to the test often means teaching the knowledge and skills needed to succeed on tests, as opposed to teaching the knowledge and skills that a test aims to measure. This can result in the use of a limited variety of teaching and learning strategies, which may exclude dynamic planning, instruction, and assessment strategies that do little to prepare students for standardized tests. Fourth, many teachers routinely participate in practices they do not support and which they recognize are not in the best interests in their students. Many students face tremendous pressure in high-stakes testing environments and whether or not they feel they can do anything about it, good teachers recognize the struggles of their students. This final section takes up teacher perceptions of the pressure facing students and the cost as teachers see it, to student learning and well-being.

When Things Go Missing: Classroom Time and High-Stakes Standardized Testing

I returned to Eddy's classroom each morning for the rest of the week and got pretty good at hoisting the sticky windows without being asked. Each day I mentioned how grateful I was for his time, particularly given the crunch he was facing preparing his students for the upcoming standardized test. When we finally sat down for our final interview it was the first thing I said. Eddy replied: "It's no problem. It actually opens up my life. I don't mark as much, planning is absolutely minimal right now, and even when I see fires that need putting out, I can't really do it if I want to. It's not really teaching." Thinking back to my own time as a high school teacher, I knew what he meant. Although I never administered or prepared students for a standardized test, examination periods were among the easiest times of year, characterized by relatively minimal preparation and time to catch up on marking. For me, like Eddy, testing had the potential to be distinct from teaching.

Chapter 1 provided an overview of the time spent on test preparation and administration. While there are reports in the United States of 60–80 school days per year spent on testing (upward of 35 percent of the school year), the Teachers and Testing Study as well as other research put this figure more commonly between 10 and 20 percent of classroom time spent on standardized test preparation, with more time correlating to more tests administered, in both Canada and the United States. Conversations with teachers flesh out this time crunch as far as its impacts in the classroom. Teachers in Toronto primarily cited standardized testing (ST) as a time issue leading up to the Education Quality and Accountability Office (EQAO) tests (written in May and/or early June each year) in grades three, six, and ten. Although Ontario has a grade nine mathematics standardized test, it conforms closely to what is already taught and just as importantly, what is already evaluated at that time of year—in some cases, it is almost a repeat of portions of the final examination. Unlike the grades three, six, and ten standardized tests, the grade nine test can be counted toward the students' final grade, a point EQAO encourages teachers to share with their students.[2] Teachers in Los Angeles were impacted more deeply throughout the school year.

Sirin, a sixth grade teacher in his 12th year of teaching at South Central Elementary, sums up the situation, saying: "look, four or five years ago things were different, but now if it's not on the CST, I cannot justify teaching it when [the assistant principal] walks into my room—we're a PI school." The CST is the California Standards Test, on which Sirin's school has underperformed by state standards since the test's inception. "PI school" refers to the low Program Improvement status of his school (a designation the school has had for years despite consistent annual gains). Sirin continues, "I was actually told I could start a history club to teach history because [the assistant principal] knew I had studied that stuff and thought it would be great for our kids." The proposed club was to happen outside of class time. Rosie (a second grade teacher in her tenth year of teaching at Southern Elementary) had started Fitness Thursdays when she noticed physical activity was being sidelined for the daily 30–60 minutes of test prep recommended by the principal. "The kids are bursting at the seams if they don't get to move—it's worse around test time so we get together Thursdays, I pump out old school hip hop and I get a work out as well," she explains. I asked if there wasn't time in the day for jumping jacks, or in-place isometrics and she laughed. "It's not like that. You go over the key terms, practice test prep books in language arts, math and science, let's take the test together, let's go over the vocabulary, how do we read the questions... that's it." Rosie raised the question of health with a school administrator, noting high rates of diabetes among the student and parent community. She suggested a school-wide health initiative targeting sugary snacks and drinks. The administrator, according to Rosie, eventually explained, "we can only do so much, the test is our problem, health is theirs."

Related to the issue of time, the question of preparation is crucial because, by design and in many cases by stated purpose, norm-referenced standardized tests are meant to provide only a snapshot (an objective measure) of students' knowledge and ability at a given time. Tests are, in principle, measures of certain understandings gained within a given period of time. Tests are, ideally, curriculum driven— in other words, content tested is gleaned from curriculum and what is taught. Test preparation that is distinct from regular curriculum-driven instruction and content is thus indicative of a schism between the curriculum and the test on the one hand, and of teaching and learning that are test-driven rather than curriculum driven, on the other. This hit home in conversation with teachers at Flower Elementary, who did not perceive testing as a high-stakes or high-pressure issue. Although I interviewed teachers from ten schools in Los Angeles, I was only able to spend extensive time in, and speak to multiple teachers from, four schools: Southern, South Central, Flower and North Hollywood. While Southern and South Central were located in one of the lowest-income areas in California, North Hollywood was located in a wealthy part of

Los Angeles, near the Hollywood hills. Flower was located in a mixed-income area.

Racially, the student population of South Central was over 90 percent Latino and Chicano (first-generation Mexican American), while at Southern, the student population was over 90 percent African American. North Hollywood students were predominantly white (90 percent) with approximately 80 percent of students identifying as Armenian. Flower was highly multiracial, multiethnic, and multicultural. Flower was unique insofar as its student population did not match its catchment area as closely as the others. With regard to race, Flower was more diverse than its surrounding area but had a lesser degree of income disparity. Teachers at Flower attributed this to the school's role as home school for children of international faculty and graduate students from a nearby university. Flower's student population was largely middle income, and the teachers often had more parent volunteers than they knew what to do with. Most students had strong academic support at home, and each of the ten teachers with whom I spoke, reported feeling strongly supported by parents.

Unlike their colleagues at Southern and South Central, teachers at Flower felt relatively little pressure to teach to or for the test. The school's state test scores for the past five years had placed it solidly among the top in the area, and testing was, as the veteran science teacher Barr put it, "not a big deal with these kids... things come up now and again and we support individual kids as they need, but that's really rare here." When I asked about time pressures, teachers reported none due to testing. Unlike Southern and South Central, at Flower there was no informal curriculum of standardized test fever (no slogans on the walls, no school songs around the Academic Performance Index [API] or the Annual Yearly Progress [AYP], and no recommended daily time for test preparation). Nadra, a Flower teacher in her 14th year, said she ran out to buy a copy of the *LA Times* the first year it published teacher names and class scores. She was nervous to see, "what am I? You know? What's my score? But our principal was amazing and said she wasn't even looking at them so we shouldn't either." I later asked the current principal about this and she suggested this approach was made possible by high test scores. She explains, "I would be in hot water if we didn't reach the scores we usually have." Nadra says, "I didn't even check mine this year–I don't know what it is." While there was relatively minimal pressure here, testing is taken very seriously by all involved. As is the case in many contexts in the United States and Canada, students are encouraged to eat a good breakfast and get a good night's sleep. By test day, as

Nadra explains, "they have that feeling in their stomach like, ooh, this is a pretty big deal." There was, however, extensive collaboration among teachers, academic freedom, and what Barr described as "the time and space to teach and learn together as a community." Conversations with faculty at Flower inadvertently deepened my understanding of Southern and South Central.

The meaning of ST was radically different in these other Los Angeles contexts, primarily because Flower teachers almost never had to teach explicitly to the test, while teachers at both Southern and South Central felt at times as if they were doing little else. This "time and space" impact on teaching methods and the classroom experience overall was consistent with the Toronto and Chicago contexts. A Chicago teacher with over ten years of experience suggests, "It's all about standardization these days. There's no room for differentiation. No time either. Project-based learning, critical inquiry, field trips, there's no time. The tests are always waiting around the corner." A new teacher from Ontario explains, "I teach the government curriculum and could cover more if I weren't spending ten-20 percent of my time preparing for the tests." Echoing this, a Toronto teacher suggests, "when you are teaching in an EQAO year, you don't have time to consolidate children's learning because you are trying to cram a year's worth of knowledge into less than eight months so that you have time to review before the test." As mentioned in the previous chapter, the stakes are increasingly high for US teachers. One Chicago teacher explains: "While I would prefer to not spend any time or at least very little preparing for testing, the reality of funding for the district and stability for my job and my school relies on results on these tests—I can't afford to not spend time preparing."

While standardized tests take up significant classroom time, the overall impact (the time crunch) is determined by not only the number and frequency of tests administered but also by the stakes attached to those tests as perceived by the teachers (a perception often not lost on the students) as well as by the degree to which the standardized tests align with curriculum. One Chicago teacher explains what she calls "special circumstances" and suggests, "I have strong and capable students and thus the privileged opportunity to ignore the tests and just take the two days for administration and teach otherwise." Note that "teaching" here means ignoring the test. The complex impact of testing also plays out as far as planning, instruction, and assessment methods. Another Illinois teacher comments: "Test prep can become very detrimental, especially when it supplants time spent helping students research, create, and present engaging projects that they're genuinely excited about and that motivate them to learn." An Ontario special education teacher suggests:

> I spend a small amount of time getting slow learners ready for grade three EQAO, but grade three classroom teachers spend huge amounts of time preparing students by mimicking the test in various assignments and sending home EQAO homework prep booklets.

The mimicking process described here is widespread, and it ensures something other than a random snapshot of student learning and ability.

In the United States, and increasingly in Ontario, ST can even take up time in nontesting years. In LA, for example, where first-graders do not take the test, many write a practice test that mirrors the grade two test. This becomes the focal point for much of the grade one year. First grade teacher Malik explains, "when it comes to testing you don't have the time to figure out what each assessment does, you just can see what standards it meets, not what it actually does as far as the kids' learning." Among the predictable results of the time crunch is a contraction of the curriculum as far as both breadth and depth.

Curricular Shrinkage and Calculated Skimming: History, Physical Health Education, and the Arts as Extra Curricular Activities

While two of the teachers mentioned earlier were encouraged to teach history and physical education (respectively) as after-school clubs, in many high-stakes testing schools, these subjects have nearly disappeared altogether from the list of regularly taught subjects. These are the extremes, of course, and teachers reporting curriculum contraction tended to describe reductions in their ability to teach outside of tested topics rather than a complete inability to address particular subjects altogether. The school day is no shorter, so it is important to look at what is displacing the arts, social studies, and physical health education (PHE).

In a 2007 report by the Center for Education Policy on classroom time use and No Child Left Behind, Jennifer McMurrer reports:

> 62 percent of a representative sample of school districts across the country increased the amount of time (a 47 percent increase in language arts and a 37 percent increase in math) spent on elementary language arts and math. These same districts decreased time allowed for science, social studies, art and music, physical education and recess. In addition, greater

proportions of schools identified by NCLB factors as in need of improvement increased time for ELA and/or math than schools not designated in need of improvement. Finally, there was greater emphasis in curricula on state tested content and skills in ELA and math since NLCB inception in schools surveyed.[3]

These findings correspond with those here, and the experiences of teachers in both the United States and Canada. One Illinois teacher explains students are "still receiving the same amount of instructional time. The focus of that time is different." She suggests that with "a focus on standardized tests, students are learning how to pick the best option, be 'smarter than the test', use text evidence, etcetera."

Marvelyn, a Toronto sixth grade teacher in her tenth year explains, "I teach a formula for taking multiple choice questions; there is usually one obviously wrong answer, one possibly wrong answer and two possibly correct answers." From the two possible correct answers she asks students to then consider which is the better of the two. Nowhere in the grade six curriculum guidelines is it written that students are expected to learn test taking strategies such as Marvelyn's, but hers is a common practice. Another Ontario teacher explains, "I teach them how to do multiple choice and respond to previous EQAO reading and writing assessment," and she relies on previous EQAO tests because they are "quicker, free and match what they will be writing in the test for the most part." This is the mimicking technique described earlier.

Mary, a 14th-year teacher in LA, explains that "a big part of test prep is teaching them to take long tests—stamina and the ability to sit there and take a test—nothing to do with the curriculum." Administrators, she suggests, "want the standard on our board, hung up, and in our books to prove that we are teaching the standards." Pointing to a Bloom's Taxonomy chart on the wall, Mary explained that fitting in the levels (moving to the stages of consolidation, extension, and critical thinking through inference and conclusion generation) becomes "almost impossible when the skills there don't move past the first stages of basic knowledge." She summarizes by explaining that: "over the years, kids are becoming worse at higher order thinking because we just don't have the space to teach what is not on the test and keep our school and our jobs." Teachers in lower grades note a major shift from hands-on to non-hands-on learning, a trend that raises well-worn questions about the degree to which standardized practices are developmentally appropriate for young children.[4]

The impact on content, on what actually gets taught, is not a value-free substitution of one set of items for another, but rather a displacement of key learning items that remain in the formal curriculum but may not make it into the classroom. As one New York City teacher explains, "I value project-based learning and critical inquiry, but you won't find these on standardized tests. They don't measure most of what matters—the ability to work in groups, problem-solving, argumentation, or developing and revising critical analysis of ideas. So we don't teach it." This, she suggests, can harm students who, "struggle more with written expression of ideas than with verbal expression... Tests don't look at real-world skills, such as team work and problem solving."

Malik describes the ways in which things can "fall off the table" due to a classroom focus on ST even in a nontesting year:

> If you look at the lower grades, even in the schedule we are given as teachers, it doesn't actually fit what we have to get done. For us, our priority becomes reading and writing and arithmetic for the test; that's it. I'm like, "if you leave here with that' that's enough—and it's enough for the admin too." My kids can all be great, can make great improvements at clarifying and inquiring and summarizing but if I send them to second grade and they can't succeed in the test it's my ass. And I have more freedom than teachers in higher grades.

When I borrowed Malik's language to ask Toronto teacher Georgia if anything fell off the table at her school, she guffawed, explaining, "Fall off? Oh my gosh, pushed off. And that's the formal curriculum, forget about the other stuff like character education and citizenship. We are encouraged to teach to the test and other content is second-rate." When asked what that encouragement looked like and how it was communicated, she explained:

> It looks like an 11 × 17 piece of paper that has our EQAO scores and a question about what we are doing to address it. With a follow up email from the admin., and most of our PD overtly talking about this stuff. It's not exactly subtle. Twenty minutes of every staff meeting goes to that column on that piece of paper.

Stecher suggests that high-stakes multiple choice testing has been linked to such pedagogical effects for some time, explaining, "By the end of the [1990s], educators began to recognize a number of problems associated with high-stakes multiple-choice testing," which included "narrowing of the curriculum to tested topics and excessive time devoted to test preparation, that led to inflated test scores."[5]

Table 4.1 Standardized testing and the narrowing of curriculum, Illinois and Ontario teachers

As a result of standardized testing, I cover a narrower range of topics than I would otherwise.

	Ont. English	Ont. French	Illinois
Strongly Agree	19.1%	45.6%	27.2%
Agree	38.4%	30.8%	35.5%
No Opinion	19.9%	9.5%	14.9%
Disagree	15.9%	10.3%	17.4%
Strongly Disagree	6.6%	3.8%	5.1%

Survey results suggest that this practice may be widespread, as Table 4.1 illustrates.

Almost 60 percent of surveyed English Ontario teachers agree or strongly they cover a narrower range of topics as a result of ST, while the rates for Illinois and French Ontario teachers are nearly 73 percent and 76 percent, respectively. The more standardized tests a teacher administers, the more likely she is to agree that as a result of ST, she covers a narrower range of topics than she would otherwise. For many US teachers, the standards are the focus of the curricular contraction. Barr, a veteran teacher of 22 years at Flower where testing pressure is relatively low, describes his strategy for teaching beyond the standards in the following exchange during a morning interview in his classroom:

> *Barr*: "I teach history backwards, from now going back to 1850, and this is a one shot deal for students to get this."
> *Interviewer*: "Is that because of the curriculum?"
> *Barr*: "No, it's because of the standards in grade five and later, there is no room for this kind of teaching and learning within the standards in other grades beyond elementary. I have spoken with so many people who teach middle and high school and they told me this stuff wasn't happening there—so I feel like this is the one shot we get to give them this material."

Anticipating the contraction to come, Barr enriches his elementary program, exercising a privilege afforded by the Flower environment described earlier. Langley, a 23-year veteran teacher at South Central describes an altogether different situation in her school:

> Children don't learn nursery rhymes anymore, but they are tested every six weeks. I call what we end up doing calculated skimming. We touch upon

a broad range of things a half an inch deep. Our thing is exposure, and it's short term. When I was coming through school I learned Shakespeare and now you have to be in an honors program to learn a soliloquy.

The calculated skimming suggested above is a skill in and of itself, and the half an inch deep curriculum can leave a lot of kids drowning. One Chicago teacher explains that in his school students are taught, "two math lessons each day in order to cover the entire math curriculum in time for state tests in March," at which time teachers "move ahead to the following year's curriculum." He suggests that, "many students who don't grasp concepts immediately are left behind." A colleague agrees, commenting, "there is no time for supplementary lessons for those who do not understand the first time." Contraction, or skimming (even the calculated kind), can thus powerfully impact teacher ability to attend to individual student needs and pacing, a phenomenon discussed further in Chapter 6.

After suggesting that honors programs are increasingly reserved for economically and racially privileged students, Langley goes on argue that an ST focus can powerfully impact the way children learn to think. She observes:

> These kids are getting bits and pieces and none of it fits together except what is being tested. I have kids who are counting on their fingers, and I call them out sometimes if I see it repeated and say "it's going to be five, you can just say five" but that is exactly symptomatic of testing-driven instruction because they are not learning to think mathematically, they, because we are driven by the test, are learning specific answers essentially, to specific questions predicted to be on the test. This is different from teaching them how to think, from them learning number sense.

This simple but powerful description illustrates a major cognitive shift demanded by and resulting from test-oriented teaching and learning (TOTL). A tenth-year Chicago teacher seconds Langley's concerns about the impacts of curricular contraction and student thinking, adding that this impacts student curiosity and ability to learn through exploration. She explains:

> Everything we do is geared to drilling into them how to think—not critically, but in ways necessary to ace the standardized tests...For instance, in reading there are about six main areas of knowledge and these things are taught to the exclusion of all else...They're only using a fraction of their brain capacity, they're certainly not being allowed to

learn by exploration and questioning, and they are definitely not being allowed to relax and cultivate their own curiosity—and therefore build knowledge—about the world around them. I feel very sorry for them.

Los Angeles teacher Mary suggests that curricular contraction can differ by severity and by grade. When asked if any specific areas of the curriculum were more likely than others to fall away as a result of ST, she explains:

> A lot of the extras like art, social studies, history—and man, history is so important. In fifth grade we test science, but some of the other grades don't, so they often tend not to teach it because it's not tested. I get it, they're busy but on the fifth grade test 60 percent of the science piece is fifth grade science and 40 percent is fourth grade science, even though those fourth grade standards are not tested in fourth grade.

This produces tensions at times between instructors at different levels, a phenomenon not limited to the impact of ST. Mary explains, "it sets us up for low scores" And says that "fourth grade teachers have to get tested on the writing standards whereas we in fifth grade don't." Although differentiated from year to year, the contraction is consistent across grades as far as TOTL. Mary explains, "they give us the blueprint guide with test question release, which is test question prep, and it becomes the bible for the second half of the year. After testing is over it is actually fun to be a teacher again." For Mary and many others in the classroom, it is the teachers who are essentially being tested, and in this high-stakes ST environment, extras have come to include PHE, art, social studies, and history.

On a more subtle level, the contracted curriculum can edge out some hidden pieces of the teaching and learning picture. A Chicago teacher observes that "standardized tests don't measure maturity and emotional growth, and many people don't realize that teachers spend quite a bit of time helping students with these." The emotional support of students, a veteran Toronto teacher suggests, "is especially hard in the EQAO years, partly because they often need more of it around the test, and partly because we have less time to offer it.", The impact of contracted curriculum on students is profound, and can disproportionately affect students who may benefit most from not only "extras" such as the arts and social sciences but also from emotional supports and pedagogical practices that identify and sustain individual learners. Any parent whose struggling child has been helped by a teacher knows that one-on-one consideration and support of children are among the most important elements of teachers' work—it is typically through these subtle and often untestable practices that teachers make the biggest differences in the lives and learning of children.

The interview and survey results illustrate that standardized test-centered classrooms are often characterized by increasingly limited curricular depth and breadth. Marginalized subject and teaching focuses (which may include everything from history, to character education, to providing emotional support) are displaced by test-oriented activities that include test-taking skills alongside a more intense focus on tested items. The tested items generally fail to cover the entire curriculum and the test-taking skills are not part of the curriculum at all. Contraction can cause tension between teachers within and across grades, and the pace of learning demanded by the contracted curriculum can leave students in the dust (and some groups of students far more than others). Time constraints lead to curricular contraction, "calculated skimming," and other unwelcome teaching decisions. As a whole, these widespread pedagogical shifts in teaching and learning constitute a revision of the pedagogical form.

Teaching and Learning in the Standardized Classroom: What Does the Finish Line Teach about How to Run?

It is clear that large-scale assessments impact the attitude, activities, and pedagogical approaches of teachers and the experiences of students.[6] Accepting that what gets tested gets taught, it follows that widespread ST has widespread impacts on teaching. Stecher suggests that high-stakes testing "sends signals to educators (as well as students and parents) about the specific content, styles of learning, and styles of performing that are valued," signals that are translated into action when "teachers respond accordingly, emphasizing in their lessons the content, styles of learning, and performing that are manifest on the tests."[7] Linda Darling-Hammond and Frank Adamson take this one step further to suggest that: "... testing in most states is less focused on higher order skills than it was in the 1990s, even though it now functions as the primary influence on curriculum and classroom instruction."[8] One Toronto teacher powerfully sums up the findings of these leading researchers, arguing: "Teaching students how to write a standardized test is like teaching them how to put a hubcap on a car on an assembly line." Results here support these conclusions and suggest a radical change in how teachers teach.

The time and curricular constraints discussed here ultimately come out in pedagogical practice. One Chicago teacher frames this process, stating: "Standardized testing returns us to the limiting and narrow style of teaching that assumes that a 'standardized student' exists. It puts school practices in direct opposition to all relevant, current and respected pedagogy." While the results of ST are, in theory, designed to improve teaching and learning, teachers surveyed overwhelmingly suggest this is not the case, as Table 4.2 illustrates.

Seven percent of Illinois teachers agree or strongly agree that the results of ST are used effectively to improve teacher practice, and the rates for English Ontario and French Ontario teachers are 9 percent and 16.8 percent, respectively. Many teachers feel that the time-consuming tests offer little new information about their students. Ninth-year Toronto teacher Karen explains: "It fills up our PLCs[9] [Professional Learning Communities] but admin seems to not notice that we have this info on kids from other sources–including other standardized diagnostics." In a pattern that runs parallel to the curriculum question above, teaching strategies driven by testing tend to displace non-test-driven strategies. Among the first casualties are critical approaches, including anti-discriminatory education, critical pedagogy, feminist education, and curricular approaches such as people's histories and the recognition that multiple perspectives are needed to understand various elements of the curriculum. A second-year Chicago teacher suggests, "standardized testing creates the myth that there are always correct and incorrect answers."

Nuno, a 12th-year teacher, who taught at one of California's largest schools for eight years, moved to a progressive charter school in order to do more social justice work. Nuno is committed to critical pedagogy and found that "because of test-focused teaching, critical work with low SES kids was becoming impossible." Although he struggled against a "conservative department head," the real barriers, he discovered, were

Table 4.2 Degree to which standardized tests are used to improve teacher practice, Illinois and Toronto teachers

In my belief, the results of standardized testing are used effectively to improve teacher practice.

	Ont. English	Ont. French	Illinois
Strongly Agree	0.4%	4.1%	0.2%
Agree	8.6%	12.7%	6.8%
No Opinion	6.7%	12.0%	6.9%
Disagree	38.0%	39.4%	37.9%
Strongly Disagree	46.3%	31.8%	48.1%

the socioeconomic challenges present in the community. He did go on to do more critical work in the charter school; however, this was made possible not by a progressive administration, but by "a student community not constantly twisting itself up for the test; [they] had high results every year and that—not the department head—allowed for critical pedagogy" to once again guide his teaching. Importantly, we see the test meaning different things in different places, a thread that runs through the questions of time and curriculum as well. The more privileged school population at the charter spent less time on TOTL and more time with critical approaches than the low-income students at Nuno's previous school.

In addition to more alternative and critical approaches, the pedagogy of standardization also displaces student-centered learning approaches to teaching and learning.[10] Based on the pioneering work of Carol Ann Tomlinson, student teachers across North America have been trained for over a decade in a method called differentiated instruction (DI),[11] which calls for teachers to adapt their pedagogy to the strengths, challenges, and interests of individual students. A DI approach considers four domains: content (what is being learned), process (the various ways and means through which this learning happens), product (the work students do as a result and as a demonstration of learning), and environment (the physical, social, and emotional climate of the classroom and school). Applied to the in-service learning of teachers, ST is powerfully impacting each of these domains. These approaches are often accompanied by the use of inquiry and exploration in student learning, as well as project-based learning, which unlike multiple choice assessment, can capture a great variety and depth of student learning and achievement (often over a longer period of time). As Table 4.3 illustrates, for many teachers there is a negative correlation between ST and their ability to use DI.

Table 4.3 Standardized testing and its impact on assessment and instruction, Illinois and Ontario teachers

Standardized testing impacts my ability to use diverse assessment and instructional approaches (such as differentiated instruction and multiple intelligences) as follows:

	Ont. English	Ont. French	Illinois
Makes It Much Easier	0.6%	1.0%	1.0%
Makes It Easier	2.1%	3.4%	5.6%
Uncertain	26.4%	29.9%	23.5%
Makes It More Difficult	42.3%	37.4%	43.6%
Makes It Much More Difficult	28.7%	28.4%	26.3%

Rates of teachers for whom ST makes using diverse approaches more difficult or much more difficult are as 69.6 percent (Illinois), 71 percent (English Ontario), and 65.8 percent (French Ontario). Rates of teachers for whom ST makes using diverse approaches easier or much easier are as follows: Illinois, 6.6 percent; English Ontario, 2.7 percent; and French Ontario, 4.4 percent.

One Chicago teacher fleshes out what this looks like in his classroom:

> While I always make it my goal to use student-centered instruction and assessment, prepping for standardized testing does not allow for this type of instruction because it is "standardized" and therefore, it is made to fit a mold that no one child fits into. So, I have to force my students to become like a student they are not accustomed to being, which is terribly disheartening and frustrating for them and takes the joy out of teaching and the joy out of learning.

In addition to an obvious discomfort with moving away from what many consider to be best practice, teachers notice the impact on the learning dynamics and the student experience on a daily basis. They also notice what gets pushed aside by the use of these limited strategies, as another Chicago teacher explains: "I do sometimes use the results to group my students for differentiation, though standardized tests don't assess creative intelligence, so those types of instruction often get overlooked." Another Chicago teacher explains: "it's hard to differentiate test prep," while an Ontario grade three teacher puts it plainly: "inquiry based learning and time dedicated to project-based learning are abandoned because of testing." Although differentiation may be possible to limited and differing degrees in standardized classrooms, it is clear that its absence is widespread, and increasingly so. Many teachers are unable to attend to student-focused teaching and learning activities as a result of ST.

In place of these approaches, pedagogy that focuses on preparation for ST often becomes, as we might expect, standardized. Toronto teacher Karen explains: "A lot of cutting edge stuff involves teachers exploring with the students in knowledge and learning, and then test teaching is totally prescriptive for the teachers—and then of course for the kids." By the end of an EQAO year, she suggests, the test "creates a cloud over everybody's head with students stressed out and teachers teaching to the test—which from what I understand about these things means this isn't really measuring what it's supposed to." Karen is referring to the systemic preparation of students for what is incorrectly billed as a random snapshot to parents and the media by testing bodies.

The following exchange with John, an eighth-year teacher in Los Angeles, picks up this sentiment:

> For years I was like, "I know what my kids need and if as long as they are improving to the best of their abilities we were good." I am competitive though, and I want to keep my job. If the guy next door is bringing up scores I need to as well.
>
> *Interviewer*: Is there a difference, or a gap between what your students need to improve and the teaching and learning that happens in and around test prep?
> *John*: "It's night and day man, night and day. One is about the kids—I can individualize my teaching. Test prep is factory farming."

Toronto teacher Sarah echoes these sentiments, explaining that around test time "kids are not doing any MI or DI it's just literacy and math as pen to paper work." This is particularly troubling to her as a teacher of English language learners (ELLs) because, "that differentiated approach is best practice within ELL teaching, so I can't tell you exactly what the tests don't show about these kids but I can say it is a whole hell of a lot—often the best parts." She points out that many students struggle with standalone pen to paper tasks but do better when these come in conjunction with other modes of expression. She tells the story of one of her "favorite students of all time":

> We were doing a project on the Acadians, and he built a model of one of their desalination devices and easily breezed through the math and sciences pieces of it, because it was applied. He presented it and described exactly how it worked, mathematically and scientifically with no notes, perfectly. If I had said just write about it he would have been stuck. After he did all that, then he could write about it. When I think about it, testing takes us to the opposite of best practices.

In Ontario and Illinois, one of the most common replacements for these "best practices" is the use of old tests, or test items to prepare for upcoming tests—mimicking, which would have left the student described above unsuccessful. In Ontario, where the overall role of testing pressure is generally much less than that in California and Illinois, the use of standardized tests from previous years is nonetheless a common strategy for test preparation with students. This extends the instructional opportunity cost of the test even beyond the test-taking period. In Ontario (where the grades three, six, and ten EQAO results do not count toward student report cards), this is driven, in part, by the need for teachers to create formal reports near the time when the test must be taken. It is nearly impossible and highly irresponsible to not assess student work ahead of a written report card or progress report; faced with the concurrent responsibilities of test preparation and gathering marks for students, teachers often resort to marking the practice tests. This makes teachers responsible for giving all students opportunities to succeed on this measure, so they understandably prepare their students for the practice test (although it is no longer a practice test but a formal evaluation), a strategy that has the added bonus of preparing them for the EQAO. This radically extends the use of the narrowed curricular and instructional focus demanded by TOTL.

One Ontario teacher explains, "when I had grade three for six years I embedded test prep in the learning, for example, using the exemplars throughout the year." This is a practice that intensifies closer to test time, and it constitutes a form of test preparation (a practice few interviewed Ontario teachers were keen to name as such). A Chicago teacher in her tenth year uses a similar pedagogical strategy as, she explains, "using previous tests helps to understand what is expected and one can assess students' responses based on exemplars provided." This degree of TOTL is uncomfortable for many teachers. Sirin describes the process by which he has, reluctantly, become a teacher who teachers to the test:

> Look, no teacher or principal or assistant principal will tell you on the record to teach to the test to the exclusion of other important pieces, but every teacher knows they have to. For the first few years of teaching (and my scores went up just as much then as they do now each year) I was aware of the standards but my teaching was not primarily informed by them. We have the standards, we have this growth and the point of teaching was the kids' growth. Lots of ability to support individual kids. I wanted my kids to do well. But in the last four or five years, everything has made testing the most important thing—it's the compass that guides us whether we like it or not. So, do I think that teachers teach to the test? Hell yeah! They are looking for any little thing to get rid of teachers nowadays, so if it's CST they want it's CST they get.

I was curious about who "they" were. Sirin explains, "the district, charter boosters, some parents, the *LA Times*." This was not his original vision of himself as a teacher. He explains, "I never thought I'd be one of those teachers. I'm a progressive guy but with our superintendent, the media and everything else I don't feel like I have a choice."

As discussed in greater depth in the next chapter, this reluctance is a professional rather than labor-based concern. Teaching to the test is easier for many teachers, but it keeps educators away from what is important, ultimately leaving them with the sense that they are underserving children. Nuno comments:

> Kids are fighting in the corner, my stuff is falling off the wall, I don't always have enough chairs for each kid but as long as we are following the latest magic bullet from the district to bring up scores, everything is fine. It's ridiculous.

A Toronto teacher asks: "All we are doing is teaching to the test; how does that improve literacy skills?"

Among the most consistent concerns voiced about the pedagogy of ST were regarding its failure to serve students effectively, consistently, and in a differentiated fashion. As Table 4.4 illustrates, most teachers surveyed believe that standardized tests do not support student learning.

The similarity and low numbers across the jurisdictions are remarkable: just 12.4 percent of Illinois teachers, 10.6 percent of English Ontario teachers, and 12.1 percent of French Ontario teachers agree or strongly agree that ST enables schools to better meet the academic needs of students and to improve student learning. One Ontario teacher offers another possible use of the data: "Current standardized tests do not provide useful data that actually helps drive instruction. They do, however, assist realtors in higher end communities to sell houses." Survey respondents in Ontario and Illinois commented extensively on questions of ST and its impacts on teaching and learning, with many raising concerns about the limits of multiple-choice questions for assessing student

Table 4.4 Standardized testing and meeting students' academic needs, Illinois and Ontario teachers

In my belief, standardized testing enables schools to better meet the academic needs of students and to improve student learning.

	Ont. English	Ont. French	Illinois
Strongly agree	2.0%	2.5%	1.5%
Agree	8.6%	9.6%	10.9%
Uncertain	7.7%	11.8%	14.8%
Disagree	35.9%	37.4%	37.2%
Strongly disagree	45.9%	38.7%	35.7%

learning. These concerns are echoed by the findings of a 2012 Rand study, which found that bubble tests were rarely able to measure higher-order thinking, and indeed constrained cognitive demand.[12] Stecher points out that multiple-choice assessment comes under fire because:

> [S]timulus materials tend to be very limited (usually short passages or problem statements with simple figures or diagrams)...the demands of the format encourage test developers to focus on declarative knowledge (knowing that) or procedural knowledge (knowing how) rather than schematic knowledge (knowing why) or strategic knowledge (knowing when, where, and how our knowledge applies).[13]

While higher-order thinking is thus often immeasurable by bubble-test assessments, standardized pedagogical practices can also leave out those struggling with the most basic concepts. Malik, who teaches in South Los Angeles, explains:

> I remember a few years ago going to Open Court[14] training and a teacher from Topanga Canyon[15] was like "my kids already know all of this, this is so basic." I looked at it and said this is so good for my kids. So standardization of approaches is a really tough go and you obviously need different strategies for different kids and groups of kids.

The interview and survey results illustrate that standardized test-centered pedagogy, like standardized test-centered curriculum and scheduling, can vary and tends to emerge more intensely with disadvantaged communities of learners. The pedagogy of standardization uses fewer teaching and learning strategies, and tends toward greater repetition and reliance on previously used tests. For most, standardization pulls educators away from best practices, and fails to support professional improvement for teachers and improved learning for children. Finally, ST and related pedagogical practices fail to serve both the strongest and the struggling (in particular), increasingly narrowing and hurrying pedagogy, and ultimately serving fewer and fewer learners. We turn now, briefly, to teacher perceptions of the learners' experience of standardization.

Pressure, Silence, Cookies, and Lemon Water: Student Experiences of High-Stakes Testing

For a great many kids, standardized test days are fun. For some, these days are anxiety-free, a change from the ordinary and a chance to share in a common experience—and they get treats. At some high-performing schools, students look to outperform colleagues at other high-ranking schools. For others, however, ST comes with fear and panic. In high-stakes testing classrooms in the United States and Canada, testing days are unique. As mentioned previously, fundamental rules (like wearing hats and chewing gum) may go out the window; teachers all of the sudden will not help them when they are having trouble, and the work they are doing is neither for themselves nor their teacher—it is made for export and students often have the sense they are representing something greater than themselves. Many students experience a variety of pressures—too many, according to many teachers. Indeed, when surveyed on whether or not ST puts too much pressure on students, 93 percent of English Ontario teachers and 94 percent of French Ontario teachers agreed or strongly agreed it does. It would be reckless to suggest that ST is bad for all children, however, as discussed in Chapters 5 and 6 in greater detail, standardized tests are often developmentally inappropriate for young children (not taking into account the way young brains learn), cause widespread anxiety, and trigger other mental health concerns, and run counter to much of what we know about how children most effectively learn. Supporting what many parents in opt-out movements across the United States already know, teachers report that for far too many children, ST can also correlate with academic disengagement.

Indeed, questions of stress and confidence actually drive test preparation for some teachers, as one Ontario teacher explains: "I want my students to be prepared so that they don't experience stress, but I don't agree with EQAO, so the only value of the time I spend preparing them is for children's confidence." An Illinois teacher with 30 years of experience echoes this, suggesting that, "sometimes it erodes students' confidence to see where they place on testing and results in tears as though to say they are not good enough." Stories of tears were commonplace when speaking with teachers. A tenth-year Toronto teacher comments: "I have had numerous students cry and break out in hives because they were so nervous during EQAO." Georgia, a Toronto teacher in her 14th year, expresses her frustration with her students' experience, explaining:

> I have a student with significant anxiety issues, who did not want to be different and exempted but then got the test and chucked it on the floor. She spent the next 45 minutes in her locker refusing to come out and muttering. I wished I could have taken a photo, slapped her bar code on it, and stuffed it in her package to send to the Ministry.

Georgia further suggests that teacher thinking around students is increasingly EQAO-focused, as she discusses below:

> From the beginning of the year students are worried about it, and if the scores go up, we celebrate it at the school. The students are really worried about it and so are teachers. More and more teachers are using EQAO results to understand students. So where a colleague used to say Sabah is really interested in math to talk about numeracy, now we get the score. Or instead Sabah loves period fiction but won't read anything else, now we get her literacy scores.

A fifth-year Chicago teacher remarks on a similar school-wide effect, suggesting: "the kids at our school grow a huge amount academically but the [Illinois Standard Achievement Test] only shows if they are at grade level or not. So our school looks weak publicly but in fact it is very strong." This frustrates teachers and students alike, promoting a feeling of futility, "getting students down" she suggests.

Meanwhile, successful results (and the work needed to achieve them) may displace other important learning and community-building opportunities. One Toronto teacher suggests:

> My school has done well on EQAO but lacks a sense of community amongst students and teachers... [T]he public doesn't know it based on EQAO scores. Our school needs more character education and working together, not higher test scores and lemon water at every desk each time EQAO comes to town.

Marco, a 16th-year teacher in Los Angeles, teaches in a school that has "turned around." He explains:

> We're no longer a Program Improvement school, but we're also no longer anything—our whole identity as a school and community, I guess as a school community, has been forged around the mold of test scores, and that mold is hollow [he knocks on his empty aluminum water bottle]. So there is a high cost, even when the desired results are achieved, and this does not even mean meaningful, more or better learning.

School-wide work around test scores frequently comes with the internalization of certain meanings associated with the test, and these can impact students' sense of identity. Sixth-year LA teacher Beta provides an example: "In my first year, I had a student's mom come in really upset about a bunch of kids bullying her son—calling her BB, below basic." "Below basic" is language taken from the interpretation of standardized tests. She goes on to say that "in schools where everyone is on board, kids who don't perform can actually be targeted by other kids for bringing everybody down, not to mention the pressure from teachers and admin." When asked if some identity formation for some students is then rooted in high-stakes testing, she agreed but cautioned, "yes, but don't forget that this doesn't even get to the way whole communities get stigmatized." While Chapter 6 takes up issues of class, race, and ability in much greater depth, Beta's remarks powerfully illustrate the potential stigma facing certain students when individual and school success are reliant on the results of standardized tests.

Teachers also suggest that high-preforming students can be troubled by the tests. One Chicago teacher explains, "I've seen really intelligent students not be able to 'grow' anymore on the assessments because they already hit the ceiling. As a result, they start feeling bad about themselves." Sam, a Toronto teacher agrees, suggesting "my top students are just checked out for April/May. There's nothing for them, especially if the old tests are hard for my struggling kids and they are checked out as well." When I asked what a checked out kid looked like, she explains, "it could be everything from getting into trouble, to reading secretly—which they get into trouble for, to talking out." Reading was a common form of student test preparation disengagement identified by teachers. The irony is not lost on educators. One Los Angeles teacher suggests: "the days when I have to yell at a kid for reading Harry Potter because he will not put it down to do inference drills with me? I feel like shit quite frankly."

For many teachers, one of the most frustrating elements of the student experience is the feeling that all the stress is simply not worth it—the learning just does not make up for the pain. While I won't recount all of the details here, I have received 42 stories over the course of this study (by mail, in the survey, and during the interviews) of students vomiting before and/or during the grades three and six EQAO standardized tests (similar stories from the United States number over 70). In teachers' eyes, the cost to students' well-being can be high and the learning pay off low, as Table 4.5 illustrates.

Fewer than 8 percent of Ontario and Illinois teachers feel students learn more or much more as a result of ST, a number roughly inverse to the percentage who feel standardized tests place too much pressure on students.

While many Ontario teachers interviewed were reluctant to declare explicitly that they teach to the test, even those who claimed not to,

Table 4.5 Standardized testing and student learning, Illinois and Ontario teachers

Fill in the blank by selecting the best option from the list below: In my belief, as a result of standardized testing, students learn _____ than they would otherwise.

	Ont. English	*Ont. French*	*Illinois*
Much More	0.2%	1.2%	0.3%
More	6.8%	6.7%	5.4%
No More or Less	42.5%	56.5%	32.0%
Less	34.9%	25.4%	37.7%
Much less	15.7%	10.1%	24.5%

sometimes promoted the test's significance to their students. Elway, a veteran Toronto teacher, explains his practice:

> The only thing I tell them about the test [grade six EQAO] is that there is a tenth grade literacy test that they have to pass in order to complete high school and that research tells us that 98 percent of students who pass the grade six test go on to pass the literacy test. I tell them that in life they will have to take a lot of standardized tests and you have got to think about preparation for skills like that and the philosophy of testing. I think that most of the kids therefore, attack it in a serious manner.

Elway is not alone. Like many teachers at relatively low-pressure schools (schools that are often relatively affluent), including those at Flower mentioned earlier, Elway's students are still informed of the importance of the standardized tests. Thus, many students are impacted by standardized tests even in relatively low-pressure contexts.

Many teachers do what they can to prevent stress with students but are unsuccessful much of the time. Toronto teacher Sarah, who reports reassuring students repeatedly that EQAO is "no big deal" during test preparation in the weeks leading up to the test, explains:

> It doesn't have to be on the report card for them to think it is important and for them to freak out. At grade three and even grade six, students rarely get the full breakdown of where and how their marks from teachers come to be anyway, so the idea that a giant test does not impact their report cards can seem impossible. They don't see behind the curtain at the details, they know it is marked, and so that difference between a letter from school that has EQAO marks and a letter from school that is the report card is pretty unclear for grade threes and even many grade sixes.

Sarah's explanation, which echoes that of many of her colleagues in Ontario, may partially explain persistent student anxiety despite teachers telling students the tests do not count. In many Ontario classrooms the teachers and students refer to the EQAO as Evil Questions Asked of (or Attacking) Ontarians, a moniker the kids find funny and jocular. Although lighthearted, it is hard to say what this joke might mean to young students, but it certainly reveals a critical conversation. Although few US teachers were able to tell anyone, least of all their students, that standardized tests do not count, many are critical of ST with their students. Despite this, many teachers in low-performing schools are actively working to create more buy-in and increase awareness of the significance of the standardized tests. Mary explains:

> We're getting better at letting the parents know how important test scores are. We have two info nights each time, and we send two letters home as kind of a back-up. The scores are mailed home and then we have two info nights to walk through the results so we can think about how to bring them up as a community.

Mary works in one of the lowest income areas in LA. The community she serves would be well-served by this degree of engagement and community building in a host of areas—a rare occasion for the teaching team to come together as collaborative professionals, which happens almost exclusively around ST.

Consideration of parents can play an important role in the pressure students and teachers experience. As discussed in Chapter 5, public opinion about teaching and testing is often very different from the views held by teachers. One Chicago teacher explains:

> The public has been brain-washed to think that standardized tests are the only way to know how well a school is doing. On the other hand, they see students in their community unhappily going to school, entering buildings where their brains and experiences aren't valued, where they are not valued for what they are capable of—only what they've done.

The failure and poor performance about which so many children agonize is, teachers report, harmful to children's sense of self and can serve to invalidate the knowledge students do bring to class, encouraging them sometimes to downplay their strengths. Toronto teacher Cooper suggests, "We tell them there are other ways of knowing, and that there are many ways to be smart, but the test doesn't get at spatial or kinesthetic abilities really." A contradiction the children recognize, he explains: "What we do by giving them the test for days, kind of trumps for them what we say." Frank conversations between students and teachers about the (dis)utility of testing notwithstanding, with equal parts reluctant buy-in and dejected exasperation, the quest for the test does not rest. The impact of ST on children is far from uniform; however, and it is clear that the high-stakes standardization environment impacts many children negatively, and further, that many teachers recognize this and are often unable to stop it. The trade-off (well-being of students in exchange for test results) is for many teachers simply not a fair deal.

Summary and Implications

This chapter has outlined radical changes to classroom practice and experience, as understood by teachers with regard to educational standardization. Interview and survey responses illustrate the classroom impacts of the criticisms and conceptual high-stakes standardized testing framework developed in Chapter 3, and detail the interactive ways in which the pursuit of higher test scores is affecting the classroom and teacher practice. This study extends existing work that illustrates that the time crunch faced by teachers is widespread, and that curricular breadth and depth are contracted in the high-stakes environment. Time and curricular pressure are varied from one schooling context to another, and increased pressure tends to correlate with previous low performance, while low-pressure schools are more likely to be affluent. Most US school children attend low-income schools where pressure is likely to be higher. In high-pressure environments, the time and curriculum constraints are felt across grades, between teachers and between schools. Despite the varied impact of ST, practices of teaching to the test are widespread and come in many forms.

A significant difference between the US and Canadian contexts persists, although this may be more quantitative than qualitative. This is to say, more testing accounts for a greater pedagogical impact in the classroom and that the same pedagogical impacts are reported but to different degrees in the two contexts. Tested subject matter displaces nontested subject matter, although more so in high-pressure schools than in low-pressure schools, a finding consistent in Canada and the United States. Extreme cases in the United States have seen the arts, physical education, and social sciences relegated to extracurricular activities or functionally eliminated altogether. In addition to tested subjects, test-taking strategies are now commonly taught, while actual curriculum items may be partially or completely overlooked. Test-oriented teaching and learning, which follows from test-centered curriculum and scheduling, is widespread and relies upon a limited variety of teaching and learning strategies. The pedagogy of standardization moves away from accepted best practices, and tends to most powerfully underserve the highest- and lowest-performing students. Finally, the findings suggest that current ST regimes in both contexts are associated with widespread stress, anxiety, and struggle for students; a hefty price to pay for data that only one in ten teachers feel improves student learning.

CHAPTER 5

Not What I Signed up for: The Changing Meaning of Being a Teacher

On the back of the toilet tank in Franco's bathroom was a piece of concrete block with a small string attached to a jagged corner. A tag he had attached on a string read: "Courtesy of the *Los Angeles Times*." Franco had sent me in to take a look after I asked him about what it means to be a teacher in LA. The home décor item had come through his front window the day after his "least effective" teacher rating by the *Los Angeles Times* was published in its annual rating of teachers. An anonymous note in his mailbox had read, "Our kids deserve better than a piece of shit like you." Franco is a fifth grade teacher in South LA. At the time, he was known as the teacher who was happy to take transient students, English-language learners (ELLs), and other kids whose abilities might have a hard time showing up on a state test. Franco was "the go to guy for these students." He loved teaching them (unlike some of his colleagues) and he had preservice and professional training to support ELLs—he understood the job and did it well and with joy. Now he struggled to spread those kids around, telling his principal, "I'll take my fair share, but not more than anybody else—I'm done being that guy." Franco has moved away from doing what he does best, from serving students who most need it, and from teaching with students in mind at every turn. When I asked why he decided to keep the projectile, he explained:

> Well, its location in the house is not accidental but that was a wake-up call for me. My whole identity was teaching...teaching for students and

their success. It was a bit outside I guess but I was that guy, the guy raised down here [in South LA] who made a difference in the movie about the inner city school. The brick was it man. I was a guy who needed his job, who needed to be safe. It was Maslow's.

The reference was to Maslow's hierarchy of needs.[1] From a professional with a purpose and the ability to fulfill that purpose (the final stage of the hierarchy), Franco was newly returned to concerns of food, shelter, and personal security (Maslow's first two stages).

As mentioned in the introduction to this book, the original purpose of this study was to better understand race and racism in teacher practice in the United States and Canada. Conversations with teachers in both countries returned again and again to the high stakes of testing. From a research perspective, I felt as if I had stepped onto shifting ground—or waded into a turning tide. Teachers' work was changing fast and the testing question for many US teachers as well as Ontario grades three, six, and ten teachers was trumping more advanced questions of practice, including equity and antiracist pedagogy. The feelings from many teachers, in conversation and through survey responses, were of transition, regression, and of trying to hold on to what they had—personally and professionally. Themes of deprofessionalization, alienation, and frustration were common. While these were by no means unanimous, in the broadest strokes, the data reveal many teachers moving professionally backward on Maslow's hierarchy, handling the basics (with the standards as food, water, and shelter) and less and less frequently attending to questions of diverse pedagogical strategies, critical approaches, and a broad curriculum (pieces that may correspond to esteem and self-actualization for teachers and students alike).

This chapter takes up the relationship between the standardization of public education and the changes to teachers' professional work and lives. This is a complex set of relations governed by a host of factors. Guided by three major themes emerging from teachers' responses, this chapter is organized as follows: The first section looks at the ways in which teaching and teachers are increasingly understood and evaluated using the narrow prism of student test scores and other standardized approaches. The second section looks at the changing relationship between teachers and the public, as well as the ways the transformation of teaching is affecting public perceptions of the profession, and the rise of demoralization as teachers are pulled away from the work they feel is best for students. This section takes up the standardization of teaching itself, with teachers reporting less autonomy and fewer opportunities to exercise professional judgment in certain areas of professional practice. The third section of this chapter analyzes the sometimes painful chasm between the pedagogy of standardized testing and the best practices as understood by teachers through their pre- and in-service learning. This section includes a brief look at related research on learning theory and developmentally appropriate assessments, and takes up the assault on constructivist teaching and learning by standardized approaches.

Testing for All and Accountability for Some: Broken Lenses for Understanding Teachers and Teaching

Increasingly, standardized testing results are the key metric for understanding the efficacy and worth of teachers and teaching in the United States. In Canada, due to the use of relatively fewer standardized tests and less standardization than the United States, this phenomenon is present but not nearly as widespread. As discussed in previous chapters, test results are seductive, appear easy to understand and allow for (overly) simple comparisons of children, teachers, schools, and districts. Test results make for good headlines, political points for or against, and suggest objectivity in as far as all students often write the same test in a given jurisdiction. At its most extreme, as discussed in Chapter 4, testing accounts for 30–40 percent of time in US classrooms. More commonly, in the United States and Canada, that figure sits around between 10 and 20 percent in testing years. Given the widespread practice of test preparation, we know testing and test-related activities are often distinct from the other practices (remember the LA teacher who said she could only get back to teaching once the tests were done).

A comprehensive measure of teaching would thus include a holistic consideration of what a teacher does all year long, as well as what he does from year to year. This would be complemented by similar parallel assessment of the community of learners he serves (also looked at across reporting periods as well as grade levels). Unfortunately, just as testing has come to define learning, it has also come to explain teaching, and by extension, teachers. Despite the limitations of what standardized testing can tell us about teachers and teaching, many US states link teacher pay and tenure to students' test scores, illustrating the high stakes of testing for teachers. So-called value-added measures (VAM) often evaluate teacher efficacy by assessing the relationship between teaching and standards, with 50 percent or more of many VAM evaluations based on standardized test results.[2] The call for tying teacher remuneration and tenure to student performance is a lonely one in

Canada. Led by the Frasier Institute, a conservative think tank, the idea has gained little traction.[3] Although the research on these evaluations in the United States has found only tenuous (and sometimes nonexistent) relationships between VAM and teacher quality, these processes march on under a general banner of data-driven accountability, despite the failure of VAM to assure quality and the noted risk of driving out strong teachers.[4] In the United States, VAM and the reporting of test scores can powerfully inform popular understandings of the work teachers do. This reading of the profession, according to teachers, is inaccurate and ultimately misrepresents and diminishes the job. Among the significant issues with this misreading is the failure of standardized tests specifically (and VAM generally) to consider factors external to classroom learning. A Chicago teacher explains:

> There are too many variables that stymie a teacher's ability (even the best teachers) to become an effective teacher. Students in most urban areas, and specifically poor under-served areas, arrive with socio-economic and psychological and emotional issues that are way beyond what teachers can address. Most of my parents are not capable nor do they support homework or working academically with their children. These factors stymie even the best teacher's ability to facilitate learning because they are forced to become mothers, fathers, therapists for those students.

As Chapter 4 lays out, the very pedagogical and support practices that address the concerns raised here are often difficult and sometimes impossible with test-oriented teaching and learning (TOTL). Myriad factors impact performance and the public, including many parents, sometimes does not recognize this. One Chicago teacher explains, "most of my parents don't understand the tests... teachers cannot accurately use the data to work with students and the public hears whatever the district tells them." Again, the theme of useless data emerges, as far as teacher practice, alongside a perceived misunderstanding by parents. Discussing teacher evaluation, another Illinois teacher describes some of the many factors that can impact test results, but that go unrecognized in the interpretation of results:

> I agree that test scores should be a tiny bit attached to teacher evaluations, but not a lot. Teachers need to be held accountable, but again, it's beyond our control what happens in a student's life outside of the classroom. I don't want my evaluation to be flawed if I have students without home/parent support and guidance... students who lack this do not always perform well at school, period.

With similar concerns in mind, a Toronto teacher suggests that evaluating teachers using test scores creates a "teach to the test mentality" and adds that although "value-added measures purportedly control for factors such as attendance, economics, etc., I do not believe that the margin of error can be small enough to make the data valid." According to many teachers, truly controlling for other factors on the test would include a consideration of the home. A Toronto teacher explains, "We cannot control for the other 18 hours students are not with us and those 18 hours have a great effect on test scores—i.e. sleep, nourishment, environmental stress, emotional stability, etc."

Additionally, in low-income areas, significant improvements may not be recognized under the data-driven accountability framework, as LA teacher Sirin explains:

> Look if you have been here ten years or more, you get hip to the fact that what we're doing as teachers, especially in neighborhoods like this, we're making a lot of progress with them but it can be hard to see small and steady increases in tests scores and really big learning jumps are drowned out by the overall difference between schools like ours and the test results in Santa Monica [a wealthy area of Los Angeles County]. We've improved each year but we're still PI [Performance Improvement School]—the lowest of the low."

A seventh-year Toronto teacher echoes this concern, explaining:

> Standardized testing is not an accurate picture of what a school is doing. The test does not take into account schools who are battling severe poverty and behavioral problems. For example, our school is making massive progress in these areas but we came in as one of the 'worst schools' in the province last year. How exactly is publishing those results helpful to a struggling community?

The preceding comments highlight an important aspect of the discourse of standardization. Testing critic Alfie Kohn suggests a thought experiment and asks us to imagine all students in a given district meeting or exceeding all of the standards. He suggests this would be more likely to result in a call to raise the standards than a call to praise the teachers.[5] Like grading on a curve, norm-referenced standards usually require winners and losers. Failure for some portion of students is by design rather than by accident. In what Kohn calls "Orwellian audacity," this results in a "process of flunking vast numbers of children, or forcing them to drop out, or turning whole schools into giant test-prep factories is rationalized as being in the best interest of poor and minority students."[6]

The teaching to the test mentality mentioned earlier can also impact teachers' decisions regarding where and who to teach. A tenth-year Chicago teacher explains the potentially inequitable impact on students:

> If you want to evaluate teachers (something I strongly support) then evaluate us, not our students. The best teachers often teach the weakest most struggling students, we need that to remain true. If you're connecting student success with teacher success, teachers will only teach the rich and the white students. That is more than a little dangerous.

Like many US teachers, Malik feels testing is too blunt of an instrument with which to identify the weak teachers out there, explaining:

> We know the district does not support us, even though they say they do. Tests have become a tool to find the bad teachers, the bad schools—they miss that in real fact, they are identifying some of the teachers working hardest with some of the toughest kids.

Perhaps not surprisingly, teachers surveyed overwhelming disagreed or strongly disagreed (over 90%) with the use of student test results to measure teachers, as Table 5.1 illustrates.

While a predictable result, in interviews and survey comments, teachers consistently identified the unreliability and inaccuracy of the test when discussing why standardized testing (ST) should not be used for teacher evaluation. The best-paid teacher as determined by VAM may be the one who best teaches to the test, a practice widely understood as unsound and as not in the best interest of student learning and development. Further, the best-paid teacher may be one who best

Table 5.1 The use of standardized test results to evaluate teachers, Illinois and Ontario teachers

In my belief, the results of testing should be used to evaluate teachers.

	Ont. English	*Ont. French*	*Illinois*
Strongly Agree	0.6%	0.3%	0.7%
Agree	1.0%	0.8%	3.4%
No Opinion	2.0%	1.8%	2.9%
Disagree	10.2%	9.2%	21.6%
Strongly Disagree	86.3%	88.0%	71.3%

avoids teaching assignments that serve traditionally low-performing students. This education dystopia may have arrived in some parts of the United States already, and may not be far off in others, when considering the struggles of low-income urban schools to attract the country's strongest teachers.

A teacher in Ontario's far North (where many communities suffer from higher rates of poverty and institutional racism than their southern neighbors) argues: "We are also 'competing' with students and teachers in southern schools. It should not be a competition but it is. It is also a shell game of moving statistics around." Another Northern Ontario teacher explains, "I teach mainly Native children and they put those tests up against white kids from downtown Toronto." Even though her school's numbers are on the increase, she reveals, "I get flak and I wouldn't if I taught rich white kids somewhere in Southern Ontario—it's not low expectations, they just have fewer supports but more pressure." Indeed the pressure is on, as 18-year veteran LA teacher Michelle explains: "We have been in [Program Improvement] since NCLB started...One year we made a 70 point jump, that was one of times we hit safe harbor, but we're still PI5+." PI5+ refers to more than five years as a Program Improvement (PI) school, and safe harbor describes a school, which is improving but which is still a PI school. The military terminology is apropos of the situation. Michelle continues, "it means we're safe from attack by privatization for another year, but the thing is we want the change worse than anybody but obviously testing won't do it—it's not real accountability." This supports previous research that suggests teachers are not opposed to the purported aims of ST, specifically accountability, consistency of instruction, and high expectations; instead, they object to the means by which these ends are ineffectively pursued through standardization.[7]

Part of the deprofessionalization teachers feel is a race to the bottom in which, ironically, professional enrichment becomes harder within the pedagogy of ST. Many teachers want accountability (many are parents themselves) and want to be part of a profession that self-regulates and evolves. In constant defense-mode (at the bottom of Maslow's hierarchy), professional improvement that treats content, pedagogy, and other central areas is disincentivized—it's risky to step off the testing train (or to even turn and face the back of the train). Two of the teachers interviewed from South LA schools were able to attend a district-sponsored week-long professional learning trip to a historic US site; a site that features prominently in the curriculum they each teach. Neither was able to use what they had learned, and one was given an informal verbal warning when, ahead of an upcoming standardized test, he was "caught" teaching a piece of Revolutionary War history during time previously allotted to test preparation. Teachers have the professional knowledge they need to do the good work they want to do, but rarely are they given the necessary time, space, and professional leeway.

With regard to the way ST data are used, one Chicago teacher explains:

> Individually, many teachers reflect upon their standardized testing data and focus on areas of growth when setting goals for themselves. But as a school, there isn't time to do a cycle of inquiry around testing data in a helpful manner for every core area of content and every teacher.

Toronto teacher Karen echoes many of her colleagues in the United States and Canada, suggesting, "it doesn't tell us anything we wouldn't know if we're keeping anecdotal descriptive records" as most Ontario teachers do to support three formal reports per year or semester. She continues, "and if you're not doing that, the [provincial standardized test] is not going to change anything anyway given the fact that you are not that kind of teacher anyway." Teachers' frustration with data-driven accountability stems primarily from the widespread belief that it is neither good data nor effective accountability. It does not work and teaching and learning are getting worse in many contexts—phenomena that hit teachers harder than most.

One Chicago teacher explains, "It's important to have accountability and to make sure teachers are teaching well but too often standardized testing results wrongly accuse teachers, principals and schools of not 'doing their job.'" Another suggests: "It is essential to understand the students' strengths and areas of needed improvement, but educators are not allocated sufficient time to implement the necessary strategies based upon these assessment results." One sixth grade Toronto teacher who administers the Education Quality and Accountability Office's (EQAO) test argues, "I am less accountable to parents, to myself as a professional now that I teach in a testing year—the only measure that admin. and parents have their eyes on is EQAO scores." A reality that is perhaps less complicated but, he explains, "less satisfying and worse for kids overall." On the question of accountability, Lorraine, a veteran teacher in South LA comments:

> I think I am less accountable than I want to be as a result of the test. I drive to work every day as a professional and I used to drive home every

day the same way. Now it's about half the time. The other half I drive home alone, not making change, not thinking about my profession like a doctor thinks of his practice, but like somebody who figures out the best way to take the million tiny instructions I get and turn them into more points on a test that I don't create, grade, and can't see. Like a mushroom: kept in the dark and fed bullshit.

The feelings behind Lorraine's most wonderful turn of phrase were shared by several others. This alienation is compounded by the failure of standardized tests to tell a complete and accurate story of teachers and teaching—a professionally intolerable phenomenon for many. One Illinois teacher argues, "the stakes are so high...philosophically I strongly disagree with teaching to a test as this invalidates the test itself. It becomes a measure of my test prep abilities, not my teaching abilities."

For all of its impacts on time, curriculum, and pedagogy—all of the things it does—there are a number of important things standardized tests do not do. Specifically, they do not measure a great range of student or teacher ability. They do not separate where (or from whom) the student learned a particular tested item, and they do not consistently improve either teacher practice or student learning. One Ontario teacher explains: "It's actually a reflection of the student and of all the teachers who have taught him, not just the teacher of that year. What a load to bear for all EQAO grade level teachers." When scores go down, Toronto teacher Lana suggests, "it does not mean I worked less, or worked worst. It also doesn't mean the kids are less capable. It really doesn't say much." On scores improving, one Chicago teacher suggests, "Improving scores generally relates to teaching to the test which protects jobs, not student learning." As Tables 5.2 and 5.3 illustrate, according to surveyed teachers, test results offer neither a better understanding of schools, nor an accurate representation of teachers' abilities.

Table 5.2 What standardized tests tell the public about schools, Illinois and Ontario teachers

In my belief, standardized tests allow the public to better understand schools' program strengths and weaknesses.

	Ont. English	Ont. French	Illinois
Agree or Strongly Agree	6.2%	6.4%	7.2%
Uncertain	5.8%	7.9%	10.2%
Disagree or Strongly Disagree	88.0%	85.6%	82.6%

Table 5.3 Standardized testing as a reflection of teachers' ability, Illinois and Ontario teachers

Standardized tests accurately reflect my abilities as a teacher.

	Ont. English	Ont. French	Illinois
Agree or Strongly Agree	3.3%	10.9%	4.4%
No Opinion	6.0%	9.1%	7.0%
Disagree or Strongly Disagree	90.7%	80.0%	89.6%

Even the most avid supporters of ST should be troubled by these numbers. A disturbing gap between the policy of standardization and the experience and buy-in of educational frontline workers is revealed here. If standardized tests were doing the job, these numbers would not be so stark.

As was the case with questions concerning time, curriculum, and pedagogy as outlined in Chapter 4, teachers' experiences of VAM generally, and of being measured by test results specifically, varied from context to context. A Chicago teacher explains, "I'm on the North Side now—high scores, parents everywhere and everybody's happy—night and day from my last school on the Southside." The North Side is far more socially advantaged than the Southside. Similarly, teachers at Flower Elementary in LA felt more valued for overall professional ability and contribution to student learning than those teaching in schools in South LA, a pattern that held for teachers at high-income and low-income schools in Toronto. Again, it is clear that ST has different impacts for teachers and students in different schools—perhaps in keeping with the notion that success for some and failure for others is not only acceptable but also part of the plan.

Overall, survey and interview results reveal deep teacher frustration with testing as a measure of their professional efficacy and value. A persistent gap exists between the expressed purposes of testing and teachers' understanding thereof. Specifically, teachers feel ST fails to reflect their abilities as teachers, and at the same time, fails to inform the public about the strengths and weaknesses of programs and schools (a hallmark claim of the accountability movement). With regard to these phenomena, the Canadian and US contexts are distinct primarily because of VAM policies in place across the United States; policies that fail, as this and other research suggests, to improve the quality of teaching and learning. Despite these differences, teachers and teachers' work in both contexts are increasingly impacted by the push for data-driven accountability—hoping to hit a bull's eye with a shotgun. With little to show academically and professionally for the pedagogy of ST, the worsening relationship with the general public is that much more difficult for teachers, as the next section details.

Teachers, Demoralization, and the Public Imagination

Teachers, for the most, like their jobs but not as much as they used to. In 2001, James Popham noted that the rise of testing can accompany a decrease in public support for teachers.[8] This corresponds to the reflections of teachers interviewed and surveyed for this study, many of whom feel less respected by the public than in previous years. With falling rates of unionization and tighter job markets, many tenured public sector workers run up against resentment. Among publicly funded jobs, teachers' work is unique insofar as its central role in the development of children intellectually, physically, emotionally, and—whether we admit it or not—politically. It is also a sector, which, unlike departments of parks and recreation for example, is constantly debated and analyzed by the media, politicians, scholars, and educators. Public education is value laden; hotly debated and disputed in the public sphere. From the moment they enter the profession, teachers navigate this contested terrain in their personal and professional lives—it is part of the job. In my teacher education classes, I ask students to itemize the criticisms they have received since endeavoring to become a teacher. Common responses include everything from teasing about summers off and short work days, to joining the liberal elite, to working below their station in life, to wanting to become part of "the system." Most often, however, my students mention friends and relations playfully (and not-so-playfully) raising the specter of jobs for life with no accountability—a criticism familiar to many teachers in this study.

As suggested in Chapter 2, standardization in education has, since the nineteenth century, ostensibly attempted to account for weak teaching and inconsistent educational experiences for children. Standardization has long worked to teacher-proof the classroom to different degrees, and in the twenty-first century we are seeing this on high. As the measure of teachers and teachers' work becomes increasingly (over)simplified through the prism of test results and VAM, teaching appears increasingly simple. Ignorance of the complexity of teaching twenty-first-century learners has led many to look down upon the profession, according to many teachers. Popular representations of the lackluster teacher abound. From comic portrayals in programs (such as *The Simpsons*, *Ferris Bueller's Day Off*, and *The Unbreakable Kimmy*

Schmidt); to dramatic films in which the protagonist is a hero because he or she breaks the mold of the lazy and disengaged teacher (such as *Freedom Writers, Stand and Deliver,* and *Coach Carter*); to dramas (such as *The Wire*); and to documentaries (such as the Gates Foundation-funded *Waiting for Superman*) popular media paint a wide but shallow portrait of a profession in decline: of individuals who no longer care about students (if they ever did); of teachers too tired, disempowered or apathetic to make a difference; and of folks overpaid for doing easy work with lifetime protection on the public purse.

As a parent, teacher educator, education scholar, and former classroom teacher I have spent a lot of time in classrooms in the United States and Canada. I am the first to suggest that there are bad teachers out there who should not be in the classroom. Many of the teachers in this study feel the same way and are truly interested in robust accountability. Data-driven accountability has not, however, improved teacher quality and there is no evidence that removing teacher tenure would improve student learning overall. One Chicago teacher explains, "The idea of some form of accountability is positive, but we have all seen the excesses of this, and I don't think ST is an ideal way to achieve this." A Toronto teacher supports assessing teachers critically, but cautions, "tests are not the only way to do that." Ironically, as described in Chapter 4 and in the previous section, test-oriented teaching and learning (TOTL) pulls teachers away from collaboration, away from holding themselves accountable, and away from research-informed best practices and professionalism. Teachers point to a need to take a more complex look at accountability that moves beyond narrow measures. In the meantime, many teachers report a deteriorating relationship with the public, and find themselves defending against the sorts of imagined popular media images of the teacher.

When asked whether the public values the work she did as a teacher, and whether this has changed over the past decade, one Chicago teacher confesses: "I used to feel greatly valued and respected. Today I don't even tell anyone I'm a teacher." Another Illinois teacher suggests: "The general public only wants to hear about the results and not the process or what we have to do to get the results. 'Value' is a strong word." This reductionist view of the profession was mentioned by many including another Chicago teacher who explains, "even my friends and family members think I babysit and am overpaid for what I do." Many link this to NCLB and the current era of education reform, as one Chicago teacher suggests: "We were appreciated more before all the NCLB, teacher accountability and charter schools came along." A change is afoot in Ontario as well. One Toronto teacher explains: "I used to tell people I am a teacher, I don't tell them anymore. I am afraid of rude comments, salary questions or political conversations."

Many teachers reported feeling a less consistent sense of public support and value. Some suggested public support, as well as support from parents wavers, eroding during tougher economic times, resulting in less concern for teachers, whom they perceive to have secure employment. One Toronto teacher explains:

> People are hot and cold on teachers. We all have a few we respect immensely but regard them in general, and especially their unions, as being a blockade to change. We can see them as either saints or greedy ingrates but can't seem to see them as professionals who run the gamut like any other profession.

Others suggest the overall political climate has changed over time. A veteran Chicago teacher comments: "I feel teachers are respected less and go unappreciated due to recent negative publicity in papers about bad teachers and testing." A number of teachers suggested this change has been radical with regard to support for teachers, including two veteran Chicago teachers with over 25 years teaching experience. The first suggests, "around 2003–2004 comments from non-teachers started to become more negative. People used to tell me that they don't know how I can do it. People now tell me that having summers off is a luxury." Extending this idea, the second explains, "When I started teaching, there was no public shaming of or maligning teachers. In the last five years, there has been a virulent attack on Chicago teachers."

Teachers suggested that public support for teachers varied between different communities, and between the parents of students they teach and the general public. One Chicago teacher explains:

> Individual parents, and the parents of my specific students value what I do, however, in a generic way teachers are not viewed positively as a whole due to the sense that "there are so many bad ones," a claim based on no evidence other than anecdotal experiences and the repetition of that claim.

A tenth-year Toronto teacher suggests, "my parent community is behind us, but out there in the big wide world teachers are getting railroaded these days." There is also perceived variation between neighborhoods and home culture. "North Side residents value teachers; South and Westside residents do not value teachers," commented one Chicago teacher, while his Ontario counterpart suggested, "it all depends on the community, and it's not just who has the money—although that impacts results—it's culture and education as well." While Chapter 6 takes up the questions of home and school culture and the impact on results, several teachers suggest these impact overall parent support for teachers.

For many, the publication and subsequent misuse of test score data are major reasons for the increasingly strained relationship with much of the public. One Los Angeles teacher had his tires slashed the day after the *LA Times* published his scores, while another found his windshield smashed at school. A Toronto teacher reports having a beer poured in his lap by an angry parent whose son failed the grade ten EQAO test, with the father telling him he was a "disgrace" among other things. The following sampling of survey comments on test result dissemination in Ontario bears out the frustration with public interpretation and reading of test score results:

> The results are used as a political tool to help the government of the day look good. It does nothing to improve teacher practice. More often than not, good teachers with challenging classes are criticized for low test scores.
>
> When shared, students/parents should be made away of the relative (un)importance of the testing and the nuances in scoring EQAO.

For their part, Chicago teachers raised similar concerns, as the following comments on publishing test scores flesh out:

> Parents need extensive education about the test and what it means. They need to know much more than data—the ranking of the student compared to others in the same grade, compared to the rest of the district and the rest of the state. It is presented in such a negative way that many parents think their child is not learning.
>
> I would be happy to have these results published if the teacher keeps the same students year after year.
>
> I really don't care if my name is tied to my test scores but I can see how others might. If it's a single piece of data, then no. If you want to add the 40 percent special education list of student needs, the fact that I have 13 percent English language learners too, and that the computers are over 5 years old and the internet connections cut out and pause the test...then, sure, feel free.

Meanwhile, a number of teachers suggest somewhat sarcastically that publishing teacher names alongside student scores is only a start. One argues: "Education is a shared responsibility so if the teachers name is made public then so should the parents' names of each student;" while another suggests, "okay—as long as doctors have to publicly state how many patients got worse or died under their care and lawyers have to publish how many cases they have won or lost."

Los Angeles teachers returned many times to the teacher ratings in the *Los Angeles Times*, and in particular to questions of what it failed to capture. Julia, a seventh-year teacher, says:

> I understand they want to have some way to measure us, but you know, they are putting everything on testing, they want to base your credibility as a teacher on test scores. The *LA Times* just put something out... [Julia tears up here] and I was rated least effective. It was the most demoralizing experience. [Her colleagues] teased me here because I cried like nine times a day. Every time I thought about it, I thought, I am a teacher, this is my life. Then there is this newspaper which says I am terrible and they're just looking at the test scores. It's hard especially when you are compared to other teachers at your school. I am the teacher who likes to take the more challenging kids. I voluntarily have special education kids mainstreamed into my class whereas some of the other teachers will refuse these kids or kick them out ahead of the tests. It makes you want to not take these kids.

Julia's story, as well as those above, illustrates not only the personal toll of VAM for teachers but also the ways in which high stakes can push teachers away from teaching vulnerable students. Teachers also point to the inaccuracy of the *Times* formula in measuring improvements in low- and high-performing schools. For example, the paper measures movement from one level to another, so for a school of top performers there is sometimes little room for movement, which in turn, does nothing to accrue points for the teacher. Despite the failure to capture needed data on what and how well teachers do what they do, it can have a major impact. Veteran LA teacher Barr lays it out, saying:

> Look, if I believed what the *LA Times* says about my teaching, I'd go jump off a bridge. My uncle in Germany called me one year and said, 'it doesn't sound like you're doing a very good job with those kids. The next day my mother called me from a nursing home in Sacramento to say the same thing.

Barr's words are all the more poignant given the suicide of Los Angeles teacher Rigoberto Rueles, who was rated least effective in mathematics and average in English by the *LA Times* (a less effective than average overall rating). He took his own life only days after the VAM rating was published, and family members have suggested the two events were related.[9] Less than a month after his rating, the paper described him as follows:

> As a teacher in an impoverished, gang-ridden area of South Los Angeles, Rigoberto Ruelas always reached out to the toughest kids. He would tutor them on weekends and after school, visit their homes, encourage them to aim high and go to college. The fifth-grade teacher at Miramonte Elementary School was so passionate about his mission that, school authorities say, he had near perfect attendance in 14 years on the job.[10]

Presuming the *LA Times* has its facts straight on all accounts, its VAM ratings appear immune to the important work teachers do, which may not be measurable via the results of ST.

A tenth-year LA teacher, describing the ratings suggests:

> Public humiliation only adds to the tremendous stress we already feel. It does not improve teaching, it diminishes us. How can I create a joyful learning experience for children when I feel emotionally a wreck by public abuse. Also, it does not take into account what teachers are dealing with. My scores may have been low, because in Los Angeles, a dead body was found on campus next to my classroom.

The sum total of the high-stakes, data-driven accountability (including the declining relationship with the public, the changing classroom, and the changing job) has left many teachers profoundly sad and frustrated with their professional lives. As Table 5.4 illustrates, ST has diminished teaching according to the vast majority of those surveyed.

Table 5.4 Impact of standardized testing on the profession, Illinois and Ontario teachers

In my belief, standardized testing has the following impact on teaching as a profession:

	Ont. English	*Ont. French*	*Illinois*
Strongly Enhances	0.4%	2.0%	0.4%
Enhances	4.9%	6.6%	3.7%
Uncertain	16.2%	37.9%	16.0%
Diminishes	50.4%	37.4%	43.4%
Strongly Diminishes	28.2%	16.0%	36.6%

While 78.6 percent of English Ontario teachers, 62.4 percent of French Ontario teachers, and 79.4 percent of Illinois teachers feel ST has diminished or strongly diminished the profession, less than 9 percent of teachers, overall, feel ST enhances or strongly enhances the profession. When asked about the changes in teaching brought about by ST, one Ontario teacher pulled no punches, explaining: "This is one of the saddest parts of my career." A colleague from Chicago in her tenth year suggested that, "for every year I teach, my happiness has decreased." She continues, linking this decreased happiness to the pedagogy of ST, by saying, "The actual teaching part, where I get to give new skills to students and they feel proud of what they've learned, that part is great, but that's the smallest part of my day." This was echoed by another Chicago teacher, who suggests, "I have never felt so burned out in my life; everything is about paperwork and data for the district, not about communication with students." In the United States, many teachers feel that politics is increasingly in the driver's seat when it comes to education generally, and to their work specifically. A fifth-year Chicago teacher explains, "I am getting so tired of all of the politics, lack of respect and increasing demands on me that will not benefit my students. In other words, I am frustrated," while another says "I love teaching, however I am dissatisfied with the way education is headed and the forces beyond my classroom."

There is a dangerous temptation to see the experiences of teachers through the lens of individual or one-off situations (which fit nicely with the stereotype of the burned-out teachers discussed earlier). The work of Doris Santoro is useful for putting these widespread frustrations in perspective. She outlines an important distinction between demoralization and burn out. She argues:

> Burnout may be an appropriate diagnosis in some cases where individual teachers' personal resources cannot meet the challenge of the difficulties presented by the work. However, the "burnout" explanation fails to account for situations where the conditions of teaching change so dramatically that the moral rewards, previously available in ever-challenging work, are now inaccessible. In this case, the phenomenon is better termed "demoralization."[11]

With regard to participants in this study, understanding widespread patterns in teachers' experiences and feelings as demoralization, rather than as burnout, allows for a focus on the dramatic changes afoot as a result of educational standardization and the daily effects of TOTL on teachers. Sandra Acker's insistence that we recognize the school as workplace[12] is relevant here, and indeed it can to be taken further. In addition to recognizing that teachers can and should rightfully raise concerns about their working conditions and relations, it is also key to remember that teachers' working conditions are students' learning conditions. The impact, however, on the changing profession as described here also signals the need to look at the schools as a site of personal meaning making for teachers. Teachers are increasingly alienated from what Santoro calls the "moral reward of teaching" when they are unable to do, personally and professionally, what is right in their work lives.[13] Teachers struggle for control in pursuit of these moral rewards.

Sadly, for some Ontario teachers, wresting control means getting out of the third and sixth grades (EQAO years) as the following comment suggests: "[EQAO] basically ruins the year for grades three and six. I never wanted to teach either of these grades again for this reason." Another Ontario teacher argues that EQAO is:

> A total waste of everyone's time. Kills the joy of learning for me and the kids. I've been teaching grade three for a number of years and am getting out of that level totally next year because it is soul destroying."

This relates to findings from the previous section, which note that ST can provide disincentives for certain teaching assignments. While some Ontario teachers are working to avoid EQAO years, one grade three teacher is leaving altogether, explaining: "The job no longer exists. I will retire in two years. I'm not leaving teaching. It has left me." To be clear, no one involved in public education in Ontario should be proud of what these last few comments reveal; they are disturbing and may very possibly speak to mediocre classroom experiences for these teachers' students. Indeed, as a father, I might try to keep my children out of the classroom of the gentlemen retiring in two years who seems to have thrown in the towel. Teaching is too important to be done by someone for whom "teaching has left." If there is no joy in your classroom, you should not have one. While accountability fanatics may suggest that these are precisely the sort of teachers we need to get rid of, there is no reason to assume that these joyless and disengaged professional experiences would show up in low test scores or other narrow VAM measures. In other words, standardization will not find the bad apples or support the good ones. Further, these teachers are telling the story of change, of the transformation of the classroom and the profession as a result of standardization. That such voices have been largely absent or marginalized in the testing conversation to date is dangerous for the profession and the students it serves.

Survey and interview data suggest a worsening relationship with the public for many teachers. Within this, variations persist by neighborhood, community, between parents and nonparents, and based on culture and other considerations. While these are concerns in the United States and Canada, they are more pronounced in comments from US teachers. The publishing of test scores is a hugely contentious issue and over a dozen teachers used the phrase "witch hunt" when referring to this practice. Concerns around this issue center on the narrow picture of teachers and students offered by these data. The publication of teacher names and ratings based on student test scores (a practice not found in Canada) creates huge upset in many teachers' personal and professional lives. Many teachers report changing feelings about the profession, and teachers overwhelmingly suggest that ST diminishes teaching. In Ontario, where only grades three, six, nine, and ten use a standardized test, some teachers are avoiding teaching assignments in testing years—a phenomenon reminiscent of those in California who feel increasingly pressured to avoid teaching students predicted to score low on standardized tests. The next section considers the conflicts navigated by teachers, between high-stakes standardization and teachers' preservice and in-service professional training.

Professional Development as Painting in the Dark: Standardization as the Enemy of Constructivism

For many teachers, a great divide exists between the work they have been trained to do and that which they actually do as in-service teachers. Chapters 2, 3, and 4 have detailed the various impacts of ST, and of educational standardization more generally. The test-oriented teaching and learning outlined here is, for many, not the sort of work they hoped to do upon becoming teachers. As noted, many teachers want to make a difference—be the change—and standardization makes this challenging, alienating them from the moral rewards of teaching. But the gap here is more than that between a teacher's dreams of being a change maker and the reality of that dream gone unfulfilled. The gap is one between teachers' professional knowledge of best practices—gained in teacher training and in subsequent professional learning (including mentorship experiences) and the teaching required by the pedagogy of standardized testing. Related concerns include the teacher-proofing of the profession. This refers to prescriptive curricula and delivery methods in which teachers are speaking, generating assignments, assessing, and planning according to predetermined rules, scripts, and items (often generated by private testing companies). Teacher resistance to teacher-proofing is by no means a simple chaffing at losing classroom authority, but instead a frustration with working away from and often against the practices that the research tells them best supports student learning and well-being. Concerns range from questions of pedagogical and assessment strategies, to the age appropriateness of tests and test-oriented teaching, to the rigidity of standardized teaching and learning.

Teachers also note that despite often having less power to impact their classrooms, they are increasingly held more responsible for the test results of students. One Chicago teacher protests, "I am told what to teach; when to teach it; how to teach it; and when or if it all goes wrong I am the blame for it." Highlighting the waste of teachers' professional knowledge, one Chicago teacher argues, "Most teachers know what works and what is best for the particular group of students they have any given year. However, as policies trickle down to the classroom level, teachers' input is barely existent." When teachers do push back and attempt innovation and collaboration beyond testing-oriented teaching, many face resistance, as one Ontario teacher describes below:

> Administration, red tape, and running schools like a business prohibit my ability to teach my children. I am encouraged to provide more "data" in charts and graphs than I do actual, concrete teaching methods. When I do try to implement something I'm forced to defend it, even after it's implemented and it does work. Generally, these policies don't mimic the paper/pencil policies of the board, so they are seen as "new" and "uncertain" even if I've used them before to much success.

When asked about having significant input in and around the school, one teacher commented "'significant'" is the rub. I am welcome to contribute, but whether it is taken seriously, or even understood, is another matter."

On the question of autonomy, teachers in both in the United States and Canada felt less control in proportion to the amount of testing for which they were responsible, and as well, based on the context in which they were teaching (high-pressure contexts with low scores meant less autonomy, while low-pressure, high-performing contexts meant more autonomy). One Chicago teacher explains: "As long as I'm teaching an advanced class I have greater autonomy, but when I teach basic classes, the district and our administration take over many of the decisions."

Table 5.5 Standardized testing, professional judgment, and teacher learning, Illinois and Ontario teachers

Does standardized testing prevent you from using professional judgment, pedagogical and content knowledge gained in teachers college, and/or other learning contexts?

	Ont. English	Ont. French	Illinois
Yes, Always	8.9%	7.2%	9.0%
Yes, Often	31.8%	33.6%	39.3%
Yes, But Only Sometimes	31.1%	36.7%	30.1%
Yes, But Only Rarely	12.7%	10.6%	10.4%
No, Never	15.5%	11.9%	11.2%

Here we see, again, the differential impact of standardization and the idea that advanced learning happens outside of TOTL, whereas "basic" learning seems to surround the test. Extending the findings of the interviews, the survey results suggest ST powerfully impacts the use of professional knowledge and judgment, as Table 5.5 illustrates.

Part of this issue is the degree to which teachers are increasingly responsible for paper work around the collection of data for their administrators, boards, and districts. One Chicago teacher explains: "I rarely get to actually teach, it is paperwork, accountability and testing." Toronto teacher Marvelyn's description of a grade-level initiative at her school extends this point: "Each year all members of the grade six team are responsible for identifying a certain number of low performing students in order to chart their progress as we bring each of them up one level." She explains that this "all happens ahead of EQAO so that we have evidence of how we are making potential improvements in EQAO areas." The time spent documenting the process could be "far better used" helping a greater "number of kids and it would be far less stressful for all involved." A veteran Chicago teacher echoes these concerns, mentioning there are direct impacts for students:

> Having teachers complete all of this daily busy work to prove that we are doing what they consider our job, takes so much time away from teachers' true planning time. Using our time and energy to jump through hoops for the administrators and politicians... this is having a direct and immediate detrimental effect on our students. When teachers are exhausted and stressed, you better believe the students feel it as well.

Such circumstances led some teachers to fairly dire conclusions. One Chicago teacher observes: "We are a profession of testers, not teachers," while another asserts: "Teachers are treated as widgets; it is no wonder that so many behave like widgets." Reflecting on her grade three class in Ontario, one teacher concludes, "the teachable moments are gone."

While the preceding comment refers to teachable moments with students, teachable moments within teacher learning may be changing as well. With regard to professional learning, two major themes emerge from the survey and interview data. First, mandated professional development (PD)—which includes in-school, lunch time, after school, and professional advancement learning sessions—is increasingly focused on TOTL for those teachers who administer standardized tests. Second, training that does not pertain to the test tends to focus on issues and approaches that often come to be jettisoned in favor of TOTL. For example, topics might include equity, mental health, and curriculum content development beyond the tested subjects; while instructional strategies might include differentiated instruction and assessment, community-oriented pedagogy, and project-based inquiry.

Cooper, a Toronto sixth grade teacher in his 13th year, explains:

> Teaching has become more dictated, more and more controlled from above. Even when it's not all bad, it's top down. Data from the testing drives everything. Every year I feel more and more pressure to teach it all and attend to the test. It becomes a quality versus quantity question where the quality of what I do is not what I want, and the test is part of that. It seems like we're teaching more and more. I just feel like, can't we stop the train and get off, just for a minute... I mean we talk about community building and the arts and I can't do it as much because there is so much to do. Maybe I have to say screw it but it's hard when the PLCs [Professional Learning Communities] and other PD are focused on this. As far as students, they are assessed to death, so much that they are almost as aware as us of education language and all that. While it's good to self-evaluate, they are learning to do it the way the test does it—very narrow.

A Chicago teacher takes up Cooper's points regarding curricular contraction and the question of the changing job, arguing, "First we were writing teachers, this year our evaluation depends on reading scores, leaving content and civics behind."

Returning to the question of Professional Learning Communities (PLCs), Toronto teacher Karen explains:

> As a Model School,[14] we get all this training in PLCs—all researched-based, awesome DI stuff—and we can't use it. Our vice principal actually

said, about using manipulatives, that this might not work for the grade six team, because they have EQAO that year. So it drives PD, but that contradicts other PD sometimes.

Echoing these concerns, another Ontario teacher describes the contradiction between her teacher training and EQAO teaching, saying: "increased focus on collaboration, discovery learning, small group instruction but still throw standardized testing at grades three and six. Mixed message much?" A Southern Ontario teacher takes the question of the mixed message a little further, noting the contradictions between EQAO and Ontario education policy. Referring to *Growing Success*, the document on which all teacher assessment, evaluation, and reporting in Ontario schools is based, she points out: "*Growing Success* emphasizes a variety of assessment strategies (products, conversations and observations) and yet EQAO is a timed pencil and paper assessment. This assessment is the polar opposite of these ideas." *Growing Success* lays out a framework for understanding and categorizing assessment practices as being *of* learning, *for* learning, and/or *as* learning; suggesting that each type of assessment of learning has its place, but that a clear understanding and application of all three are needed to effectively assess students. Applied to the EQAO, one Ontario teacher argues: "Assessments for, as, and of learning serve students. Standardized tests offer no descriptive feedback or ongoing conversations about growth. EQAO tests are a testament to distrust in the system."

Another Toronto teacher suggests: "Teachers are required to participate in CILs which are always relevant to the needs of your particular students (it is usually based on the needs of the school according to the previous year's EQAO results)." CIL refers to collaborative inquiry for learning, an Ontario government–driven professional development initiative that encourages collaboration among teachers in a number of grades and subjects. It is an interesting initiative, but one that teachers mention is regularly devoted to EQAO planning. With PLCs and CILs increasingly directed by and toward EQAO results, one Ontario teacher suggests, "EQAO scores drive everything our school does—from the resources we buy to the PD teachers have to attend. It's frustrating."

While Ontario teachers pointed more consistently to an increased impact of testing on PD than their US counterparts, a number of Los Angeles teachers discussed the role of mentorship in shaping the stronger parts of their pedagogy, and suggested this important professional development was harder to pursue for both the mentor and the mentee, and that when such relationships did exists, they were increasingly facilitated in order to support increased test scores. Los Angeles teacher Malik discusses the loss of mentorship in the face of an ST focus within professional development, explaining:

> In my program we had mentors in schools as we finished our second year and they carried over into our first year of teaching. I talked to my old professor and that program has been replaced by test training for teacher candidates in college and first year teaching.

Newer teachers (those with five years or fewer of teaching experience) were more likely to note the gap between test-oriented teaching and teacher training, but not mentors. More experienced teachers pointed commonly to mandated professional development and professional learning communities, suggesting these activities are increasingly focused on the promotion of specific strategies aimed at raising test scores—often to the exclusion of other important teaching and learning considerations. More experienced teachers in Los Angeles were the only group to raise the issue of mentorship and ST.

The following excerpt from my conversation with Sarafina, a ninth-year LA teacher, brings together a number of the issues raised here. As such, it is included here at length:

> My mother was a single mom and a teacher. I remember going to PD sessions with her because she did not have childcare, and it was seeing those women working together, planning, eating, laughing, thinking about their students—referring to them by name and not only to say bad things as is so common today. That made me want to be a teacher and now it's a mad scramble to get those days and when we do, there is always a coach—usually literacy or math—telling you what to do with your assessments, or it's the principal delivering the latest rules for bringing up scores. We never get to generate our own ideas based on what our kids need. Three years ago our school won a grant to allow us four days of PD and we were able to use one of those days to look at something other than testing. That was the only time in the past five years. I do my own study when I can [outside of mandated professional development work] but I might as well be painting in the dark because I can't use any of that stuff when I get back to the class unless it directly supports the test. I remember when I was hired, they told me it was because of my experience and demonstrated expertise with portfolio based assessment—so rich assessment stuff. At our first assessment team meeting the principal, who hired me, literally said "the core of every single assessment at this school needs to be guided by getting each individual student the points bump needed to push him or her to the next level." I put my hand up

and reminded her I was hired for my diverse assessment experiences. She put down her notes and said "we wouldn't want the thing that got you hired to get you fired." In front of the whole team. I said, I wouldn't do it, that's dehumanizing my kids and reducing them to a number, in my mind and in theirs. I know where my kids are weak and I would rather spend my time working on those specific skills.

Sarafina's story reveals the ways in which autonomy, passion for teaching, commitment to students, power, hierarchy, pedagogy, and resistance intersect and interlock with questions of ST. She no longer works at the school.

Teachers also report disconnection between education research and test-oriented teaching, specifically around issues of developmentally appropriate assessment and constructivist pedagogy. Following a trajectory outlined in the previous sections, teachers struggle to reconcile their professional knowledge with test-oriented professional practice. With regard to testing and professional knowledge, one Chicago teacher explains: "I keep up on academic research, but if that research contradicts policy, well, there goes the research." A tenth-year Toronto teacher suggests that testing is "a giant brick wall and total hindrance" to both the development and use of professional knowledge that best supports student learning, while a first-year Los Angeles teacher explains teaching around standardized tests is "against my professional judgement, understanding of the research and pedagogy."

Teachers were quick to point to research, which, in their estimation, was inconsistent with current practices, particularly in the United States. One Chicago teacher explains, "we learn about child development but then standardized tests are given to K-2 students," while another says, "I'm going to graduate school for bilingual bicultural education and every day school standardized testing practices are in direct opposition to the best practices I learn." Many teachers raised concerns about the impact on students, including an Ontario teacher who argues, "the greatest loss is in early childhood where research is being ignored and academics are being stressed instead of social and emotional readiness. My sixth-grade students are very stressed over the emphasis on test scores." Teachers expressed concern about the use of computerized standardized tests as well, a direction in which Alberta and Ontario are moving and an important piece of the Common Core State Standards Initiative (CCSSI). Toronto teacher Marvelyn questions the Ontario transition to online testing, "moving the EQAO online is a funny decision, especially for the grade threes. Do we really need more screen time for these guys?" A Chicago teacher raises a similar issue: "Standardized testing interrupts my instruction, administering tests that are unfair and harmful for my students. Several of the tests are 45–60 minutes long and on a computer which is inappropriate for young children." A second-grade teacher from Chicago argues, "none of the standardized test that I administer to my students are appropriate for their cognitive abilities."

They're not making this up. As is frequently the case, teachers recognize from classroom practice, much of what the research on these issues bears out, specifically with regard to developmentally appropriate assessment for young children. Indeed, a host of leading researchers point to what amounts to a crisis in early years education, specifically around testing and high-stakes assessment before grade four, and the persistent use of assessments that do not reflect what we know about cognitive development.[15] A 2009 *Harvard Education Letter* reporting on the findings of a variety of academic studies on developmentally appropriate instruction and assessment in the elementary years suggests, "teachers need to address young students' social, emotional, and physical needs as well as their cognitive development" and that a variety of research studies raise concerns about a lack of physical activity, a need for better connections between students and teachers, inflexibility on the part of teachers and standards, and a narrowed curriculum.[16] In 1991, Powell and Sigel noted the challenges of assessing young children and the necessity of age and developmentally appropriate measures:

> Young children are not good candidates for taking traditional tests. The reliability and validity of test results are greatly compromised by the child's rapid changes in development, fluctuations in the intensity and focus of interests, and the unfamiliarity of the assessment situation. (p. 194)

This extends the 1989 research from Bredekamp and Shepard who offer the following recommendations to protect young children from inappropriate expectations, practices, and policies:

- Delay standardized testing of all children until third grade or later.
- When using standardized achievement tests for purposes of accountability and school and district comparisons, use sampling techniques instead of testing all children.
- Schedule such testing in fall, rather than spring, so that teachers will not "teach to the test" and the scores cannot be used for teacher evaluation.[17]

Note that these recommendations, as well as widespread research supporting this work, predate No Child Left Behind by a decade. Suzanne Lane outlines three reasons for the mismatch between assessment and what we know about cognition and development (1) the disciplines of psychometrics and of cognition and learning have developed separately and are just beginning to merge, (2) theories of the nature of proficiency and learning progressions are not fully developed, and (3) economic and practical constraints affect what is possible.[18] While these concerns might best apply to creating standardized measures that are appropriate, many teachers quarrel with the limits of standardization writ large.

Among the various critiques raised, teachers point to testing and TOTL's failure to include the following considerations: individual characteristics, strengths and challenges of the learner; questions of context; collaborative work between students (as well as between schools and communities); and discovery, or exploration-based learning. These practices and considerations are related to constructivism, a theory of learning that argues knowledge emerges from a combination of experiences and ideas. Constructivism[19] emerges from the works of Jean Piaget, Lev Vygotsky, John Dewey, and many others, and has been the backbone of pedagogical training in teacher education programs for nearly a half century in Canada and the United States.[20] Widespread practices including reflective and reflexive teaching, differentiated instruction, and arts-informed teaching fall under the constructivist umbrella, as do more critical approaches including critical pedagogy, holistic education, and culturally relevant and responsive pedagogy.

The exclusion, or sidelining, of these practices can be particularly harmful for traditionally underserved students, including low-income and racially minoritized students—unjust educational practices in unjust contexts. To be clear, although low-income and racially minoritized students are the majority in US and Canadian urban schools, constructivism is not merely an approach for certain children or groups of children. It is a fundamental conceptualization of how human beings learn and know, with implications for how teachers teach. Constructivist approaches tend to consider learner self-regulation, student safety, and healthy attachment, as well as a recognition of representational thought and exploration (allowing students to express their ideas using multiple forms) domains that research suggests are crucial not only for learning but also for children's well-being.[21]

Constructivist teaching also allows, when possible, for applied learning and for students to arrive at answers, rather than memorize them. For example, the student learning to count, who is also curious about how many teeth lions have, would count the teeth on a picture of a lion's mouth rather than practice rote number recitation and learn the average number of teeth lions have from a text. The test-centered practices outlined in Chapter 5 rely increasingly on didactic practices that are teacher-led, narrow, and, by teachers' own description, ineffective for learning beyond the test itself. The central failure of testing and test-centered teaching is the failure to support learners on an individual basis. Russian psychologist Lev Vygotsky suggests that individual students learn most effectively within a zone of proximal development (ZPD), wherein, guided by a teacher, the student is challenged neither too little nor too much (disengaged by neither the boredom of something too easy nor the frustration with something too hard). This simple yet powerful idea will make sense to most people who have spent time with kids. When spending any extended time with a child, it is hard to not teach him something—hard not to become an instructor of some kind. In personal interactions with children, we answer their endless questions based on who is asking (prior knowledge, interest, context, etc) not based on their date of manufacture or on what standards apply to that particular batch of learners. This is the impotence of ST and test-oriented teaching, and it speaks to a fundamental and dehumanizing aspect of our current education systems.

Summary and Implications

Teachers are increasingly on the defensive as professionals and as human beings who care about their work and have dedicated their lives to educating children. In many cases, they are struggling to defend their jobs, their schools, their pedagogy, their students, their knowledge and ability, and the profession as a whole. Teachers sense their worth and efficacy are increasingly understood through narrow measures prescribed by various value-added measures (VAM), which often rely on an overuse of student test results to determine teacher quality. Test-oriented high-stakes teacher evaluation incentivizes test-oriented teaching and learning. Many teachers favor accountability for the profession but note that data-driven accountability does not reliably measure or improve teacher quality—a conclusion that supports extant research. The high-stakes environment has, for many, diminished the profession in and out of the classroom. Teachers report variation as far as pressure, based on context—on where and whom they teach—with high-pressure teaching contexts characterized by low test scores, and low-pressure contexts characterized by high student test scores. This same variation applies to a worsening relationship between teachers and the public, although teachers report additional variations such as neighborhood and home culture in dealings with parents. Although VAM are not used in Canada, teachers administering Ontario's EQAO tests report similar changes to the profession and to the relationship with the public as those in the United States, but to a lesser degree. With some embarrassed and some feeling merely unsupported compared to previous years, teachers struggle against the near-archetypal image of the entitled, tenured, and benignly hapless public school teacher. Many have become alienated from the moral rewards of teaching as they feel increasingly unable to effectively support the success of all students.

The culture of standardization, meanwhile, drives many teachers to avoid certain schools, students, and grades. Teachers report that test-oriented teaching and learning runs counter to best practices learned in teacher training, professional development, and (in some Los Angeles contexts) mentorship-based learning. Mandated professional development increasingly focuses on strategies aimed at raising test scores; a practice that embeds major contradictions between teachers' sense of what is best for students, and what is best for test scores. Finally, teachers have major concerns about the degree to which standardized measures are developmentally appropriate for their students. These concerns support a number of major research studies that suggest a failure of large-scale assessment to appropriately work with the cognitive and developmental needs and abilities of young children. The findings from this chapter combined with those in Chapters 3 and 4 illustrate the widespread jettisoning of constructivist practices in the classroom, which include a variety of practices that support all learners and which are particularly crucial for supporting the success of racially minoritized and low-income students.

CHAPTER 6

A Lack of Accountability: Teacher Perspectives on Equity, Accuracy, and Standardized Testing

Although the rationale for standardized testing has, for decades, included the call to ensure equality in educational delivery and content for all students, there is little evidence that standardization improves education outcomes for low-income students, racially minoritized students, or English language learners (ELLs). Achievement gaps for these groups have in many cases remained the same or grown with increased use of standardized testing, as have the divides between individual schools and districts. For over a decade, research has linked standardized testing to inequality in education in the United States and Canada.[1] Equality in education is often understood through the prism of equity, which recognizes that fairness requires, at times, treating students differently in order to ensure every student has equal access to successful educational outcomes. Treating everyone the same way, regardless of their strengths and challenges, can increase rather than mitigate inequality. At its most basic, an equity approach would never ask students to run a race when some have shoes and others are barefoot, or demand students with mobility impairments participate in a foot race against those who have no mobility impairments. Taken a little further, an equity approach would consider the results of the race (even one in which all students have shoes and similar mobility) in light of opportunities for training, a healthy diet, coaching, and other contextual factors impacting the individual. Taken even further, an equity perspective might challenge the notion of competition altogether (not the question of comparison but that of competition). Schooling is not a competitive sport after all, and while it is unclear at what age it becomes acceptable to rank children and place them in competition with one another, few of us think of certain small children as needing to come first, and others needing to come last, as a necessary part of healthy development and learning (and if we do, we tend to imagine our own children coming first).

Norm-referenced testing, however, requires winners and losers, and in both the United States and Canada we see its developmentally inappropriate use with young children. At its very core, despite perhaps early intentions to the contrary, standardization runs counter to equitable education outcomes. Questions of equity and of educational justice were raised repeatedly by teachers who powerfully fleshed out the persistent and diverse ways in which issues of class, race, culture, and language become operationalized as markers of advantage and disadvantage on standardized tests for students, schools, and teachers; a cadence of educational inequality sketched on the backdrop of standardization.

This chapter addresses equity as it concerns teachers and teaching, as well as students and learning in four major sections, based on themes emerging from the study. The first section looks at the persistent and deep gaps between standardized testing (ST) results and those of other assessments of students and schools. It also takes up teacher perceptions of ST as a tool for understanding student learning and teacher ability. The second looks at the intersection of equity and accuracy in teacher perceptions of ST. Teachers identify a host of equity-related phenomena, which, given the high-stakes use and impact of testing, raise questions about the validity of standardized testing. These include the failure of standardized tests to account for issues of race, class, language, and various environmental factors that shape the terrain of student learning. The third section looks at the plight of equity-centered inclusive education approaches, which directly and indirectly address issues such as race, class, gender, ability, sexuality, immigration status, and religion in students' lives, in the face of teaching-oriented teaching and learning (TOTL). This section takes a closer look at the specific impacts of TOTL on learners with exceptionalities and ELLs, and at the experiences of these students surrounding the test itself. The fourth section looks at the differing levels of pressure faced by teachers and students in different contexts. Picking up on a theme emerging in Chapters 3, 4, and 5, this section illustrates the inequitable teaching and learning conditions facing teachers, from school to school and district to district. In high-pressure contexts, some teachers help to increase student scores using a variety of methods, from helping students during the test (as reported by some teachers in this study), to changing student answers after the fact (a phenomenon well publicized as a result of various cheating scandals but not reported personally by any of the teachers in this study). With major implications for accuracy, such practices and pressures are far less common in schools with high test scores, a differential that impacts the student experience as well.

Sometimes Things Just Don't Add Up: Accuracy and Standardized Testing

Teacher concerns around accuracy focused on questions of both reliability and validity. In broad strokes, and as mentioned in Chapter 2, reliability refers to repeatability and how likely the results are to be effected by chance (were the test to be given repeatedly, the results should be the same), while validity refers to whether or not the information the test gives us is dependable for the jobs we ask it to do. Stecher explains that: "Validity is not a quality of tests themselves, but of the inferences made on the basis of test scores."[2] So, the question of validity hinges on the accuracy of what the tests tell us about students, teachers, teaching, schools, and districts. Stecher is among a number of researchers for whom validity is necessarily connected to how data are used.[3] Therefore, reliability without validity is possible (a scale that gives you your correct weight each time you step on it cannot tell you if you are too heavy), but validity is not possible without reliability (a broken scale is not a good tool to help you reach a healthy weight). Stecher suggests that a proper determination of validity includes first, "a variety of types of evidence to assess validity of inferences from a given measure"; second, "comparisons among scores from similar and dissimilar measures"; third, "patterns of correlations among elements that go into the total score"; fourth, "comparisons with concurrent and future external criteria"; and fifth, "sensitivity to relevant instruction."[4] Teachers point to an absence of such thorough processes for determining the validity of ST data. Inferences, meanwhile, are often wild and widespread, including claims of "low" students, ineffective teachers, and "loser" schools.[5] Given the high stakes of ST as well as the inferences based on the results thereof, questions of reliability and validity can undermine the legitimacy of standardized measures.[6]

Although a great deal of testing inaccuracy identified by teachers centered on complex questions of equity, some also raised concerns about the basic trustworthiness of the results of ST. At its most basic, many teachers feel testing fails to measure students' academic ability, as Table 6.1 illustrates.

Table 6.1 Standardized tests as a reflection of student academic ability, Illinois and Ontario teachers

In my belief, standardized tests offer an accurate reflection of students' academic ability.

	Ont. English	Ont. French	Illinois
Strongly Agree	1.6%	1.0%	1.6%
Agree	7.5%	5.4%	6.9%
Uncertain	8.1%	7.9%	11.9%
Disagree	35.9%	41.2%	41.1%
Strongly Disagree	46.9%	44.4%	38.5%

Although measuring academic ability is among the primary purposes of ST in our schools, fewer than 10 percent of teachers surveyed feel standardized tests do so accurately. One Chicago teacher explains, "it is highly accurate for some students, highly inaccurate for others, and a scattershot guess for most." Many felt that results misrepresented student ability, a validity issue, as one Toronto teacher explains:

> The math EQAO in grade nine tests reading skills more than it does math skills. Often during non-standardized tests, some students who have reading deficits require clarification of a word here or there, or need the teacher to point to the most critical word in the question. These students then can often answer the question with ease. On EQAO, they are only allowed verbatim reading, and only if they have an IEP [Independent Education Plan]. No clarification of words, or of awkward question wording is allowed. Students who might otherwise be able to answer the question might get zero because they didn't understand one word.

Teachers suggest ST frequently fails to measure student and school improvement within and across grades, a phenomenon that can conceal great teaching and significant learning. One veteran Chicago teacher points out that standardized tests are only "one measure" and "the not only thing that should be considered." She explains that "often people only look at the end score and not where the child was in the beginning. Students may have a low score while having made significant progress during a given year." An Ontario teacher echoes these concerns:

> When EQAO includes children who did not write as a zero score and then publish those results in the paper, all the public sees is reduced scores that do not in any way reflect the reality of what goes on in the classrooms. Trying to teach to all the needs in the classroom is extremely

difficult and the public has no idea about strengths and weaknesses of the school aside from the EQAO marks.

While inferences made by the public may be invalid according to many teachers, others suggest that in-school use of the data may also fail to recognize important gains, as another Ontario teacher suggests:

> Unfortunately, our administration doesn't understand sample size (or statistics in general). A few years ago we dedicated an entire year of PLCs [Professional Learning Communities] to trying to raise our EQAO scores because they had "dropped so significantly" from the previous year. This despite the fact that fewer students failed the EQAO and the fact that both the school mean and median were higher than the previous year.

While such concerns regarding interpretation and inference were widespread, Ontario teachers repeatedly pointed to an inconsistency between student achievement on EQAO standardized tests, and student achievement on other assessments. Toronto teacher Georgia explains, "Every year there are major inconsistencies between my grade level reading assessments and the EQAO results, and EQAO is never lower." When asked about this issue, her colleague echoes this concern, explaining: "It depends on the year, sometimes it's just one, but overall DRAs [Developmental Reading Assessments] are always lower," meaning the EQAO pegs students at a higher reading level. DRAs are a Pearson standardized test administered and graded by teachers. Another teacher explains, "We had one student more than two years below grade level get grade level EQAO level two." Level two is roughly a mark of "c." This phenomenon is widespread, according to sixth grade teacher Ben:

> When I have kids who I program for two grades below and they score at grade level on the test, this to me raises big questions about accuracy and what these tests actually tell us. Talk to any teacher and you'll hear the same thing. I have had some really weird results where stuff is marked as a level three [a B level grade] which I would not consider passing. It's sketchy. Also, there is no place to think outside of the box, literally or figuratively.

Lana, a 12th-year Toronto teacher agrees, explaining:

> What I don't understand is that the EQAO a lot of the time does not match the CAT4[7] or the diagnostics I do, and we have talked about this as a team because we have all noticed this. They send us scoring guides

and other resources to help us prep students, but they do not describe the results of particular kids and these often don't really match with other specific outcomes of students.

As mentioned in Chapter 3, of the four EQAO standardized tests Ontario students write, the ninth grade mathematics examination is most closely aligned with other assessments around the same time of year. Despite this, teachers report inconsistency here as well. One Ontario teacher explains: "We mark the grade nine math EQAO tests as part of our course marks. It seems sometimes the marks reported by EQAO are very different." This means the classroom teacher is marking a very similar same test as the EQAO evaluator and coming up with a different grade.

Issues of student results disproportionately impacted by small errors or single questions missed, as well as those of subjectivity in marking, fall into the category of reliability; adding to the host of issues associated with testing, teaching, and learning. The final section of this chapter picks up the threads of reliability and validity with regard to teacher practice, but this chapter turns first to the intersections of equity and accuracy as related to ST.

Blurry Snapshots: The Intersection of Equity and Accuracy

Related to accuracy, teachers raised concerns about mental health and learning exceptionalities, language proficiency, race, socioeconomic status, and questions of school choice (although not the kind we are used to hearing about). As far as learning exceptionalities and mental health, students' experiences can be divided into temporary and nontemporary issues. Temporary issues refer to those that present primarily (although not necessarily exclusively) around the standardized test. Nontemporary refers to issues that are present at other times for students, but which may become unaccommodated issues leading to student disadvantage in and around the test. The most common temporary concern relates to students who suffer anxiety about high-stakes testing, a well-documented phenomenon described in the previous chapters. One California teacher recounts:

> In San Diego when I was giving my first grade students the STAR [Standardized testing and Reporting test] test my brightest students were crying at the overwhelming-ness and uncertainty of such an inappropriate task for six year olds.

She suggests that after this, students were "highly unlikely to write a strong test that day."

The following dialogue with Toronto teacher Fran illustrates the sometimes unintentional ways in which pressure is placed on students:

> *Fran*: "I know that some grade three and grade six kids get so anxious about the test, some don't care but many do. I had a girl vomiting in my classroom. This all impacts how they perform. Even when the teachers sometimes make an effort to not make a big deal in obvious ways about it, kids get stressed, again not all of them but many. I hear them talk about at the start of grade four, already saying they can't believe they have to take it again grade six. I had a grade four having an emotional breakdown when she found out they had to write it again in grade six, and it is so sad."

When asked why kids were experiencing anxiety even though teachers are not pushing the significance of the test, she explained:

> They often have intrinsic anxiety about big tests, it might be parents but I can't say. Despite not making a big deal about it they do feel a pressure, and we use old EQAO questions all year, so perhaps without meaning to that pressure on teachers comes through to the students. The teachers themselves don't want to be seen as failures. So for kids, if they have to prepare all year they know what it means and for many students this does not drive up the test score.

When pressed again about the question of pressure, and reminded that EQAO results do not count toward the report cards, she points out, "they are far more concerned with EQAO than the report card. Many grade threes don't even look at the report cards, don't think about them but EQAO is on their radar beginning in grade two."

Not all temporary struggles are related to anxiety or mental health issues. One Toronto third grade teacher explains: "Last year one of my best students was constipated during the test and got a bad score. I guess she is a terrible student and I taught her nothing!" Other issues that arose for some students only during test time included headaches, upset stomach and diarrhea, sleeplessness, challenges focusing, and challenges sitting still.

On the question of student anxiety around the test in particular, given its widespread persistence—from nerves, to hiding, to vomiting, to passing out—and given how many folks are aware of these experiences for children, it is remarkable how little is being done to support students. Children suffering with high levels of anxiety around the test tend to perform worse, and the presence of test anxiety can pose problems for the overall academic career of some students.[8] As the teachers in this study report, this is a widespread problem. Found in children as young as seven, research suggests that 10 to 40 percent of students experience test anxiety in some form.[9] These numbers increase for females, racially minoritized students, and students with disabilities.[10] While many might think a little pressure is good thing, a lot of pressure (particularly in the younger grades) is most certainly bad thing for many. It is difficult to pin down the exact number of children who experience anxiety or other issues around testing; however, if this many children were made sick by a medicine or vaccine, it is highly debatable whether it would be required for all children. Indeed it might even be deemed criminal, even if it saved the lives of many others (a claim that, as of this writing, has not been made about any public school standardized test).

Nontemporary issues are more likely to include learning exceptionalities and chronic mental health issues, for which standardized tests do not adequately control, according to many teachers. One Illinois teacher argues: "Students who have post-traumatic stress, or other stresses at home do not fully show their ability on these tests," while another suggests, "my students with depression and/or bipolar can and often do have bad days and they just can't bring their best." This can be a vicious cycle for students, with test-related stress compounding other issues. Another Chicago teacher suggests, "For ELLs, exceptional learners, low SES students and students with testing anxiety these tests are a nightmare."

The narrow format of standardized tests is a challenge for many learners who have accommodations and/or modifications outlined in independent education plans (IEPs) based on their learning strengths and challenges. One Ontario teacher observes:

> EQAO is dependent on writing style and ability, evaluator's subjective thoughts, and evaluator's preferences—oral responses are not permitted, even with an IEP which allows for scribing, resources are limited. You are taking a blurry snapshot of the learner.

Another Ontario teacher suggests the EQAO, "does a poor job of modifying for LD, DL, MID students,[11] yes it can accommodate for them sometimes, but it does not modify as clearly stated in their IEP." A colleague shares this concern: "My kids are all on modified curricula, and they need accommodations with that. EQAO is not adapted to reflect their modified expectations, and they are not allowed certain key accommodations, even with a psychologist's recommendation."

One category of learning exceptionality is that of high performing or what some call gifted learners. Veteran Toronto teacher Cooper points to some of the challenges facing these students:

> Sometimes I find the higher thinking kids in my class who are very creative often don't do as well on the test, specifically when they express their thoughts or opinions on the test—and my gifted guys will often provide answers that are too smart for the test and the scorers have no way to give a mark for answers which do not fit the choices they are working with.

The often narrow lens of testing can thus exclude evidence of student ability, particularly for learners with exceptionalities. Apart from any issues of reliability, these findings suggest in many cases that there may be limitations to the validity of results for understanding the abilities of certain students when compared with those of others in norm-referenced standardized tests.

There's No Raining Cats and Dogs in Spanish: Cultural Bias

Additionally, teachers report that questions of equity and accuracy are also relevant with regard to the content of the tests themselves. Teachers note the presence of cultural bias on testing questions, and as well, the failure of ST and teaching to account for unequal levels of student and school support. Few of the teachers surveyed believed standardized tests adequately controlled for racial bias as well as bias based on socioeconomic status, as Table 6.2 illustrates.

One Toronto teacher claims: "I've never seen an EQAO assessment that reflects the multicultural students that I teach," while another suggests, "these tests measure what the province already knows...socioeconomic

Table 6.2 Standardized tests controlling for race and income bias, Illinois and Ontario teachers

Percentage of teachers who agree or strongly agree that standardized tests control for race and income bias

	Ont. English	Ont. French	Illinois
Bias Based on Race	12.6%	19.6%	21.86%
Bias Based on Socioeconomic Status	11.21%	17.8%	20.35%

status of students determines everything." The implication that wealthier schools generally do better on EQAO is true and the same holds generally, for the testing results in the United States. Teachers from Ontario and Illinois had dozens of stories and examples of culturally inaccessible content on test items. The following sample from Chicago teachers highlights the persistence of inappropriate content in testing questions:

> It seems inappropriate to ask students to read and write about topics that they may have no experience of and then evaluate them against students that are familiar with the topic. For example, read and respond to a story about a camping trip.
>
> Many times passages are about things my students have absolutely no background knowledge on because some may have never been exposed to such things such as sledding or polo.
>
> My inner city kids in building projects did not know what a chandelier was on one of the state test.
>
> We live in a large urban district, these tests often have images that do not reflect where we live. Also, there are reading passages about things that would not happen in a large city. (Ex. reading passage about downhill skiing. We don't have mountains near us nor do these urban students have the means to travel to a ski resort.

Ontario teachers note a parallel failure as far as inclusion, test item language, and cultural vocabulary:

> I teach in an inner city school located in one of the lowest income areas in the province with a huge ELL population. Many of my students struggle with the contexts of the questions. For example, there have been questions about scuba diving on EQAO. Most of my students have no idea about scuba diving. Another question referred to tents and camping. My students remember tents as their homes in refugee camps.
>
> Anyone who has read a test can see that they are biased. When questions ask students "describe the life cycle of a pot-hole" students who are young or don't have cars are at a disadvantage. I have also seen questions about hockey and ice skating, terms which immediately alienate students who don't play, immigrants who are not familiar with those terms, and those who have not played.
>
> These tests were written by people who have no understanding of the knowledge and experiences of disadvantaged students. Example: A large number of our grade threes had no idea what a resort was.
>
> A grade 3 student especially can have an off day or misunderstand the question, or have limited experiences. One question one year asked grade threes to answer questions about a "cafe menu." There are no cafes

in their neighbourhood, and only one pub with a sit-down menu. If the menu had been organized like a board at a fast food joint, they would've felt more comfortable with it. In another question they had to choose the right unit of measurement to describe the distance from their house to "the forest." All of them wanted to know which forest? The trees in the park behind the school? Wilderness outside the city?

Oddly, Illinois and Ontario teachers reported examples of outdoor activities in test questions in 32 separate comments, 22 of which made specific reference to camping.

Like all teacher remarks included here from the survey, this is just a sample of many more similar comments. Michelle, veteran Los Angeles teacher, explains the challenges facing students who are unfamiliar with certain English idioms:

> There is no raining cats and dogs in Spanish, right, and the tests are full of these types of things and there are really no test prep strategies for us to get them ready for that, or even context clues in the test itself.

The issue here is twofold. First, the use of dominant expressions, idioms, and references (to activities commonly participated in by middle and upper class communities) results in children with certain cultural experiences being at a disadvantage when it comes to the test because they simply may not know what certain phrases mean. Second, the sociocultural curriculum of the test is, for many racially minoritized and low-income students, not their own. Such testing content can alienate students from the content and context of their education. So, where a student speaking Spanish as a first language does not understand the expression "raining cats and dogs" and the low-income African American child speaking English as a first language does, the language and references may still refer implicitly to white, middle, and upper class norms. Toronto teacher Georgia suggests these issues are most visible in tokenistic attempts at inclusion, explaining, "a name change is often as far as they go, like putting a black kid on a cereal box that used to show only white kids. It doesn't even control for different kinds of learning." She goes on to compare these approaches to "national secretary's day." The disadvantaging of low-income and minority students is, of course, the corollary to the potential advantaging of their colleagues whose language, culture, daily life, and expressions are present on standardized tests. This invisible advantaging sets up wealthy white students for academic success.

"The Tutoring Bias": Testing, Learning, and the Income Gap

Many parents provide expensive tutors for children, further upending the playing field in what one Chicago teacher describes as "tutoring bias" wherein "wealthier students, more than not, are tutored outside of school in language and math, and this advantage can't be registered on the test while the kid next to him, with more ability, does worse." In Chicago, New York City, Los Angeles, and even Toronto many tutoring companies specialize in standardized test preparation. This investment can pay off, with long-term advantages for some children. Another Chicago teacher explains:

> This is why the achievement gap does not close! Rich kids keep buying extra help to seem academically more gifted. Seriously affluent parents spend thousands of dollars to hire tutors for their second grade kids before they take the IQ test. The IQ test is what qualifies students to be considered GATE [Gifted and Talented Education], which qualifies students to get more enrichment classes and be in AP [Advanced Placement] and honors classes later. It's a very classist system.

Economic inequality exists at the school and community levels as well. Per-student funding in the United States can vary by up to $1200,[12] meanwhile, commenting on data from a recent Center for American Progress report, the *Huffington Post* reports:

> Schools that enroll 90 percent or more non-white students spend $733 less per pupil per year than schools that enroll 90 percent or more white students. These "racially isolated" schools make up one-third of the country's schools. Nationwide, schools spend $334 more on every white student than on every non-white student.[13]

While funding formulas in Canada tend to be far more equitable, when private fundraising is taken into account—moneys, which in Ontario have funded school libraries, sports, recreation facilities, and a host of curriculum enrichment supports—a gap between high-income and low-income schools has emerged. For example, Toronto's wealthiest school raised $654 per student in the 2012–2013 school year, while during the same period, Toronto's school with the lowest per-student fundraising brought in $8.25 for every child.[14] At the national level, federal funding of on-reserve schooling for Indigenous children tends to be far lower than provincial and territorial averages.[15]

In Los Angeles, annual school booster drives in wealthy areas can raise close to $500,000. Nadra, who teaches at Flower Elementary with what one of her colleagues describes as a "solidly middle class student population," explains that Flower's booster, "brings in about $100,000 because we are not a relatively rich area." She comments, "folks always ask how the scores are so high, most scores that high come in whiter richer schools. I think it is school culture." Though Flower might be the poor cousin of LA's rich Westside schools, its recommended donation for parents is $500. While school culture is the key for test success at Flower, in contrast with schools that raise little or no money in East and South LA, Flower is very well supported. As described in Chapter 2, societal equity, as well as equity between schools and districts in national and subnational jurisdictions are among the most important predictors of overall educational success. Despite rising inequality in Canada, race and wealth gaps in education and society as a whole remain smaller than those in the United States, a consideration, which may be informative for understanding Canada's consistent out performance of the United States on international education measures. Despite differences in school culture, well-funded schools tend to have higher test scores than schools serving low-income populations.

Environmental Factors and the Test

Teachers also point to additional environmental factors that may impact students' ability to show what they know on high-stakes standardized tests. One Chicago teacher explains:

> I had a very bright girl that came on testing day and her brother had been shot and killed the night before...would that be a day to get an accurate reflection of ability? That is one of hundreds or thousands of real scenarios.

Another suggests a host of factors impact kids daily, which simply cannot be accounted for. She explains: "When children are homeless, hungry and in a dysfunctional family have a hard time concentrating on a test they are not going to "score" at the level they should or could." Another suggests:

> Student attendance in an urban setting is not a factor compared to what happens at home. If my students came to school every day and had parent involvement and didn't have to take care of siblings I'm sure I would

have much better results. It's like expecting a plant to grow by giving it sunlight but not water."

While the teacher's choice of words implies at best a misunderstanding, and at worst a complete disregard for the learning that happens in every home—including a sense responsibility and time management skills that develop from caring for little siblings—his comment highlights the relationship between what happens outside and what happens inside the classroom; a variety of educational research has illustrated the impact of home-school dissonance for racially and economically marginalized children and families, in which the cultural norms of school are at times inconsistent with those of the home.[16] In these cases, the knowledge of the home is potentially inconsistent with the formal and informal curriculum taught in schools. This teacher's remarks are focused on standardized test results, and there seems little room in his standardized classroom for the home learning of certain students. Surely there is "water" in every home to complement the "sunlight" from every class. A fifth-year Chicago teacher explains:

> Great teachers teach all kinds of students. The ones who can score high may not have learned from their teachers but from their lives. The ones who score low may have made great gains which are not visible on tests that do not test what the curriculum of the classroom or the curriculum of their lives teaches.

This comment suggests that the standardized classroom can thus exclude certain learning and knowledge from the sphere of what is recognized, validated, and rewarded in schools. This extends a long-standing practice of excluding the cultures, narratives, struggles, and lived realities of many low-income and racially minoritized communities—speaking to the exclusion of the "curriculum of their lives" from what counts as worthy an important in our classrooms.

For Pacheone and Kahl, test validity means: "evidence obtained from the assessment provides support for the interpretation of the evidence to the extent that the interpretation is stronger than any other alternative explanation (e.g. internal validity)."[17] The host of issues raised by teachers suggests major problems with questions of validity given the widespread use of testing to assess student and teacher knowledge and ability. Teachers suggest many English language learners and students with learning exceptionalities often write standardized tests at a significant disadvantage. Questions of test-centered illness, including the scourge of anxiety powerfully impacting kids in both countries, were chief among teachers' concerns. Teachers also note the race and income politics of the test, pointing to inaccessible and culturally exclusive language (including vocabulary, idioms, and expressions) as well as to the promotion, implicitly, of white middle-class norms in which many students cannot see themselves represented. Students with certain Canadian and US cultural knowledge are advantaged in comparison with their peers, even though cultural knowledge is not (explicitly) part of the standards.

In summary, this extends existing research on the failure of large-scale assessment to control for unnecessary linguistic complexity and cultural bias.[18] Teachers suggest that questions of money play out powerfully around testing. At the student level, some students receive expensive tutoring while others go to work from a young age or care for siblings. At the school level, a significant funding gap impacts the student experience at every turn in both the United States and Canada (although to a far lesser degree in Canada). Teachers identify a host of other factors which may impact student test scores including hunger, parental time and support, and crime in the community. Finally, teachers note the mismatch of home culture with that of the standardized classroom, paralleling an entrenched chasm between school and home culture that is particularly deep and wide for low-income and racially minoritized students.

Collateral Damage: The Consequences of Testing-Centered Teaching for Inclusive Education

In addition to the equity-related questions of accuracy raised with regard to the current widespread (mis)use of testing results, teachers also note that equity-centered practices are more difficult within standardized teaching and learning. Finding ways to include all students in the content of their schooling and learning is getting more difficult, and while equity is increasingly central to many teacher education programs, that learning often stops at the in-service level with professional development increasingly focused on raising test scores. Teachers note that when questions of inclusion and testing are taken up, it is usually with a focus on tokenistic inclusion, and increasingly, on the removal of unclear terminology from the test rather than on integrating multiple cultures, perspectives, and politics within test content and language. Chapter 3 looked at the revised pedagogical form of standardized teaching and learning, and pointed to the reduction in student-centered teaching strategies, including differentiated instruction. Among the the central offerings of such approaches is the focus on the individual strengths and weaknesses of students. Inclusive approaches such as critical pedagogy, feminist education, antiracist education, antihomophobia education, culturally relevant and responsive pedagogy/teaching (CRRP/CRRT), and community- (or place-) based learning center the learner and the community as starting points for critically reading and making change in the world. Moving beyond liberal approaches, critical education suggests that reading the world precedes reading the word, and that education should be a process aimed at collective societal improvement.[19] ST can thus powerfully deter the very consciousness-raising education that might be required to counter educational standardization.

One Chicago teacher explains, "Our critical race work, and CRRP is gone, in a school of 90 percent African Americans we don't have time to talk about racism." Other teachers noted a similar squeezing out of critical work. Toronto teacher Ben comments, "Twice we have had to cancel character education assemblies where we talk about equity issues because EQAO was being written. That's how the grade six test impacts the grade seven and eight programs." Ben illustrates the spillage of the grade six standardized test onto grades seven and eight at his middle school. When asked about the impact of testing on equity-centered teaching at her school and in her practice Fran says:

> It's huge overall. It's a lot more focus on reading and writing and math. We do a lot of total staff PD around how are we going to teach particular skills which are on the test—this was time that would have at least in part been looking at community and equity items. Everything we have to do as a staff generally reflects EQAO scores now. All of our focus has to be EQAO data driven. Over the years, I have found ways to integrate those things into my programming without losing all the other parts of what I do, but it has really taken a little while and it is still a struggle.

She notes that this "struggle" to do equity work while swimming in the water of high-stakes testing is a solitary one, and optional: "I do it because it's important to me, no it's not a staff thing and the admin doesn't have this as a priority." To recap, the pathway to equity practice sketched here takes years, is done in isolation, and is not recognized or rewarded by the administration whose main focus remains raising test scores. Though Fran is a grade four teacher (not an EQAO year) she is still in some ways teaching to the test.

Marvelyn notes this is widespread and sees a change over the past decade in students coming into middle school, saying:

> This happens from K-6 in. I notice when kids come to me they have these specific skills, and not others, because they have been focusing in these even in the younger grades on literacy and math but no community building, no critical thinking. It definitely makes a difference when everybody focuses on similar things—it gets easier if you don't mind letting go of certain parts of the learning, and that is a benefit, but it gets thinner as well, and the pieces you are proud of get harder to find.

Marvelyn's description relates to the moral rewards of teaching described in Chapter 5, and to the potential demoralization, which so many teachers experience. She is also tracing a more widespread impact of the EQAO, noting its increased influence in grades other than the three and six testing years.

A veteran Chicago teacher notes these trends can be particularly disengaging for racially minoritized students:

> I used to rely on cultural events, and on struggles in the community to engage my students, now I am a translator of standards that have nothing to do with my group of mainly brown and black kids, and they are less engaged as a result.

"Translator of standards" refers in part to the idea of teacher-proof teaching described earlier. He also suggests the narrowed standards fail to connect to students, where community-oriented teaching once had. Los Angeles teacher Mary tells the story of a cancelled program that focused on teaching and learning for and by African American students:

> We used to have the Academic English Mastery Program which transformed language results and engagement for our African American kids, but that got cut because it wasn't seen to be helping enough kids with test scores. This program taught teachers and students about language and the history of language, looking at what language meant for slaves, from the slave ship to life in America. We were learning and teaching about the difference between home and academic language in a way that valued both—it was so amazing and we cut it.

Los Angeles teachers described numerous cancelled programs that supported ELLs, students with limited US cultural reference points, low-income students, and racially minoritized students. Although education in LA, like many US cities, is a political hotbed of competing policies and politicians, the guiding light and through-line of policy change has been a focus on increasing test scores over the past decade.

With a host of new responsibilities on their plates, and testing increasingly at the center, equity is pushed off the table with many teachers feeling there is simply no time to get there. Eighth-year Toronto teacher Jessica explains:

> When we come together as a staff, we don't have time to get at questions of equality. As far as equity there really isn't time. There is so much pressure to bring up student scores, and improve performance that as much as I want an equity piece in the middle of what we do, it would at this point really feel like just another thing, not that it's not important, just that it is hard to imagine doing anything else on top of everything we need to do around testing.

As mentioned in Chapter 3, teachers' responsibility continues to expand with no time to accommodate these changes and little support for meaningful implementation of various classroom pieces. Only the most mandatory items are attended to consistently, and while testing is mandatory, equity is not. Los Angeles teacher Brian breaks it down as follows:

> If you have got 90 minutes to get through all the material that needs testing and race is not in the standardized test, there is no way you're going to talk about race. Time is the teacher's most precious commodity and in my admin's eyes, talking about race does nothing to help our school. ST allows for one understanding of the world and to do social justice work that won't do.

When asked about the steps to increase accountability (e.g., EQAO often reviews test questions to consider issues of cultural bias) some teachers were highly critical. Georgia suggests:

> Taking out "John" and putting in "Ali" does not make a test inclusive. Even saying someone lives in a project, and giving this character an African-Canadian sounding name. This is still not taken up as an issue or barrier, but as a permanent condition, a cultural condition; and this is supposed to be an equitable test.

Veteran teacher Lori raises a similar issue about the depth of criticality found even within equity-oriented changes to test items, explaining:

> Questions of cultural inclusion can happen at the most basic lower level thinking modes, where students are actually using often diverse texts by diverse authors, but there is no real critical thinking about power. This might tick the box of "compare multiple sources" or "summary," but it does not get at relationships to students' own experiences, or the ability to contest ideas, to agree and disagree. So the texts might actually be more inclusive on the face of it but the work does not generate real critical thinking that actually has to do with their lives, their experiences or their struggles or their successes.

Lori and Georgia offer a vision of inclusion that extends beyond representation to a critical reading of the world and a framework for deep understandings of injustice connected to student learning and development. These themes are central to critical education and are, according to many teachers, nowhere to be found even in processes geared toward more inclusive testing.

Often, even in cases where equity is a stated priority, testing takes precedence (and resources). Georgia, who has worked at various Toronto Model Schools (a program designed to support low-income and racially minoritized students), explains:

> We have more testing at Model Schools than most, and in the original purpose of Model Schools, there was a social justice thread and that has disappeared in many Model Schools, and certainly the three that I have taught in. Instead the focus is on bringing up CASI marks.[20] CASI and EQAO are huge right now, and we are under major pressure. Every staff meeting we develop our school improvement plan and bringing up EQAO scores is a really big part of that. We have people come in from Model Schools, from the board and from the ministry to talk about bringing up the scores.

Equity, according to Georgia, is thus subverted by the testing focus. Her comment also points to intentional to-the-test-teaching, which, remember, is not supposed to be happening as EQAO promises a random snapshot. Georgia continues:

> My admin openly said to me that he wants his strongest teachers in grades three and six. Also, grades broken down by gender. Our PLC's were test-driven as far as math, and they didn't use to be. Even my

MART[21] training has focused on bringing up math EQAO scores. Past tests are analyzed and the number of questions on each single curriculum piece is tallied, and our teaching is expected to be weighted according to the expected test weighting. So stuff is left out that is not on the test, left for [after the test in June], and you know not much happens in June. Anti-racism? June. Islamophobia with a 90 percent Muslim group? June.

According to some teachers, this downward pressure on equity practice and the increased push to raise test results is guiding the way schools are valorized by virtue of their test scores. Toronto teacher Jessica recalls her principal bringing a newspaper article to a staff meeting and announcing, "next year we move up or else everything will change here." The article listed the school's EQAO score drop and had comments from local parents. Public perception is increasingly important, as Fran explains: "People look at the scores when they are choosing schools and we have to consider what this tells us when the tests themselves are culturally biased and cannot accurately measure populations as diverse as ours." When asked about this phenomenon, Toronto teacher Gracie echoes these concerns: "Yeah, for sure. It's absurd. It's like an audition with parents as the audience, or as customer and admin eats this up whether or not what it takes to raise scores is good for kids." A process that reminds Gracie of her time teaching at a private school in which: "student results needed to make the school look good to prospective customers, sorry, parents." In all of this she explains, "the most under-served remain the most under-served, specifically ELL and spec. ed. kids."

As mentioned in the previous section, ELLs and students with exceptionalities face specific hurdles as far as testing when it comes to accuracy, and the same holds true for teaching and supporting these students in and around the test. In some cases, resources are even pulled away from supporting ELLs in order to focus on raising test scores. Lynn, a Toronto middle school ESL teacher of seven years, explains:

Work with sixes then becomes totally test-focused at the teachers' request for the last half of the year–looking at test taking strategies for ELLs. At least though, we get to keep doing ESL. At our feeder school, their six dedicated ESL positions were all assigned to test prep with low students for the month leading up to testing—these are dedicated positions with funds allocated specifically for ELL instruction and none is happening during this time. So ELL programing becomes test-focused, or eliminated because of the test.

In addition to the flagrant misappropriation of funds, Lynn also reports the way test pressure is transferred onto the shoulders of students:

> It is a really stressful thing to put someone through, and most of my kids can't speak English but do know EQAO. There is an air of "what if we fail Miss?" There is a panic for sure. Also, for many ELLs multi-day exams are make or break in their home countries, and even if we say "look this is not a big deal" they have this frame from home about tests deciding their future, and parents from these countries tend to buy in more intensely in this way as well.

Teachers also suggest that inclusive teaching and learning strategies that are central to the success of ELLs are displaced by test-oriented teaching. Lori, veteran ESL teacher from North Hollywood, puts it bluntly: "The introduction of standardization in testing has killed project work. All the stuff we know that supports ESL learners, as well as newcomers, is all impossible with standard-aligned curriculum and teaching." Los Angeles teacher Laura explains, that for ELLs, "wording on the test can cause major problems some years. There were many years in which a word threw the kids in a different direction" raising the question of reliability and validity as far as the test results for some ELLs. On the stress a poorly designed test can cause students, Toronto teacher Ben comments:

> I teach mainly ESL and special education kids and the test is not designed for them to succeed. For ESLs the language and terminology is way off and inappropriate, and for spec. ed. kids they struggle and stress only in many cases to perform very poorly and wait for those results in grade seven to feel terrible about themselves.

A Chicago teacher echoes this concern regarding the experiences of students with exceptionalities: "My special education students only feel disheartened because there is so much on the test that they do not know how to do." One Ontario teacher explains teacher practice around testing can ultimately contribute to students feeling disheartened:

> I taught in a school with terrible scores, but we were really good at working with kids with special needs, those arriving with limited English or without previous schooling, or family violence or upheaval. Our grade three EQAO scores looked awful, but the DRA [Developmental Reading Assessments] scores showed that by grade three more kids were at grade level than in kindergarten and grade one and those who were still behind

were less behind than they had been in the previous grade. The push is then away from these kids and toward what will bring up tests and these kids felt terrible.

Impacts of test-oriented teaching and learning are particularly relevant for ELLs and students with exceptionalities.[22] Teachers recognize this issue and many see it as a profound injustice, a part of their teaching that breaks their hearts and acts as a barrier to the moral rewards of their teaching—a barrier perhaps parallel to that faced by ELLs and special education students when it comes to test-centered teaching and the emotional toll of ST.

This section has fleshed out the constraints teachers face in the use of equity-centered practices. These effects are felt in the classroom and in the staffroom, as teaching and professional development with a focus on equity becomes more difficult in light of high-stakes standardized testing (HSST). Teaching and learning geared to include low-income and racially minoritized students is sacrificed for standardized instruction and content, with questions of context excluded from content and delivery. Teachers report disproportionately negative effects and impacts of standardized testing and teaching for ELLs and students with learning exceptionalities. This change in professional practice is, for many, a shift away from what they consider to be the in the best interests of students whose access to success is already strained. As the next section details, and as discussed in previous chapters, teachers experience these pressures and changes to different degrees and in different ways based on a host of contextual factors.

One Teacher's Ceiling Is Another One's Floor: The Inequitable Impacts of Testing on Teachers and Pedagogy

A persistent theme over the past three chapters has been the differential effects of standardization on teachers and teaching. This section dives a little deeper into this issue with a focus on this inequity as experienced by teachers; discussing some of the consequences for teacher practice and the ways in which teachers feel pressured to boost test scores. Teachers' work aimed specifically at improving scores ranges from the multiple ways teachers teach to and for the test to helping students cheat, to cheating themselves by changing answers on student tests. To be clear, none of the teachers in this study reported changing student answers. The analysis undertaken here intends not to weigh in on the ethics of these practices but instead to point to differences in pressure and incentives to undertake such practices, and as well to highlight the related potential validity issues raised by these pressures and practices. The most obvious example of inequity in this regard comes between teachers who teach testing years and those who don't: Los Angeles teacher Michelle asks: "Some teachers will never be ineffective because they teach kindergarten and first grade, is that accurate?" While a Toronto teacher comments, "I'm safe, I teach grade two." Conversely, some will be deemed ineffective no matter what their students do. In Florida, there can be negative consequences for teachers if their students fail to make predicted test score improvements. In 2014/2015, Florida teacher Luke Flynt had four students predicted to score above the maximum score, making it mathematically impossible for him to do his job to the satisfaction of local VAM. One of his students actually scored perfectly on the test, but her score counted negatively toward his evaluation.[23]

Many teachers teaching the same grades in the same cities have radically different jobs. At its most basic, low test scores equal high pressure, while high test scores equal low pressure. Although there are exceptions, this rule applied to many of the teachers who participated in this study. One Chicago teacher suggests:

> My students do well on standardized tests because they are generally from affluent homes. That is the only indicator that consistently matters with most standardized tests. Therefore, I am in a lucky situation. I can ignore a lot of teaching to the test and test prep stuff, and can focus on real teaching and learning issues. When I taught on the South Side we had to live and breathe the test.

The South Side of Chicago has a far higher African American population and far more low-income students than the North Side. The "luck" mentioned here refers to not having to teach to the test as much as he would if he were not teaching wealthy children. Another Chicago teacher explains, "When I moved to the South Side, my husband said I had changed jobs, that [teaching there] should have a different verb to describe what I do." One frustrated Toronto teacher comments on these drastic differences:

> I had 35 kids last year, with mental health issues (depression, suicide attempts, cutting, family alcoholism), learning disabilities, 35 percent IEPs, social issues (bullying) and serious gaps in their learning from previous grades. How can the results of standardized tests possibly reflect all of the progress they did make that year, compared to a nice, calm, class of 25 in an upscale neighbourhood without these issues? If anything,

I worked harder, longer hours, and made a greater impact than [I did] in a school where the scores are always 99 percent.

A veteran Ontario teacher comments: "the public doesn't recognize the differences in communities: new Canadian communities versus upper-middle class communities and what this means for our work (it's much harder and more of it) as teachers who administer the EQAO." Toronto teacher Jessica explains, "teaching poor kids, non-white-kids, low EQAO communities, they get more teaching to the test than rich white kids, and the white kids may not even need the DI stuff as much but they get that good stuff."

Los Angeles teacher Sirin explains, "The kids who most require the stuff we're trained to do—look man, I am an equity educator by heart and by training—they get test prep. They get the canned curriculum." While he likes where he teaches, he notes the difference between his work and that of teachers in wealthier communities, "when I go to PD with teachers from Santa Monica and they are happily telling stories about all their experimentation, their happy mistakes, I'm like yeah right, that can never happen in my school." The preceding powerfully brings to mind the moral rewards of teaching, from which many teachers serving low income and racially minoritized are alienated when engaged in TOTL with low income and racially minoritized children. In many cases teachers are ready and keen to do critical work with kids who may need it most but ST gets in the way.

While teachers serving all student communities reported teaching to the test, this work involves different techniques and is performed with different levels of intensity—based on where teachers work. At her low-performing school, Georgia explains that students are told to "write something, even of it is nonsense, and this is a formal strategy because writing nothing brings down the school's marks." Like Marvelyn's strategy for taking multiple-choice questions based on typical choice creation patterns (described in Chapter 4) Georgia's approach has nothing to do with content learning, and instead focuses on using students' time and attention to increase marks rather than to learn. Neither teacher is happy with these practices and both recognize they diminish the validity of what test results can tell us about these kids and their learning (both teach in low-income, racially minoritized communities).

Teaching to and for the test abounds in multiple forms that do focus on content as well. In so doing, teachers face a variety of motivational issues with students. One Chicago teacher explains:

> I teach to prepare them as much as I can but standardized testing is boring as hell and my students hate it. On one standardized test I had a couple of students tell me they were not taking the test because they did not want the people downtown to think they were stupid.

The teacher's frustration here parallels the students', with this comment pointing to the emotional toll on students as well as teachers. Teachers in high-pressure schools frequently have to sacrifice their pedagogy to keep their jobs, when scores are tied to teacher remuneration and school funding. At its most extreme, teachers feel the pressure to prevent the withholding of funds and even school closure—a pressure on teachers that often bleeds into the student experience.

For teachers, this pressure can often punish good work, as Los Angeles teacher Cheryl explains:

> I have a friend who works in an East LA school, and because she has her bilingual credential she always, every year gets all the newest kids who score the lowest—and they want to link that to her pay. She tutors every recess and lunch, and does reading groups all summer with her kids. Working with these populations could actually cost her money—or her job.

I was able to track down this friend. We met one day at her school and she indeed had a constant informal tutoring clinic running in her classroom. She was one of the first teachers to tell me about the *LA Times* ratings. She told me how she was always given the temporary and transient students. She asked her principal why and was told she was the best the school had. She humbly explained the principal had listed her accomplishments with marginalized students. As the stakes are raised around her, this teacher's teaching success may be held against her as far as test scores and remuneration, despite her widely recognized professional excellence. Indeed, like the late Mr. Rueles, she was identified by the *LA Times* as least effective, and said she cried for almost two days after a parent delivered a copy to her door.

This systemic failure to recognize good work extends to understandings of schools as well. Veteran Los Angeles teacher Mary explains:

> The *Times* basically ranked us as one of the worst schools in LA, the lowest of the five categories. But we grew [between 60 and 90] points that year and they had us as the worst. What is that? Parents read that, even kids sometimes and they don't see the growth, just the ranking.

One Chicago teacher explains: "The public only gets the idea that certain schools, usually in wealthier neighborhoods, will guarantee their child academic and even social success. This helps to keep separate children of different economic means." An Ontario teacher suggests:

> It misleads the public. Schools with high ESL & ELL (essentially new immigrant populations) look like bad schools with bad teachers and the wealthier schools look better and appear to have better teachers, thus perpetuating stereotypes and a warped understanding of what quality education and teachers look like.

The experience of one teacher at one of those "better" schools in Toronto lends support to this argument: "My school has a high amount of high SES students so we have very high scores which is used to promote our school and ultimately our teachers." A veteran Chicago teacher points out that such pressure and perception can lead to manipulation of the system:

> Teachers in more difficult schools or with more challenging or special needs kids are disadvantaged. In districts where pay or job is linked to scores, it creates an incentive to keep less "desirable" or needy students out of the school. Many schools in the US are already gaming the system this way, and they don't see anything wrong with it.

Teachers in the United States also report that students predicted to produce high test scores are increasingly sought out by some schools, a finding reported by wider research,[24] which speaks to the notion of less and more desirable students and teaching posts. Los Angeles teacher Mary explains: "We even get kids sent back to us from schools who take our kids at the start of the year to get their Title One funds, and then they set up closed enrollment nearer to test time and send them back."

This is another version of school choice, in which schools choose students rather than students choosing schools. Sarafina comments: "If you have a few empty rooms, charters can come and co-locate and with no resistance those schools can cherry pick our best kids which kills the scores for everybody else." This advantages teachers at the schools doing the cherry-picking, and can worsen the test score ghettoization of some schools, powerfully impacting public perceptions of teachers.

Beyond questions of race and class, high-stakes testing can also have differential impacts on teaching based on school and community culture. Marvelyn, another Toronto teacher, explains:

> My school is 95 percent non-white, and probably 99 percent very low income. Most of my dads [the fathers of her students] are very well-educated in their home country, having written standardized tests there—and those tests mattered—[the tests] decided your academic stream, if you went to secondary, post-secondary and got good jobs—which to come to Canada, most of them did. Our school is improving but still fairly low on EQAO, but the parents are fanatical about the test.

As is the case in many low-income, visible minority communities, small test preparation businesses have popped up in the neighborhood of Marvelyn's school, tutoring students using EQAO tests from previous years, often using drill and kill instruction. She explains:

> This does nothing for the overall learning of students, and if I were teaching at my son's school which is far more heterogeneous than [my school] it's mixed but mostly white middle class kids, I would not have any of this on my radar. I compare, just chatting with the teachers there, and the scores are high and there is little emphasis from the privileged parents there.

At Marvelyn's school, questions of culture, origin, history, and gender play out in teachers' work and testing, reminding us that despite important patterns, school culture is unique to every school. Los Angeles teacher Nadra takes up the question of school culture, suggesting disadvantaged students (who are in the minority at her school) are academically driven by a combination of home and school expectations. She comments:

> Even among our pretty small population of Title One kids, who don't have parent time, work space at home, and who may have no crayons and no pencils, they do whatever they can—they are driven and school success is key for them and their families. Parents at my old school [which served mostly low income and racially minoritized students] would argue with me that it was my job to practice multiplication with their students. I would never hear that at this school.

Mentioned earlier, Nadra's school is Flower Elementary, which, on its last booster drive asked for $500 per parent. While not as wealthy as some schools in LA, Flower likely brings in far more money than most LA schools. At any given time, the school is full of parents helping out, and booster money enriches programming in every classroom. While there is little doubt these resources would benefit all Flower students, including those qualifying the school for Title One funds, home and school culture, and the link between the two, are of course important factors in student achievement and school experience. For example, research suggests many Latino families may have different expectations of what parental involvement in their children's academic life should look like,[25] which may go a long way toward understanding Nadra's experience at her previous school that had a high percentage of Latino and Chicano students. Variations exist for a host of reasons and these can impact teachers and teachers' work.

One result of the testing burden teachers carry in high-pressure schools is the decision by a very small minority to help their students succeed through acts of cheating, large and small. An Ontario teacher describes one of the more moderate strategies: "In past years we have left posters up in our class. I know one teacher whose window faced a portable and he did chalk graffiti outside that his kids could see from inside." Perhaps with incidents such as these in mind, some teachers suggest that having teachers involved at all will bias the outcome. When asked about whether standardized tests were accurate or produced good data, one Ontario teacher suggests a step already taken in many US jurisdictions:

> Maybe if it were a true standardized test, not given by the classroom teacher and in a neutral environment. I am aware of certain teachers and admin that cheat due to the pressures put on them by higher socio-economic parents and perception of them as teachers. Take the bias out…remove the teacher from the equation and have a third party administer if they really want good data.

Teachers also report helping students, particularly ELLs and learners with exceptionalities. Jessica says, "I've done it, my friends who teach three and six have done it. I have had [ELLs and special education students] in tears more than once, it's the least I can do." Another Ontario teacher explains, "I have seen manipulation of EQAO by teachers and administrators. I have seen tests copied, windows covered to conceal coaching and I know teachers cannot refuse helping their students sometimes."

With a nod and a wink implied, one Chicago teacher explains, "The only goal was to get good scores so we were not put on probation. We got good scores because two people were assigned to go over the tests to 'erase stray marks.'" Cassandra, a teacher in Los Angeles, explains:

> Now, in LA, they sometimes analyze eraser marks on every test of every student. The first year they started this I had six tests sent back for review... I won't say more about that, but I did have a number of [teacher] friends whose... how can I say it? Whose kids' tests were found to have too many, too large or the wrong color of eraser marks. I am very happy to not be thinking about that anymore.

She's not thinking about it anymore because now she is at a low-pressure school. Her friends were all at schools serving "mostly black and Latino kids in crazy neighborhoods." In Ontario, a small number of teachers identified practices in which teachers marking a specific test more than once per year (per student) would adjust their grading to demonstrate improvement that may or may not have been there. Georgia explains: "When I first started teaching a mentor teacher of mine said to mark the first CASI harder than the second one," in order to show student improvement.

In addition to the substantial issues of validity raised here, these practices threaten to disadvantage struggling learners even further. Illegitimate satisfactory scores threaten to mask areas of need and can prevent students from receiving the support they require. One teacher who, like the vast majority of participants is adamantly opposed to cheating, suggests that this worry gives the test too much credit: "If test results translated into teacher practice that immediately supported individual learning, teachers would have far fewer objections to standardized testing." Although Ontario teachers in this study note a variety of different strategies used to bring up test results, there have been no widely publicized cheating scandals. In the United States, however, the occurrence of cheating by teachers is widely reported.

Among the most famous cases comes out of the Atlanta Public Schools system, a scandal that involved 40 schools and saw the indictment of 35 educators in 2013 under charges generally reserved for organized crime using the Racketeering Influenced Corrupt Organizations (RICO) Act. In 2015, 11 educators were found guilty and five were sentenced to prison. They were found to have held erasing parties and picnics, and to have coordinated a widespread effort to raise the test scores of their low-income and primarily African American students. All of the educators sent to prison were African American. The question of undue pressure cannot be overlooked here, and indeed the indictment reads: "Over time, the unreasonable pressure to meet annual APS [Atlanta Public Schools] targets led some employees to cheat on the CRCT [Criterion Referenced Competency Tests].[26] With this in mind, justice has been served only on the very smallest of fish within a larger food chain of unjust education practice and policy. These unjust educational practices are products of unjust educational contexts. Mike Bowers, former Georgia Attorney General who led the investigation, recalls interviews with accused teachers, explaining some, "fainted during the interviews and it would break your heart." Bowers tells the story of one teacher, who explained:

> My kids, third graders, can't read or write and I spend my days combing hair, brushing teeth, getting clothes, getting shoes and making sure they have a place to go at night and here I am sitting in front of you admitting cheating knowing I am going to get fired... and lose the best job I will have ever have.[27]

This tragic picture reveals a system rife with tangled priorities, to say the least. Although it is impossible to say for sure, it is unlikely that all of these same teachers would have made all of the same choices in another teaching environment.

Whereas these practices play into a poverty of low expectations for low-income and racially minoritized students, they emerge from "unreasonable pressure" on certain teachers as even their indictment clearly states. The differential pressure mapped out by this chapter runs through all aspects of teachers' work associated with testing and test-related activities. Teachers experience and thus understand their work differently based on where it takes place and with whom. "Lucky" teachers face less pressure than unlucky teachers: a framework that makes working with kids of color and working-class communities personally undesirable for many and professionally dangerous for many more.

Summary and Implications

Survey and interview results powerfully flesh out the persistent ways in which issues of class, race, culture, and language become further enlivened as markers of advantage and disadvantage as a result of ST. Teachers raise issues of validity as far as the use of test results to understand teacher and student ability. Research suggest ELLs and students with exceptionalities face unique and substantial disadvantages in and around ST, and that widespread health and well-being issues—including anxiety—which present around testing, are harmful for students and may impact results. Race and income are consistently reflected in test results (including issues of "tutoring bias," unequal school funding in the United States and unequal school fundraising in the United States and Canada) and teachers point to persistent issues of cultural bias, unnecessarily complicated language, and other content issues that do not correspond with curriculum and/or standards. A variety of environmental factors impact student success on standardized tests, and teachers feel increasingly unable to assess or address the individual needs of the most marginalized students. Inside the classroom, critical teaching approaches are disappearing in favor of TOTL, a change that is for many teachers a shift away from best practices.

Professional development is increasingly moving toward boosting test results (displacing equity-centered PD and practices) and, in some cases, where equity issues have been identified and related support has been provided (e.g., the misuse of ELL funds in Toronto), these resources are diverted for test preparation. Teachers' widely varied experiences suggest that not all teaching assignments are created equal, and that some teachers enjoy low-pressure environments, while others grapple with high-pressure teaching assignments. These differences exist within and across schools and districts. Teacher accountability, understood through student test scores, disincentivizes the teaching of disadvantaged kids, and can lead teachers and schools to target high-performing students to the exclusion of those less likely to succeed on the test. In its most extreme form, the educational climate of high-stakes testing has produced cheating scandals across the United States. In both contexts, teachers report various strategies aimed exclusively at boosting student standardized test scores (citing pressure and student well-being). To be clear, only a very small number appear to engage in such acts. Apart from any ethical considerations, teachers indicate these practices emerge more frequently in high-pressure contexts, illustrating a pattern found in this and the previous chapters.

CHAPTER 7

Implications: Synthesis of Findings, Resistance, and Alternatives

Introduction

In twenty-first-century schooling, standardized testing (ST) has as much to do with politics as education. In the United States, the Common Core State Standards Initiative (CCSSI) may produce the largest and most complex web of ST in all of history, while simultaneously, parents in record numbers are pulling their children from the tests and public outcry has reached fever pitch across the country. In Canada, a much quieter push and pull is under way. Like other phenomena related to ST, the differences in resistance as well as political bolstering seem quantitatively (rather than qualitatively) different in Canada. The conversation about testing in Canada is a much smaller (and calmer) version of that in the United States. In Ontario, which is heavily invested in ST, teachers and a small but growing number of parents are pushing back with students opting out in small numbers. This appears, roughly, to correspond with less testing and with relatively less teaching to the test than in US contexts. While Ontario teachers primarily expressed concern with questions of the changing classroom and the changing job, many US teachers read the testing landscape with an eye toward politics as well, and many identify a hidden curriculum of testing as far as the profession.

One Chicago teacher explains: "Public school systems are imploding because the people at the top don't want to listen to the people in the trenches," while another suggests: "test scores are a way to transfer responsibility to teachers alone—they talk about accountability but none for boards and states. Society (in the United States) has changed a lot." Like countless parents, academics, and other stakeholders, many teachers perceive a war on education as we know it involving a devaluing of teachers, a slow transfer of public education into quasi-private hands, and the destabilization of a profession, which for decades has been providing good jobs for a largely female workforce. One Chicago teacher comments:

> I work at a "highly successful" charter school. Clearly, our drive for high test scores is being used to advance the privatization movement as if we have some special magic instead of being a school that draws from a wealthy neighborhood.

Los Angeles teacher Nuno suggests: "Race to the Top is part of a larger push to support the growth of charters, and the focus on testing is a push for me, away from teaching, away from serving my community." As we walked to a local bodega after our interview, Nuno and I passed a well-dressed man with a clipboard standing just off of school property. He asked if we had any concerns about the school. He was just beginning to introduce himself when Nuno cut him off, saying "hey man, I'm glad to see they found a Latino to match the surroundings but you can step out of my way right now, I teach here." The well-dressed man stepped aside with a confident smile and we walked on. The man, according to Nuno, worked for Parent Revolution, a group that works to flip underperforming schools using parent trigger[1] policies for which the group itself successfully lobbied. The gentleman, Nuno claimed, "must be newly hired because there was outcry in the community that the reps were all white, so I heard they actually set people up to live in the communities and they get people who look local."

Parent Revolution claims to support parents' and students' rights groups, and operates in a number of states, working at the school, community, and state levels to effect change in policy. Its work focuses on school choice and on making measurement tools available to help parents and students make these choices.[2] The organization is funded in part by the stridently anti-union Walton Foundation, and was, until 2014, headed by Ben Austin (formerly of Green Dot Charter Schools).[3] This is the water in which many US teachers are swimming. The significance of testing runs through teaching life. When we reach the bodega, Nuno introduces me to the owner, who provides free snacks during test time for students, "if they promise to try their best." In Oklahoma, a MacDonald's restaurant in Muskogee offers free breakfasts for students during test time. According to the Academy of Nutrition and

Dieticians Foundation, almost half of US children go to school without having eaten a proper breakfast, and at test time, this is a problem many schools, businesses, and other organizations appear resolute on mitigating.[4] Teachers note that hunger doesn't just show up at test time but is present all year long for many students. Today's most dramatic action and attention in education reform do not attend to equity or real professional improvement, but are focused instead on assessment practices that do little for children and ultimately serve to hold educators accountable to scores rather than to children, parents, communities, or tax payers.

Some teachers suggest the only interests consistently served by ST are testing companies and real estate agents. A Toronto teacher warns:

> The [Education, Quality, and Accountability of Office test] results of my school are used on real estate websites to lure potential homebuyers. In other words, if you have high results as a school, you will increase the attractiveness of the neighborhood. What about the schools that don't perform well? I think that publishing the results increases class division. If we drop the tests what will we do about pushback from the real estate agents?

Although obviously intended as a joke, recent comments from Nicole Brisbane, state director at New York Democrats for Education Reform, indicate these concerns may not be immaterial:

> "Schools are one of the biggest differentiators of value in the suburbs... How valuable will a house be in Scarsdale when it isn't clear that Scarsdale schools are doing any better than the rest of Westchester or even the state? Opting out of tests only robs parents of that crucial data."[5]

Education is a US $4.625 billion business,[6] and much of the growth of this figutre over the past decade relies on the slow but steady privatization of a public asset (a pattern found in prisons and other social services) in which well-paid, tenured, and skilled teachers represent a serious challenge to the bottom line.

To varying degrees, teachers recognize that their profession and work are ground zero of a massive struggle in public policy. After a brief synthesis of the findings and implications of the preceding chapters, this chapter turns to a discussion of resistance to ST, and to a look at a series of assessment alternatives to ST. The first section looks at various forms of resistance undertaken by teachers, parents, and increasingly politicians aimed at curbing, decreasing, and in some cases eliminating the use of standardized tests in public schools. The second section, informed by additional research, teachers' voices, and teacher visions of accountability sets forth a series of alternatives both for assessment policy and teacher practice. This is followed by a close look at the future of Common Core in the United States and of the Education Quality and Accountability Office (EQAO) standardized tests in Ontario.

Synthesis and Implications of the Preceding Chapters

After providing an introduction to the current use of testing in the United States and Canada, this book has investigated the impacts of ST with a focus, first, on the redefinition of high-stakes standardized testing (HSST); second, on the impacts of HSST for classroom practice; third, on the changing nature of teachers' work under HSST; and fourth, on questions regarding equity and accuracy raised by teachers in this study.

The notion of high stakes, as fleshed out in Chapter 3, refers to ST and the widespread use of its results as a governing principle in and of our education systems, our schools, and our classrooms. High stakes can exist in the absence of a particular test that determines a teacher's or student's path. It is an atmosphere rather than the consequences of one evaluation; an atmosphere that is palpable at the national, regional, board, school, teacher, student, and in some cases parent levels. Each chapter has illustrated the varying degrees of pressure applied and experienced in different parts of this high-stakes environment, creating significantly different school life experiences for teachers and students than their peers experienced only a decade or two earlier. This radical change was undertaken in the United States with the passage of the No Child Left Behind Act (NCLB) in 2001, and in Ontario, much more slowly, with creation of province's testing body, the Education Quality and Accountability Office (EQAO) in 1996. Though teachers in the United States and Canada who administer standardized tests experience many of the same pressures, the two contexts are markedly distinct. Canada's use of testing is moderate, whereas the United States tests more than any other country. While the look and impact of Common Core remain to be seen (Common Core will no doubt be an important site of contestation at local and national levels) high-stakes large-scale assessment is deeply embedded in the life of US education. Canadian jurisdictions, meanwhile, may follow a variety of paths with some (such as Ontario) looking more and more American, and others following the research from jurisdictions such as Finland which thrive with minimal standardization and very little high-stakes assessment.

Among the myriad consequences of HSST is a revision of the pedagogical form, a move to test-oriented teaching and learning (TOTL), which is characterized by curricular contraction (of both breadth and depth) as well as a focus on tested content to the exclusion of untested content. In particular, the arts, physical and health education, social sciences, and in some cases science education are marginalized. TOTL relies on an overly narrow toolkit of teaching and learning strategies, to the exclusion of student-centered practices such as differentiated instruction, whole child education, and other critical approaches. Test-oriented teaching and learning moves away from teachers' understandings of best practice, and often fails to meet the academic needs of both the highest- and lowest-performing students. Teachers also note that TOTL is associated with widespread stress, anxiety, and struggle for students. TOTL is not only harmful for some children but also pedagogically unjustifiable at times; a waste of teacher ability and a squandering and snuffing out of student potential.

HSST is changing the work and work life of teachers. In the United States, testing is a widely used tool for measuring teacher efficacy and worth, a fact that incentivizes TOTL. Teachers want accountability that improves their service to students through high standards and necessary supports, but suggest that high-stakes testing has not and will not accomplish these aims. While in-service professional development is increasingly focused on raising student test scores, teachers often use less and less of the professional knowledge gained in their preservice training; particularly the application of constructivist-based teaching and learning strategies that emerge from the science of education psychology and have guided teacher training for a half century. Meanwhile, the relationship between teachers and the general public is changing. Many teachers feel less supported than in previous years, and many feel the profession has been diminished by standardized tests.

Echoing widespread concerns of many researchers, teachers in both contexts raise major concerns about the developmentally inappropriate use of standardized tests with young children. Under HSST, teaching is increasingly deprofessionalized; teachers are alienated from the moral rewards of the work (serving student growth using expert knowledge to effect positive change); and relationships on which successful education depends become strained, routinized, and distant as testing increasingly directs interactions between teachers and the communities they serve.

The study illustrates the ways in which HSST and TOTL can contribute to the further educational marginalization of low-income and racially minoritized students, of English language learners (ELLs), and of students with exceptionalities. While race and income are reflected in standardized test results, these factors are also issues within the tests themselves, with inaccessible language, references, and expressions.

These same culturally specific test items can be confusing for some ELLs, who along with students with exceptionalities, can experience higher rates of test anxiety than other students. Anxiety itself is widespread and can affect student performance. ST can fail to account for a host of environmental factors that may bear on test results. These concerns suggest a host of validity issues as far as the ways in which ST results are used. Teachers also find it increasingly difficult to address the individual needs of the most marginalized students. Further, critical approaches to teaching and learning are progressively more difficult to implement within TOTL, despite the importance of such approaches for shedding light on various forms of injustice facing marginalized school communities. Professional learning and resources targeting marginalized students are often displaced or re-allocated in service of boosting test scores, and teachers who are evaluated based on those scores risk being professionally punished for working with students, communities, and groups who "test low."

Teachers identify a variety of strategies for boosting student scores, and note they use these strategies not only because they face pressure but also to support students (often marginalized kids) who are having a terrible experience with the test. There is wide variation as far as HSST pressure and TOTL in teachers' work (from one class, school, neighborhood, and/or jurisdiction to the next) a variation that constitutes an equity issue for teachers. Taken as a whole, the pedagogy of standardized testing is remaking education in the United States, and is poised to do so in Ontario absent an alternate vision of teaching and learning.

Resistance

From comedian Louis CK, to former US Assistant Secretary of Education Diane Ravitch, popular resistance to ST is widespread in the United States. Public distaste for publisher Pearson Education, the world's biggest testing company, has exploded in the wake of criticisms of Common Core State Standards Initiative and Pearson's central role in the development of its products for student and teacher testing. Reports have been critical of Pearson's highly routinized grading of standardized tests by workers sometimes hired on Craigslist.[7] Recent revelations that Pearson secretly monitored the personal social media activities of students taking New Jersey's Partnership for Assessment of Readiness for College and Care test (PARCC)[8] have done little for the company's reputation (although its bottom line remains very healthy). This type of test fever is uniquely American. No countries test as much (or at such a cost) as the United States. Some countries have outlawed school ranking based on test scores[9] and, while students face extreme academic pressure in countries including South Korea and Japan, the United States is unique in that it may be doubling down on questionable practices with the Common Core. Canadian jurisdictions appear more measured, although widespread resistance to the grade three and grade six tests is building with entire classes opting out in various schools, on the one hand, and EQAO showing no signs of going anywhere soon, on the other. In this light, and in broader comparative perspective, the US push for ST (while good business) is truly radical, unprecedented, and unexplainable without the market logic of education conceived of as big business. Resistance is mounting among teachers, parents, and in a few cases, academics and politicians.

Teacher Resistance

Collectively and individually, teachers have pushed back against standardization for nearly a century. Teachers' unions and professional associations have called for more moderate use of testing and are often vocal in their disapproval of current testing regimes in the United States and Canada (with, for example, policy papers in Ontario and anti-testing television commercials in New Jersey). At an individual level, teachers resist in countless ways every day. While most do not resist the tests themselves directly, many work to subvert the effects described in the previous four chapters. The push back against ST comes in and out of the classroom. A veteran Chicago teacher suggests: "I choose learning over test taking. I do not teach anxiety or boredom," while a junior colleague comments:

> My Masters degree in technology and curriculum development is sadly being used the majority of the time for test preparedness. I still use every teachable moment I can squeeze in to help my students discover the depth of the Internet and the skills that they need to bring that part into their projects but I fight to not let the test takes over.

This work is too rarely praised when it does not lead directly to improved test scores. Many teachers note the challenges of resistance and the professional pressure against it:

> While I frequently do what I believe is best for my students' diverse learning and emotional needs, I resist, it is much to the chagrin of my administrators and I have been reprimanded countless times for not using more harsh disciplinary action. I prefer to take into consideration the difficulties my students have with understanding social language, delayed development of age-appropriate social skills, impulsivity, sensory integration dysfunction, etcetera; all of which can greatly affect how each of them reacts to his/her environment. It is a battle I am willing to continue fighting for the rights of my students, as I trust my own professional knowledge and judgement, and my intuition when it comes to how to most appropriately handle situations in an effort to validate students' thoughts and feelings, while also gently providing them with alternative choices.

These comments imply choices. In the purest sense, every teacher decides the degree to which he or she teaches to his or her conscience. Some face much more challenging choices than others, however, depending on tenure status, remuneration, and whether or not he or she teaches at a high- or low-pressure school (considerations that vary by jurisdiction, school, community, and classroom).

The increased use of test results to assess teachers' work makes this resistance—this teaching that may not show up on a test score—a professional and political risk, which can strain the relationship with the public. One Ontario teacher explains:

> I think there's more awareness of teacher appreciation now, but I also think that there's been an increase in teacher bashing when teachers explain other learning has happened but scores go down. I attribute this to teachers speaking out more about their needs and standing up for their rights in the classroom. Many look at this as teachers whining.

Here, the narrative of entitled teachers held accountable by tough standards comes into direct conflict with the service of students' learning and teachers' best practices. One Chicago teacher suggests this lends itself to a larger, inaccurate, reading of teaching and teachers: "Test scores to evaluate teachers are a successful soundbite implanted by the right: Schools are failing because strong unions protect ineffective teachers. Progressives haven't been able to replace this with a more nuanced (and valid) concept." Los Angeles teacher Sirin suggests: "that's the rub, best service to students can be a liability, but we have to teach back, be bigger, and be committed to the work more deeply—that's my resistance—I tell parents every day." Teachers from a Los Angeles school that was part of this study participated in a rally (with parents and students invited) after the *LA Times* published its school rankings. In other jurisdictions teachers have boycotted various standardized tests. The best known and perhaps most lauded of such cases was at Seattle's Garfield High School in 2013, when teachers successfully refused to administer the Measures of Academic Progress test (MAP) and it was subsequently deemed optional for students in the district.

As far as pedagogical responses, in Ontario, teachers regularly criticize the test with students creating a "we're all in this together" sensibility in which, as a group, classes struggle through the testing. These group criticisms of EQAO often help to create common understandings and can serve as community-building experiences. These in-class forms of resistance are complemented by a host of other activities. Many Los Angeles teachers quietly criticize the narrative of school identity as being entirely test-based, challenging students to see themselves as "a heck of a lot more than a number, or a test score," as Mary explains. Most teachers do not identify the preceding as intentional forms of resistance, however, or even as intentional responses to ST. Further, although some teachers do identify their decisions to help students do better on tests as a form of resistance (practices documented in Chapter 6, which range from answering questions during the test, to leaving up posters that may help children in the classroom while writing the test) they report doing so at times without having originally planned to, often in reaction to a feeling of concern for one or more students.

Forms of Teacher Practice as Intentional Resistance

Teachers resist the professional and pedagogical pressures of HSST using various rationales for their practices. From among the teachers who identified making conscious decisions about intentionally resisting in some form, four approaches emerged. Borrowing from Alfie Kohn, we can term the first form of resistance the better-get-used-to-it approach in which teachers are resigned to teaching to the test because they feel it is unavoidable and ultimately a disservice to students to not prepare them for testing success. A second form is the superheroes (and villains) approach, in which teachers feel they can and should do it all: meet the needs of the standardized test and provide enrichment to students as needed to round out what students need to know using a variety of instructional strategies. The third form of resistance can be termed the consequences-be-damned approach, in which teachers largely ignore test pressures and push forward with independent (research-informed) visions of best practices. The fourth tactic is the choose-your-battles approach, in which teachers teach to the test as needed in class but are active in educating about testing in other contexts.

Better Get Used to It: (Very) Passive Resistance
Teachers engaged in the better-get-used-to-it approach do little to challenge the centrality of high-stakes testing but they are conscious of many of the issues with which HSST is associated, and often share these critiques with students. One Chicago teacher explains: "Students need to be prepared for the test, not for what I wish the test was," while another suggests, "I tell them it is a necessary evil but that there is no avoiding it." Toronto teacher Marvelyn comments, "I have no problem telling them this is basically in addition to everything else and when they say it doesn't connect [to the our classroom activities], I say 'you're right' but we have to do it." While this may not be much of an alternative, the critical conversation with students may have significant impacts on the public conversation about testing. Ontario students explaining to parents that their third grade teacher calls the EQAO "evil questions asked of Ontarians," as mentioned earlier, may indeed provoke doubt about the tests among parents and other stakeholders.

Superheroes and Villains
Superhero teachers have no time for this approach. Indeed, for many superheroes, better-get-used-to-it teaching is the mark of the villain. One Chicago teacher comments, "Many people go through the curriculum like a checklist. Again, not seeing the big picture. We can get to the big ideas in many ways. There is room there." The "room" refers to adequate time and space for good teaching and learning, and as well for bringing a critical lens to the test itself, despite the pressures of HSST. One Chicago teacher explains:

> I do not base my ability to differentiate the instructions or scaffold my students based on standardized testing; I use my own set of assessment tools to measure that especially authentic assessment and portfolios which speak more to 21st Century Learning and the results are fine.

In Los Angeles, Sarafina has little patience for those who feel handcuffed as far as the time constraints of testing, commenting: "We as teachers need to look at the standards and analyze them critically. The time argument is bullshit. I tutor students after school if I am forced to teach to the test." Another Los Angeles teacher, Ernesto, agrees: "there is no excuse; if you are committed [to critical education] you have to work beyond the standards and be critical of the standards—I used to tell my students one [curriculum] for the test and one for your lives." These teachers see the game and play it, recognizing that high scores are a prerequisite for critical work in the classroom with students. Sarafina suggests that, "Bad ass teachers know they have to make the principal look good" in order to do the "critical pieces of teaching and learning." Anything less was unacceptable for the superheroes.

Charlie, an assistant principal in Los Angeles, contends that teachers claiming an inability to teach beyond the test is intolerable, and that in 180 days there is no excuse for not creating rich and dynamic classrooms and curricula. He explains:

> Unpacking standards and turning them into dynamic lessons takes courage, takes know-how, takes resources, takes steering by the admin and good leadership—as an assistant principal this was the biggest challenge. I used my specialization and that of the teachers I supervised to collaborate, mentor and create clear paths to bring up teachers who were behind. If, after that, after a clear attempt to work with their learning styles in multiple ways and multiple times they cannot do it—whether it's laziness, deadwood, or even their own abilities for whatever reason, then they have no business teaching, but I can tell you I had no one who could not be brought around to unpack standards and turn them into dynamic lessons.

Charlie's is a seductive argument. Listening to him, it seems committed teachers and dynamic leadership are all that's required to get the most out of standards while improving the profession, enriching context, and improving instructional quality. The process he describes, however, is uncommon; as are those mentioned by Sarafina and Ernesto.

A caution about superheroes: As a teacher educator I would invite all of these exceptional educators to provide guest lectures in my class. As a parent, I would happily place my children in their classrooms. And, as an education researcher, I am profoundly interested in learning how their admirable practices might inform other teachers in the field. To wit, these are star educators whom I deeply respect. The work they describe, however, is largely unsustainable, nonreplicable across the system, and unrealistic when expected over the course of a teaching career. To be clear, these teachers do amazing work (not unlike characters in movies about great teachers—movies often set in LA!) but they also point to their best teaching as having taken place when they had no children, when they were relatively young, when they were content to work 60–80 hours per week, and largely in isolation—suggesting their work was exceptional and in many cases unconnected to colleagues and lacking collaborative support. Ironically, these teachers, who were among the most critical of all of those in the study as far as social justice and equity, would no doubt be applauded by neoliberal education reformers—an irony they recognize. Read with a neoliberal lens, each of these teachers is a model of successful practice in their respective school: they worked the hardest, brought up scores, and demonstrated that bad teachers (villains) were the culprit when it came to student success (rather than testing-centered teaching and high-stakes assessment).

For various reasons, within survey and interview responses, teachers ascribing to a superhero approach were all either in their first ten years of teaching and were tenured, or were no longer full-time public school teachers. The superhero represents the ideal imagined teacher, an ideal reaction to standards: student-centered, selfless, and wholly concerned with the work. This quickly meets with two major problems: First, this sort of work is untenable over the course of a career. Recognizing that teachers' best work often comes between their eighth and twentieth years of teaching, superhero expectations may drive down retention rates and keep good people out of long-term expert professional practice. Second, these teachers are radical outliers. Their work is not the consequence of high-stakes testing. While the ideal imagined teacher has long been the superhero, high-stakes testing cannot be judged on how it should be used, or how it should impact the classroom. Instead, it must be understood by virtue of its actual impacts on teaching and learning. The excellent work of these educators (the types of teachers that make me want to be a better educator) does however, raise important questions about how to nurture high professional expectations while providing the time and supports needed to meet them consistently over the course of a career.

Consequences Be Damned
Consequences-be-damned resistance pays little heed to making the principal look good, and generally throws caution to the wind as far as student test scores as a measure of their professional ability. Many

teachers adopting this approach are former superheroes, who had to choose, as Toronto teacher Georgia said, "the standards, or the kids and good teaching to be proud of," recognizing that doing both simultaneously was not possible. Lori, a 24-year veteran Los Angeles teacher, works outside of her mandated PD, going to college language course preparation conferences, and does, "whatever the hell she wants" in order to support her students for college language readiness. This involves aligning language learning with resources developed outside of the standards that may have long-term proven outcomes for students but which are "not aligned with state and federal standards." One Chicago teacher explains: "Often I ignore the 'prescription' if it isn't working for my kids, and do what works based on my own research and experience, and that of the other people I teach with." An Ontario teacher comments:

> They can do what they want with our scores but I no longer let it get in the way. If I still have real curriculum to cover the month before EQAO, my kids will not see a booklet, or do any test strategy until we are through; through in a rich and whole way—the grade three curriculum.

For many, the consequences-be-damned approach relied on independent research and understandings of teaching and learning that run counter to test-oriented teacher practice, as one Toronto teacher explains:

> I am completing my doctorate with a focus on assessment, and there is absolutely, nothing, anywhere, by anyone in the literature to suggest that EQAO and other standardized measures boost the learning of children (or for that matter offer valid measures of pupils' ability beyond simple comparative measures). So for me, teaching for any of those assessments is not going to happen. If my grade ten English students cannot pass the [the grade ten Ontario Secondary School Literacy Test] which in 2014 will still be using multiple choice test items, then we have bigger problems.

To be clear, even in Canada where test scores have no impact on remuneration and no value-added measures (VAMs) are in place, this is a radical position. The consequences-be-damned approach comes, for many, with inherent risk. Los Angeles teacher Farabundo, suggests: "At a certain point I made up my mind, and I was like, no, something has to give, and it might be my job, and it was my job." He was teaching critical histories of the Spanish American War, and ultimately lost his job at an urban high school in LA. Despite being a tenured teacher he was ultimately terminated, noting he felt "unsupported by the union," and that his "colleague-friends" disappeared when he challenged the test.

Similar to superheroes, teachers using the consequences-be-damned approach faced consequences, and weathered these storms based on tenure status, based on how close they were to retirement (Lori noted her principal knew it wasn't worth coming after a 24-year veteran who was going to be gone in a couple of years), and based on the context in which they were teaching. Superheroes Sarafina and Ernesto both taught at low-income schools with large racial minority student populations. Their voices are unique here insofar as the superhero approach was more common among teachers in low-pressure teaching environments. Similarly, the teachers using the consequences-be-damned approach did so with greater ease at schools with high test scores.

Choose Your Battles

The fourth approach, choose-your-battles, was reported by only a handful of teachers in the United States and Canada, and in many ways was a response to each of the previous three approaches as far as recognizing the challenges of time, pressure, and politics. One Chicago teacher explains: "I do standards in class, but I am against them. I blog about standardized testing, I attend rallies and am part of [name of activist teachers group in Chicago]. That's my pushback." Another Illinois educator, heavily involved in her union explains, "the fight is not in the classroom, it's at the DOE, or on the picket line, changing minds that way." Describing a similar approach, one veteran Ontario teacher comments: "it's an equity question and it's not the kids' job to navigate the politics of EQAO. I don't support it, am part of [a small anti-EQAO organization] but the kids don't know that." This is work kept away from administrators and the teacher's board. She explains, "I use separate email and all of my social media activist stuff hides that I am a teacher in my board."

The preceding comment speaks to a theme that arose for a few teachers using the choose-your-battles approach, namely the idea that challenging the test in the classroom was professionally inappropriate. Los Angeles teacher Malik explains:

> My fight or whatever, against standardized testing is as a citizen, not a teacher. I can quit my job—and I might actually—but you don't take up that question in class or ever with kids. I have professional activity out of the class, even with parents once and a while, having frank conversations that [standardized testing] is bogus, but no, never with kids.

Teachers engaged in choose-your-battles resistance are thus all engaged in pedagogical projects but they fall outside of the classroom, and represent an interesting crossing of borders (from teaching to activism) as well as a protection of that border (keeping the in-class teaching separate from the activist teaching).

These four overlapping forms of pedagogical resistance illustrate a range of activities and thinking about pedagogy and the contestation of standardization in education by teachers. Taken alongside more extreme measures (including boycotts and various forms of boosting scores) as well as policy-based pieces such as union policy papers, a broad picture of teacher resistance to ST emerges in the United States and Canada. To be clear, not all teachers fit into these categories—in fact, most participants do not report intentional resistance at all, as far as contesting the impact of high-stakes standardization. While nowhere near unanimous resistance is, however, widespread and varied. These contemporary forms of intentional and unintentional resistance (from boycotts, to in- and out-of-class criticisms and critiques, to the policy opposition by teacher professional associations) build on nearly a century of teacher resistance in various forms, to educational standardization; work that has tackled questions, which range from student learning, to race and racism, to working conditions associated with ST.[10]

Parent, Political, and Academic Resistance

Teachers are not alone. Parents and students are at the center of resistance to ST and they are changing the conversation about testing in every part of the United States. From large-scale coordinated national efforts, to state, district and city-based actions, folks are destabilising the ST movement. Indeed, from an age of standardization, we have entered an age of resisting the test. Facebook group pages serving as information sources include groups such as Parents and Kids Against Standardized Testing and Opt out of the State Test—each with thousands of members. UnitedOpt uses a variety of resistance strategies and has sponsored annual Occupy the Department of Education gatherings in Washington, D.C.; Save Our Schools has held rallies and conferences in Washington, D.C., and Philadelphia. Local grassroots groups like Change the Stakes in New York City, provide information, advice, and support for parents choosing to keep their children away from testing, with their numbers rapidly increasing in recent years. While the number of students opting out varies from year to year and from place to place, hundreds of the thousands of children opt out of testing each year in the United States. In New York State, some areas reported a 50 percent opt out rate in elementary schools in 2015.[11] This unprecedented public disobedience is impacting the utility of ST data, destabilizing the ST metric.[12]

Just as standardization applies different levels of pressure to teachers based on where (and how) they are situated, opting out of ST is easier for some than others. Families with multiple secure pathways to higher education and/or professional success for their children have had an easier time pulling kids out of school and away from standardized measures (measures long-billed as great equalizers for low-income and racially minoritized students). While there are important histories of education resistance and activism within marginalized communities, opting out has, until recently, been mainly the choice of those with means, those with cultural capital and those for whom equitable schooling is an ideological rather than material struggle (i.e. rich white folks). At schools in South Los Angeles, teachers pointed out that many of their students' parents were reluctant to opt out because they were undocumented, and did not want any interaction with officials of any kind (including principals or assistant principals). Many marginalized communities have thus not felt entitled to stir the pot for risk of negative consequences for children and/or parents. This has changed somewhat in recent years, however, and the loose coalition against testing in the United States now includes a diverse group of families. As this movement grows, joining becomes less risky—less high stakes—for families that rely on public schools as the only path to success for their children. The opt-out movement increasingly represents a broad political spectrum as well. The passage of Common Core represents an extensive centralization of education policy at the federal level, which has raised the ire of many with libertarian sensibilities. Widespread criticism of Common Core from US Republicans has broadened the movement. In a rare and powerful moment, teachers unions, students, libertarians, wealthy parents, working-class families, teachers, and civil rights groups (even the American Civil Liberties Union) have come together and are beginning a mass destabilization of standardization-based reform in the United States.

This has left some politicians struggling to figure out which way to jump, and has created a hot button no-win situation for others (in the lead up to the 2016 US presidential election, prospective candidates from both parties were asked about their stance on ST). Teacher evaluation—using test scores and other VAM—has been a key mechanism for fighting teacher tenure and other worker protections (priorities for many neoliberal Democrats and Republicans alike). As a popular and widespread issue that includes wealthy parents from Malibu and Long Island alongside parents from Chicago's South Side and South LA, politicians are having an increasingly difficult time juggling unpopular policy and the potential loss of an important tool for free market, neoliberal reform (a policy direction embraced on both sides of the aisle).

In addition to teachers, students, parents and (a few) politicians, academics have cautiously joined the fray. While research on ST has for decades raised serious questions about its validity, reliability, impact on students, and a host of equity issues, some scholars are stepping into the activist arena as well. At the 2013 American Educational Research Association (the world's largest education conference) academics created and distributed hundreds of handheld protest signs to audience members present for US Secretary of Education Arne Duncan's invited talk. One side of the signs asked attendees to consider the research on standardized testing and its impact on US children. The other read, in bold letters, "Not in My Name." Throughout the speech, dozens of participants around the packed room held up the "Not in My Name" side of the sign, in response Secretary Duncan's comments on testing and schools. During one of the Secretary's stories about his time in schools on Chicago's South Side (among the areas hardest hit by Duncan's own education reform policies) an audience participant played Coolio's "Gangsta's Paradise" (featured in the movie *Dangerous Minds*), which prompted both positive and negative reactions from those nearby. Outside the hotel, blazer-clad professors marched with teachers who were protesting the Secretary's speech. While many teacher educators are pushing back against teacher testing (an important corollary to student testing) some researchers have suggested a boycott of academic journals that promote ST data as an adequate tool for measuring education outcomes. While this is only a small number of academics overall, this growing number may be important as part of a broad coalition of those resisting standardized education.

In the Canadian context, where provinces and territories use far fewer standardized tests, there is relatively little resistance to ST. While the same academic critiques of ST apply in Canada (as they do in most places ST is used) there is scant critical analysis of standardized tests used in Canada, and while school trustees may address questions of ST in local debates around election time, there is little widespread discussion among politicians. Teachers unions have come out against testing regimes (e.g., in Ontario and British Columbia) and as documented here, teachers note a variety of resistance techniques. There is no widespread opt-out movement in Ontario among families; however, many parents do opt out their children. The process for opting out can be a murky one and, in practice, it can differ from school to school. While the EQAO Administrators' Guide makes clear the very limited circumstances in which exemptions are permitted, in a handful of Ontario schools, entire grade three classes regularly do not write the test. Following the pattern of other comparisons between the US and Canadian contexts in which greater use of ST correlates with greater impacts on the classroom and the profession, resistance in Canada is qualitatively similar (similar criticisms, concerns, and actions) but there is much less of it. And, to speculate, there is likely much more satisfaction with, if not support for, ST in Canada than in the United States. The stakes are not as high and testing is a much smaller part of life in schools.

From teachers and parents, to academics and politicians, resistance to high-stakes standardization in education is widespread and growing. Teachers report a variety of forms of active and passive resistance, while US parents are leading a nationwide opt-out movement that threatens to bring down the entire house of cards. Academics are slowly adding activism to scholarship and many politicians may be rethinking high-stakes testing. Resistance in all its forms is characterized by a tension between agency and structure. Like other phenomena related to testing, the way people participate in and experience resistance depends on where they are situated. Teacher resistance is powerfully impacted by job security, by union support and seniority. It is also impacted by whether or not teachers are working in high- or low-pressure schools. Superhero teachers mostly worked in high-income contexts, and consequences-be-damned teachers were mostly very secure in their positions and were no longer seeking any forms of advancement (in other words, minimal consequences). The parent-led opt-out movement, although increasingly diverse, has been an easier sell for middle-class white folks than poor and racially minoritized communities. Here too, a question of context, of where one is situated, comes in to play in which those with the most advantage can most easily risk resisting. These comparative variations aside, critical conversations about large-scale HSST naturally merit discussion of alternatives. Based on the Teachers and Testing study, as well as related literature, the following section looks at alternatives to current large-scale assessment regimes.

Alternatives to Standardized Testing

Education systems can be informed and improved by the isolated practice of superior teaching but cannot be reliant on these practices for the successful education of all students. The potential success of the current testing regime in the United States relies on an imagined army of superhero teachers, a fantasy no more realistic than one in which we pretend the current system is working and that teachers and schools are just fine as they are. American education is in deep crisis with regard to the current use of large-scale ST. Radical change is needed and for better or worse, it is on its way. The overhaul of education begun with No Child Left Behind continues on high with Common Core. It is unclear whether federal standards will be a site of possibility for better teaching and learning, remedying our deep social chasms; or whether more of the same is on the way with ever-narrower visions of teaching and learning ushering in even more teacher proof-teaching and test-driven pedagogy.

Much of the Canadian context stands at different crossroads. Not nearly as far down the standardization road and with greater variation between jurisdictions than the United States, Canada's use of ST is significant but not extreme. While Ontario appears to be doubling down, recently investing a great deal to take standardized tests digital, other jurisdictions are reconsidering and/or pulling back on large-scale assessment. Given the regional variation, and absent a federal mandate such as Common Core, it is likely ST policy will continue to vary by jurisdiction. Despite the fundamental differences between these two countries and their multiple jurisdictions at the state, provincial, and territorial levels, they face the same initial question: How much ST, if any, is appropriate in K-12 education? Roughly, the possible answers are the same in each context: none, less, the same amount, or more.

No Standardized Testing/Less Standardized Testing

Given the fairly strong support for the elimination of ST from Ontario teachers (indeed this was a frequent suggestion from teachers in the study) and the ongoing controversy surrounding EQAO, a moratorium on ST is an unlikely but not unreasonable possibility in this context. With school funding and teacher pay unlinked to test scores, and with the results not used as part of students' overall grades (with the exception of some grade nine mathematics EQAO results) very little would need to change if the province's four standardized tests were eliminated.

Conversely, the elimination of ST in the United States would likely be politically challenging and widely unpopular. Prevalent resistance to ST in the United States comes in response to the frequency and use of results rather than to the existence of ST writ large. Though many successful education jurisdictions (including Finland) survive and thrive with little or no ST, this would be a major challenge to a US system that depends heavily on test scores to understand what is happening in schools and school systems.

In both contexts, less testing is a more realistic alternative to the current regime than the elimination of ST altogether, as teacher professional associations have long called for. Possibilities include testing students less often, testing students in fewer grades, and testing only a sample of students in a given grade or level. The move to random sample testing, as the Program for International Student Assessment (PISA) uses every three years, would represent the biggest shift in both the United States and Canada. First, this approach generally does not link results to particular students, schools, or even districts. Second, it makes teaching and learning to and for the test, far less likely. In the United States, a reduction in the number of tests each student writes in a given year is more realistic; and in both contexts, further recognition that ST is developmentally inappropriate for children under nine may lead to less ST of young children.

The Same Amount of Testing/More Standardized Testing

Continuation of the status quo is unlikely for much longer in either context. Change is a constant in education policy. In the United States, given the nationwide resistance to ST, Common Core may use the centralized curriculum to reduce the total number of tests students write (even though they may cover a broader range of topics). In Canada, things are in flux from one region to the next. For example, jurisdictions such as British Columbia may reduce their use in coming years, while Ontario is investing in a digital platform for EQAO. Among the many responses to the charge that what gets tested gets taught is to broaden what's tested. The Common Core is indeed an expression of this logic on a massive scale. EQAO testing is unsatisfactory and a great many people know it; the testing body's press releases are increasingly defensive and increased student and teacher stress has only further muddied the tests' reputation. Accordingly, ST in Ontario has reached a crucial juncture: is the solution to unsatisfactory tests, satisfactory tests and more of them, or instead eliminating or reducing the tests altogether?

A decrease or elimination of the use of ST in either context raises the question of whether or not additional measures are needed in place of standardized tests. And, if so, what might those measures be? Though teacher participants in this study speak to each of these questions and scenarios in some detail, they offer no consistent or unanimous guidance on this issue overall. When asked about alternatives to ST, well under 10 percent of teachers from both contexts support keeping testing as is. Despite these across-the-board low numbers, teachers have a limited common vision of what testing should or should not look like. While 78.8 percent of English Ontario teachers feel there should be no standardized tests, that same number drops to 48.6 percent and 54.9 percent for French Ontario and Illinois teachers, respectively. Teachers do, however, identify a number of priorities as far as assessment. Before looking at the US and Ontario contexts specifically, this section first considers the consistent themes related to assessment identified by teachers in interviews and survey comments in both countries. Taken as whole, a picture of teacher assessment priorities emerges that considers student learning, teacher accountability, and ensuring that the positive elements of testing are retained in any future large-scale assessment.

Teacher Visions of Alternative Assessment

For many, relationships are at the center of successful teaching and learning. Explaining the high graduation rates at his school, one Chicago teacher explains, "This is so because we know learning/teaching is a human relationship—caring for and nurturing this relationship. The current reforms upend this relationship." The success of learning depends, many suggest, on sharing experiences, as another Chicago teacher explains:

> Education is a long, slow process of mistakes, reflection, re-assessment and risk-taking. This can't be done in monthly or annual bits and pieces that are valued against the month before and after or the year before and after. It's a culmination of experiences. Teachers are there to share and foster those experiences, not to brow-beat kids for not making it to a standardized notch at arbitrary timed periods.

The iterative process described here, and facilitated by ongoing low-stakes opportunities for mistakes and stumbles is crucial, Toronto teacher Marvelyn says, "to deep learning, out of which students might gain new interests and possibilities for who they are as a learner." High-stakes teaching and learning can not only "turn kids off" but can also lead students to self-identify as incapable in certain areas. Marvelyn explains, "Some students will say 'I'm not a math person, or I'm not a science person.' I don't hear this when they are inquiring using math and science, only when they can't do pen to paper activities." As illustrated in Chapters 4 and 5, many teachers are familiar with the necessary complexities of rich assessment, and are thus frustrated with the narrow measurement strictures demanded by by ST and TOTL.

In place of ST, teachers suggest a variety of other assessments and assessment focuses. A veteran Chicago teacher suggests: "Portfolio's would be a much better option but no one has the time to view them every year all year long." In place of annual measures, another Illinois teacher comments, "Students should have exit portfolios at the end of their sixth and eighth grade years." These would provide key diagnostic information for seventh and ninth grade teachers. On the question of authentic assessment, which avoids the high-stakes of ST as far as the student experience, another Chicago teacher explains:

> If we truly wanted to assess the ability of students throughout the nation and compare them amongst their same aged peers, we would gather work samples from throughout the year that were completed when students were not given any sense that they were being assessed or that the assignment was going to be used for any purpose different from any other assignment. That way, these authentic pieces of student work would be a more accurate reflection of individual student performance and give an opportunity for students who demonstrate their abilities through different means than filling in bubbles on a test form, to truly show what they know.

Such an approach would dramatically change the student and teacher experience of large-scale assessment. For reformers bent on ranking and comparing students, this "authentic" measure might provide far more valid and reliable data on student ability. It would also, ideally, address the persistent issue of ST as a one-way street for students in which they work hard to prepare, work hard to take the test, and then receive no timely feedback (often the following school year) and no descriptive feedback at all. A Toronto teacher comments:

> Students are forced to learn the entire year before the end of May. If we have to do the tests, they should be done in the fall of the next year, it sits in a warehouse all summer anyway, and students might actually learn from them if feedback was provided.

On long-term assessment complemented by consistent feedback, one Chicago teacher suggests: "I think day to day assessment and observation offer a more accurate reflection," while another adds: "Progress monitoring with frequent feedback, which measures change over time is a more accurate reflection of students' abilities and actually supports their growth." A third-year Toronto teacher reflects, "teachers college was all about not relying on assessment of learning and instead making sure that assessment is for learning, EQAO, and now the teaching around it, is not educational." Assessment of, for, and as learning is a framework spelled out for Ontario teachers in the Ministry's *Growing Success* guide to assessment in the province's public schools.[13] Teachers are required to understand how assessment can take place "for" and "as" learning, and are encouraged to use assessment that does not teach (i.e., assessment "of" learning) only when needed.

Many teachers feel ST fails to tell them anything they do not already know, and that what ST does tell them, is readily available through other measures. One Chicago teacher explains, "Many students do not do well under pressure. They should be given the chance to show what they know in other ways, which I know teachers do but has not been reflected on their evaluations," while another adds, "the grades I already give are a better reflection of student performance, these need to be used—even if they need to be improved—to measure students if we want accuracy and student learning." Testing, according to many teachers, is a misallocation of scare education resources. A young Ontario teacher explains: "Real literacy comes from good teaching and enriching texts in the classroom. The EQAO money would be better spent allowing me to by new books and technology to support learning," while a Chicago teacher argues: "it's going to take leaders with the courage to spend this testing money on real learning—trust the teachers and the kids—radical I know."

Part of the opportunity cost of ST (beyond dollars that might be better spent) is the squandered possibility of improving teacher practice. Los Angeles teacher Sarafina explains: "Good teaching is really challenging, it's big decisions each day and we need big professional judgement for those decisions." TOTL pulls teachers in another direction. Mary explains, "We're busier than ever, but we're not necessarily getting better professionally—it's like a collar we wear that keeps us a certain way." Test-centered collaboration is usually top down, and as reported in Chapter 5, teacher accountability and professional development can actually be hindered by TOTL. The "radical" idea mentioned above of trusting teachers is a necessary first step to holding them accountable to high expectations. Teachers can only act like professionals if given the opportunity (leeway, respect, and supports) to do so. High-stakes testing takes things in the opposite direction. Andy Hargreaves and Michael Fullan suggest:

> Teaching is hard. It's technically difficult, for example, knowing the signs of Asperger's, differentiating instruction, learning all the skills to deal with difficult adults. It requires technical knowledge, high levels of education, strong practice within schools, and continuous improvement over time that is undertaken collaboratively, and that calls for the development of wise judgment.[14]

Hargreaves and Fullan's work on the concept of professional capital suggests the current climate of standardization (including VAM) can often fail to account for, to nourish, and to develop teachers' work in these areas. Absent, then, are measures of teacher ability in these areas, as well as teacher opportunities for professional growth. Hargreaves and Fullan identify "three kinds of capital that comprise professional capital: human capital (the talent of individuals); social capital (the collaborative power of the group); and decisional capital (the wisdom and expertise to make sound judgments about learners that are cultivated over many years)."[15] While human capital (understood here as individual talent) is central to standardized education, social and decisional forms of capital are disincentivized at best, and in some cases even frowned upon. On the basis of extensive work with a variety of education systems around the world (including the United States and Canada) these authors suggest that the sort of teacher deprofessionalization bred by high-stakes standardization (including teacher-proof teaching, assessments in which the individual strengths and weaknesses of teachers and students are overlooked, and teaching and learning practices that fail to consider a host of contextual factors) ultimately fails students, schools, and the profession. Teacher visions of assessment involve high professional expectations of teachers as decision makers, working closely with colleagues and students.

The Future of Common Core

The future of ST in the United States is tied for now to the future of Common Core. Adopted by all but a handful of states, it is the way forward for US education, despite widespread opposition from a diverse group of stakeholders. It is fundamentally remaking US education; impacting curriculum, teacher training, student assessment, teacher assessment, and all aspects of pedagogy. It is poised, as well, to fundamentally transform the teaching profession. Testing is the tainted lifeblood of many American schools and its total demise will not be coming to a neighborhood school anytime soon. The question facing twenty-first-century US education is not "should we proceed with Common Core?" It is instead: "how can education stakeholders push for assessments (under Common Core or any other approach) which do not harm children through undue stress; which do not narrow content, pedagogical approaches or teachers' professional growth; which hold teachers, as professionals, to high standards; and which address the fundamental social gaps which have been a definitive part of education in the US for over a century?"

From teachers to parents to students, US education stakeholders are primed for a reduction in the use of ST (of how many tests students write, of how often students write them, and/or of how many students write each test). Given the political appetite for data-driven accountability, however, better measures (with which to compare, rank, and file students) may be a realistic—although not an ideal—place to start. Linda Darling-Hammond's work (as well as that of others) on performance assessment provides one path forward. Performance assessment (often made up of smaller, performance tasks) offers potential remedy for some of the major limitations of ST. Understanding accountability beyond tax payer return on investment, Darling-Hammond suggests good assessment improves learning rather than simply measuring it.[16] Performance assessments measure a greater variety of student skills and offer a greater number of entry points for student success than standardized tests. They also generally assess students over a longer period of time than standardized tests, and typically incorporate inquiry and exploration more often than standardized tests. Teacher professional knowledge and decisional capital with regard to local and regional contextual factors is central to good performance assessment, and research suggests that unlike VAM, rich performance tasks improve the quality of instruction.[17] Curriculum-embedded performance components might incorporate more locally developed and curriculum-related tasks into the measures currently touted as providing accountability. Applied to Common Core, this could mark an important reintegration of teacher knowledge into large-scale assessments.

Performance assessments as a central part of Common Core, however, may be a tough sell. According to Linda Darling-Hammond:

> The challenge ahead will be for states and districts to prepare to implement new [performance] assessments given the many challenges they entail. On the one hand there is substantial consensus that US assessments

must evolve to meet the new expectations for student learning. On the other hand there are countervailing pressures regarding funding, time, and traditions that stand in the way of assessment changes.[18]

Further, performance assessments can become high stakes for students, teachers, districts, and states based on the significance attached to the results.[19] Additionally, unless explicitly guarded against, performance assessments are not immune to standardization. Brian Stecher suggests: "As performance tasks become more complex (i.e., as process skills become richer and content knowledge more open), it becomes more difficult to develop scoring criteria that fully reflect the quality of student thinking."[20]

Another concern of teachers and other stakeholders is equity. No alternative to ST will, by its very structure or medium, solve the education gaps that so powerfully characterize US education. For example, multiple-choice questions on their own neither create nor eliminate race-based advantage or disadvantage in education, and the same holds true with performance assessments.[21] This raises questions for teacher training where, for example, the portfolio model is widely used but too infrequently linked to potential future professional practice. The role of teacher education may also be central in linking progressive future assessment practices (of, for, and as learning) to particular articulations of Common Core standards with an eye toward equity-centered practice.

Among the most important questions raised by the possible implementation of performance assessment as an alternative to standardized tests, is whether widespread implementation of high-quality performance assessment is likely given the cost proclivities; the challenges of the bureaucracy needed to hammer out nuanced assessment practices; and the recent history of bubble test fever. To date, much successful performance assessment has been developed at the local state level. Because Common Core is based on a national vision of assessment, questions certainly arise about the ability of these assessments to be adapted based on local context and knowledge (including knowledge of teachers).

Figuring out a way to ensure that students construct rather than select their answers may not go far enough in addressing the concerns of countless researchers, educators, and parents about educational standardization generally and standardized assessment in particular. I recently visited a Toronto kindergarten class where students were outdoors all year long (even through the Canadian winter). Surrounded by little fingers covered in soil, structures built of bark, and cheeks rosy from constant activity I was reminded that inquiry is human, intrinsically exploratory, and indeed that this beautiful learning would likely have to stop in order to assess it (there were no real "products"). I can muster no excitement at the prospect of thoroughly qualifying and quantifying these activities all in the name of measurement (even good measurement conducted through performance assessments, which closely mirror the real-life moments in which the measured skills and knowledge will be applied).

Education gaps (or debts, as Gloria Ladson Billings suggests[22]) are among the only constants in US education. The American system is simultaneously plagued and blessed with perpetual, albeit partial, reinvention. Whether or not the twenty-first-century educational change will reflect the voices and professional wisdom of teachers in the pursuit of growth for all learners remains to be seen.

The Future of EQAO

Like their counterparts in the United States, Ontario's education policy makers are facing an important series of decisions in the coming years as they inevitably move in one direction or another on the use of ST. In articulating alternative visions of assessment, a number of Ontario teachers identified positive elements of testing, which they felt should inform any subsequent large-scale assessment regime. One Toronto teacher comments: "Over time, patterns can arise. Those patterns should be looked at more courageously by any alternatives." Toronto grade six teacher Elway has administered the test for nearly a decade, marked it for the province four times, has sat on numerous committees at EQAO (one that looked at bias in questions and performance), and has been a question writer for the test. He suggests EQAO brings staff together for effective and thoughtful collaboration, commenting:

> Rarely as a staff, do we look at the results as connected to any one student. It is more a planning piece which helps us to mold our pedagogy, connect our pedagogy and reflect on our pedagogy, a reflective process with which a majority of teachers engage. We noticed for four years running that our geometry marks were low each year and we puzzled over this. Eventually we realized that we were following the text book and that geometry was last in the textbook, even though it is a complex skill. So we moved our geometry instruction so that most of the school does it in the January/February area and our marks went way up. So most of what we are doing is at the teacher planning level rather than the teacher student level.

This sounds good, but we are left to wonder what used to be taught in January/February and when it's taught now. Elway acknowledges that even strong teachers struggle to balance what is best for students and what is best for a teacher's professional standing and well-being as far as test results. Elway uses old EQAO questions on tests but does not tell his students about it. He suggests that teaching to the test is a slippery slope that leads to disengaged kids and that the knowledge base in his "privileged white school" allows for teachers to avoid the slope because there is relatively little temptation to teach to the test at his school.

Ontario teachers note that EQAO has been a demonstration of what effective collaborative practice might look like, but criticize the overall aims of this practice. Georgia explains, "if we could be this concentrated and organized and focused as a staff on equity we'd have an amazing school." Marvelyn, suggests, "okay, EQAO has shown we can accomplish a goal, now let's turn that goal to assessment that is actually useful for teaching and learning." Another Ontario teacher comments:

> Teachers always teach to the best of their ability. The key is to invest in building teacher capacity. I think EQAO has done its thing and demonstrated higher level thinking questions thereby supporting improved teacher practices. We get it now so let's move on. The world is a different place [than when EQAO was implemented] and its run its course. Thank you and bye bye.

The notion that the EQAO may have been a good thing at one time which has now run its course was a common sentiment among Ontario teachers, owing mainly to improved teacher understandings of assessment in the past decade.

This common understanding among many teachers that EQAO, specifically at the elementary level may have served its purpose, should not be overlooked by education policy makers in Ontario. At a minimum, given the host of concerns raised in this book and elsewhere, and given the widespread concerns about the use of standardized testing for children under nine, use of the grade three EQAO test should be immediately halted in its current form. There was never a public outcry for data-driven accountability in Ontario, indeed standardized tests were not part of the original recommendations which led to EQAO's creation. If numbers on performance are needed in the absence of the grade three EQAO, a variety of province wide-performance assessments would be ample replacement. If common large-scale assessment is necessary, then surely it is worth doing properly and in a way that provides a more holistic and complete picture of student learning. If EQAO cannot use assessments which teachers support; which research demonstrates adequately control for bias; and which are used to generate valid conclusions about our students, teachers, and schools (requiring a consideration of the way results are used) then the province should consider pulling back on province-wide assessments until such time as it can proceed on more solid ground and in the interests of all Ontario students. The consequences of the current Ontario standardized testing regime for teaching and learning are simply too grave to continue with things the way they are now.

In addition to the elimination of the grade three standardized test, the grade six, nine, and ten standardized tests should be reconsidered in light of their impact on classrooms (including student learning and teacher practice). The demand for, and necessity of, each of these assessments should be clearly established and made public. For example, the grade nine mathematics EQAO is often a mirror of tests already given in the same class at the same time of year. A clear and adequate rationale for this standardized test needs to be made available to all stakeholders. If such measures are deemed necessary, the integration of performance assessment tasks should be undertaken within each test. At a minimum, any revision of province-wide assessment in Ontario should closely consider a variety of student inputs over a longer period of time, based on a greater variety of student strengths and abilities. If any of the current EQAO measures are preserved in their current form, the province should consider testing a sample population and should get teachers out of the EQAO-preparation business. In the meantime, parents and the general public need to better understand that teaching to the test is a widespread practice in Ontario, and that claims of EQAO being a random snapshot of an individual student's learning are false. Further, claims that these tests are low pressure, unimportant or somehow do not matter, must be disposed of quickly. The pressure (including variations therein) facing Ontario students and teachers needs to be widely recognized and addressed. Finally, parents need to know their rights as far as testing, and should be informed that many families are opting their children out of the grades three, six, and nine tests.

As this book was going to print, many Ontario elementary teachers refused to administer the spring 2015 EQAO tests, as part of a job action resulting from a labor dispute. Just as importantly, they withheld all test-related teaching and activities. The cancellation was announced by the union just as test preparation was at its peak in many classrooms.

Overnight it was gone. In grade three and grade six classrooms across much of Ontario that spring, teachers had almost a month on their hands. In quick conversation with eight of the teachers interviewed for this study originally, I had the chance to ask what they were planning on doing with the time. Almost all of their answers were examples of student-led, curriculum-relevant, and inquiry-based activities about which, teachers reported anecdotally, the students were thrilled. Most mentioned planning some type of outdoor activity after a long winter, and every single teacher described some form of deep and engaging learning (none mentioned watching movies in class, which often rounds out testing days and weeks).

As a jurisdiction, Ontario is a top education performer with some of the best trained teachers in the world. Assessment and evaluation practices have improved tremendously since the introduction of EQAO standardized testing. Teachers have a long history of professional engagement in the province, and are fighting to maintain their work and place as education experts, as committed advocates for children, and as productive and contributing citizens. Empowering teachers in all of these areas supports student learning in the classroom. Equity within and between schools is among the major comparative strengths of Ontario's education system, and any future vision of large-scale assessment must work to support and improve on this. In practice, this will require special attention to ELLs, to students with exceptionalities, and to students in the applied stream.

In Closing

US and Canadian teachers' visions of assessment identified here are varied, insightful, applied, and student centered. While there is no shying away from teacher accountability, there is also no need for high stakes in any punishing form (for students or teachers). Teachers' voices can guide us toward more appropriate strategies (including peer-group research projects, student work portfolios, oral and written communications, and students as instructors), which far surpass the abilities of standardized tests to determine and measure learning and achievement. Teachers offer a vision in which individualized classroom assessment must take priority system-wide; using assessments developed at least in large part by teachers that encourage learners to apply what they have learned to tasks relevant to their lives and local contexts. Planning, instruction, and assessment should consciously consider the empowerment of students as individuals and as part of a collective, to work toward critical consciousness and the building of capacity for social and political change. Learners are best guided by frequent, real-time support, and timely feedback from teachers, peers, and where possible, community members, and outside experts.

Teacher visions of assessment are often research-informed and thoughtful, noting what should be kept and mobilized from their experiences with ST, and what needs to be jettisoned in order to best support whole-student success for all learners. Unfortunately, these articulate voices and visions are too often ignored or deemed untrustworthy and self-interested. Teachers—understood as experts and professionals of whom the public can have high expectations and who are responsible for professional evolution and holistic growth for all students—must play a central role in educational change in the United States and Canada. A failure to center and consider these voices will not only alienate teachers from teaching but also prevent a wealth of professional knowledge from reaching our classrooms and our students. Treating teachers as recipients of education policy from on high is an absurd yet common practice. While political courage and vision is needed to move away from ST in its current forms in both the United States and Canada, the bold policy maker will be well-supported by decades of education research, thousands of frontline education experts (teachers), and countless parents and students.

It is clear that the very idea of accountability as a public interest needs to be reexamined to consider more closely what education stakeholders actually want and require from our public schools and teachers. Teacher insights into the impact of HSST indicate that ST answers questions no one is asking. In US jurisdictions, it may provide a solution to the neoliberal dilemma of empowered and protected workers but on the whole it is not improving education; indeed in many cases HSST is a hindrance to teacher practice and student learning. While the standardization movement may claim to be responding to legitimate concerns in education (social learning gaps, underfunding, and ineffective teachers) this response is no more logical than answering the front door when the phone rings. Teacher voices are a central and required component of any worthwhile large-scale educational change initiative. Teacher insight and buy-in are crucial to high standards for all children and adults in our schools; they are also sorely needed to ensure that assessment practices offer paths to success for all students.

Education policy makers in Canada need only look at educational success in global context (avoiding a focused gaze straight south) to recognize that further educational standardization will do little to preserve Canadian educational success and that standardization has failed, overall, to improve teaching and learning in Canadian schools. US education policy makers (in government and the private sector) will do well to think beyond the borders of recent history, and to consider a future in which the United States does not use more standardized tests than any other jurisdiction (ever) in the world. The United States is home to unparalleled educational innovation. Focusing these energies and capacities on assessment solutions that serve all students, a true vision of the commons without a built-in expectation of some failing as a matter of structural course, may hold the key to a poststandardization US educational renaissance. In the meantime, replacing narrow, make-or-break high-stakes tests with low-stakes, frequent, holistic, and student-centered assessments based on high expectations of students and teachers alike would be a good start. In both the United States and Canada, consideration and integration of teacher visions of assessment will be a central piece of any successful step forward.

Appendix: A Note on the Survey

The survey was developed, translated, and field tested in Toronto and Los Angeles in early 2013. It was distributed and made available electronically to teachers in New York, California, Illinois, and Ontario by teacher associations, through university networks and through various independent teacher networks between May 2013 and December 2014. Comments from open-ended survey questions are included here in addition to commentary from interviews. The interested reader will note that comments included from interviews refer to the teacher by name, while comments from the survey do not. Comments from the survey raise important questions and serve to support the generation of hypotheses, as well as to extend and enrich the interview findings. These comments also offer context and detail unavailable through the use of fixed-choice survey responses.

To varying degrees there are limitations to what the results of any research can tell us, and this survey is no exception. There are significant limits to the statistical significance of the data. Although there are enough responses for a representative sample, given the size of the Ontario and Illinois teacher populations under study (958 from Illinois, 450 from Ontario [French], and 604 Ontario [English]), the teachers who completed the survey (the survey sample) do not make up a true random sample of teachers in these regions (population), as the study employed a self-selection methodology for the survey. Further, the recruitment methods make an exact response rate impossible to determine. Many factors weigh on the source of unaccounted for variance (in other words, differences between and among responses and respondents). Ideally, a survey like this would isolate respondents' views on the items in question, without the influence of outside factors (cutting out the noise and getting to the issues at hand), but this cannot be accounted for without a random sample methodology. For example, teacher willingness to take the survey (as well as their individual answers on the survey) may or may not have been impacted by timing and availability; by comfort level with the topic and format of the instrument; and by interest in, as well as knowledge of, the issues. Additionally, contextual factors may or may not have impacted the participation. For example, most of the surveys were distributed or made available to teachers by their unions or via union-related websites. In Ontario, there was labor conflict between teachers' unions and the government in early 2013; while in September 2012, Chicago teachers went on strike over school closures and a host of other education reform issues. The impact of these phenomena on survey results is unclear.

None of these sorts of limitations, however, are unique to this study. Indeed, they are present to different degrees with much survey-generated data, and to all studies that do not use statistically random samples. Even in cases where a true random sample is present (e.g., in government census or large-scale polling data) questions of context, current events, and other factors may or may not impact the overall results (the difference is those impacts would be neither over- nor underrepresented in the results). While the survey results presented here thus do not represent a true random sample of all teachers in these populations, there is good evidence that the survey sample and the populations are aligned. For each of the three data sets—Illinois, Ontario (French), and Ontario (English)—the survey sample and population as a whole are, to the best of my knowledge based on consultation with the Chicago Teachers' Union and the Ontario Teachers' Federation, largely consistent with available demographic and professional data (on age, gender, and race, where available) as well as with relevant professional markers including years of experience, grade level(s) taught, and number of standardized tests administered each yearly. So, the thousands of teachers we hear from in this study allow us to generate hypotheses about standardized testing and the classroom, they allow us to more deeply understand the impacts of high-stakes testing in the classroom, and they provide us with a rich backdrop against which to contextualize and understand the interviews. The quantitative findings included here are for the most part quite decisive, noting only patterns large enough to be potentially meaningful.

Quantitative results presented throughout the book come from three identified teacher populations: French Ontario teachers, English Ontario teachers, and Illinois teachers. "French Ontario" describes teachers at public French school boards throughout the province, while "English Ontario" refers to teachers at public English school boards throughout the province (French and English boards follow the same curriculum in Ontario). Although most "Illinois teachers" surveyed were from Chicago, a few identified as teaching in nearby locations. This informed the decision to use "Illinois" rather than "Chicago" to describe this teacher population.

Notes

Introduction

1. The last segregated school for African Canadian children in Ontario, Canada, was closed in 1965, while the last Residential School for Indigenous children closed in 1996.
2. Paulo Freire, *Pedagogy of the Oppressed* (New York: Continuum, 1997).
3. Chris Goering, "Opt Out? Why Parents Should Opt-In to Standardized Testing," *Huffington Post,* May 21, 2014, accessed February 17, 2015, http://www.huffingtonpost.com/chris-goering/standardized-test-optout-movement_b_5347225.html.
4. Susan Ohanian, "Let's Turn the Tables," *SusanOhanian.Org*, April 18, 2003, accessed October 3, 2014, http://susanohanian.org/show_commentary.php?id=61.
5. Eric Norden, "A Candid Conversation with the High Priest of Popcult and Metaphysician of Media," *Playboy,* March (1969): 37.
6. Arlo Kempf and Ruth Powers Silverberg, "Academic Disobedience: Engaging Michael Apple's Nine Tasks of the Critical Scholar in an Age of Standardization," in *School Against Neoliberal Rule: Educational Fronts for Local and Global Justice: A Reader,* ed. by Mark Abendroth and Brad Porfilio, 187–206 (Charlotte, NC: Information Age Publishing, 2015).
7. Arlo Kempf and Ruth Powers Silverberg, R. "Academic Disobedience: Engaging Michael Apple's Nine Tasks of the Critical Scholar in an Age of Standardization," in *School against Neoliberal Rule: Educational Fronts for Local and Global Justice: A Reader,* ed. Mark Abendroth and Brad Porfilio, 187–206 (Charlotte, NC: Information Age Publishing, 2015).

1 The School as Factory Farm: All Testing All the Time

1. Brennan is the author of *Educational Measurement*, a work the University of Iowa's Center for Advanced Studies in Measurement and Assessment describes as the "bible in the field of measurement" (2014, Center for Advanced Studies in Measurement and Assessment).

2. Robert Brennan, "Revolutions and Evolutions in Current Educational Testing: CASMA Research Report Number 6," *Center for Advanced Studies in Measurement and Assessment,* 2004: 6, accessed May 7, 2014, http://www.uiowa.edu/~casma/wallace.casma.rpt.pdf
3. For more on this phenomenon, see: Thomas Philips, "Articulating the Purpose of a Social Foundations of Education Course through Instructor Self-Interviews," *Studying Teacher Education* 9 (2013).
4. Andrew Feenberg, *Critical Theory of Technology* (New York: Oxford, 1991), 12.
5. Melissa Lazarín, *Testing Overload in America's Schools* (Washington, DC: Center for American Progress, 2014), 2.
6. Howard Nelson, *Testing More, Teaching Less, What America's Obsession with Student Testing Costs in Money and Lost Instructional Time* (Washington, DC: American Federation of Teachers, 2013), 6–7.
7. Matthew Lynch, "Education Officials to Re-examine Standardized Testing," *Education Week*, October 22, 2014, accessed October 23, 2014, http://blogs.edweek.org/edweek/education_futures/2014/10/education_officials_to_re-examine_standardized_testing.html?qs=standardized+testing.
8. For a complete and convenient table of Canadian tests (including subject matter and frequency) see Després et al., *Accountability or Illusion of Success? A Call to Review Standardized Testing in Ontario*. Ottawa: Action Canada Task Force Report, 2013, accessed June 2, 2014, http://testingillusion.ca/wp-content/uploads/2013/01/illusion_of_success_EN.pdf.
9. Education Quality and Accountability Office. *A Parent's Guide to EQAO Tests* (Toronto: Education Quality and Accountability Office, n.d.), 2.
10. Appendix One provides a brief description of the survey methods and methodology, and addresses the possibilities and limits of the research design used in the Teachers and Testing Study.
11. Lizette Alvarez, "States Listen as Parents Give Rampant Testing an F," *New York Times*, November 9, 2014, accessed November 10, 2014, http://www.nytimes.com/2014/11/10/us/states-listen-as-parents-give-rampant-testing-an-f.html?_r=0 2014.
12. Diane Ravitch, *Reign of Error: The Hoax of the Privatization Movement and the Danger to America's Public Schools* (New York: Knopf, 2013), 12.
13. Howard Nelson, *Testing More, Teaching Less, What America's Obsession with Student Testing Costs in Money and Lost Instructional Time* (Washington, DC: American Federation of Teachers, 2013), 6–7.
14. Matthew M. Chingos, *Strength in Numbers: State Spending on K-12 Assessment Systems* (Washington, DC: Brown Center on Education Policy at Brookings, 2012), 1–2.
15. Linda Darling-Hammond and Frank Adamson. "Developing Assessments of Deeper Learning: The Costs and Benefits of Using Tests that Help Students Learn" (Stanford, CA: Stanford Center for Opportunity Policy in Education, 2013).
16. Matthew M. Chingos, *Strength in Numbers: State Spending on K-12 Assessment Systems* (Washington, DC: Brown Center on Education Policy at Brookings, 2012), 10.

17. Matthew M. Chingos, *Strength in Numbers: State Spending on K-12 Assessment Systems* (Washington, DC: Brown Center on Education Policy at Brookings, 2012), 10.
18. Matthew M. Chingos, *Strength in Numbers: State Spending on K-12 Assessment Systems* (Washington, DC: Brown Center on Education Policy at Brookings, 2012), 2.
19. Matthew M. Chingos, *Strength in Numbers: State Spending on K-12 Assessment Systems* (Washington, DC: Brown Center on Education Policy at Brookings, 2012), 2.
20. Barry Topol, John Olson, and Ed Roeber. *The Cost of New Higher Quality Assessments: A Comprehensive Analysis of the Potential Costs for Future State Assessments* (Stanford, CA: Stanford Center for Opportunity Policy in Education, 2010).
21. British Columbia Ministry of Education, "Getting the Facts on FSA," N.D., accessed October 1, 2014, https://www.bced.gov.bc.ca/assessment/fsa/info/facts.htm#tdD.
22. Alberta Education, "Breakdown of Alberta Student Population," N.D., accessed November 3, 2014, http://education.alberta.ca/department/stats/students/studentpopulation.aspx.
23. Michael Zwaagstra, "Is NSTU Digging in Against Standardized Testing?," *Chronicle Herald*, October 8, 2014, accessed October 9, 2014, http://thechronicleherald.ca/opinion/1242308-is-nstu-digging-in-against-standardized-tests.
24. Education Quality and Accountability Office. *2011–2012 Annual Report* (Toronto: Queen's Printer for Ontario, 2013), 14.
25. Cory Turner, "U.S. Tests Teens A Lot, But Worldwide, Exam Stakes Are Higher," *National Public Radio*, April 30, 2014, accessed October 3, 2014, http://www.npr.org/2014/04/30/308057862/u-s-tests-teens-a-lot-but-worldwide-exam-stakes-are-higher.
26. Iris C. Rotberg, "Assessment Around the World," *Educational Measurement* 54 (2006): 4.
27. Center for International Education Benchmarking, "South Korea Overview." (Washington: Center for International Education Benchmarking, 2012), accessed October 3, 2014, http://www.ncee.org/programs-affiliates/center-on-international-education-benchmarking/top-performing-countries/south-korea-overview/.
28. Center for International Education Benchmarking, "South Korea Overview." (Washington: Center for International Education Benchmarking, 2012), accessed October 3, 2014, http://www.ncee.org/programs-affiliates/center-on-international-education-benchmarking/top-performing-countries/south-korea-overview/.
29. Iris C. Rotberg, "Assessment Around the World," *Educational Measurement* 54 (2006): 4.
30. Organization for Economic Cooperation and Development, *Reviews of National Policies for Education: Improving Lower Secondary Schools in Norway* (Paris: OECD, 2011), 9.

31. Organization for Economic Cooperation and Development. *PISA 2012 Results: What Makes Schools Successful? Resources, Policies and Practices Volume 4* (Paris: OECD Publishing, 2013), 147.
32. Organization for Economic Cooperation and Development. *PISA 2012 Results: What Makes Schools Successful? Resources, Policies and Practices Volume 4* (Paris: OECD Publishing, 2013), 147.
33. Organization for Economic Cooperation and Development. *PISA 2012 Results: What Makes Schools Successful? Resources, Policies and Practices Volume 4* (Paris: OECD Publishing, 2013), 148.
34. Organization for Economic Cooperation and Development. *PISA 2012 Results: What Makes Schools Successful? Resources, Policies and Practices Volume 4* (Paris: OECD Publishing, 2013), 148.
35. Adapted from: Organization for Economic development and Cooperation. *PISA 2012 Results: What Makes Schools Successful? Resources, Policies and Practices Volume 4* (Paris: OECD Publishing, 2013), 148.
36. Alfie Kohn. "Standardized Testing and its Victims," *Education Week*, September 27, 2000, accessed October 1, 2014, http://www.alfiekohn.org/teaching/edweek/staiv.htm.
37. See: Chicagoland Researchers and Advocates for Transformative Education. *Research Brief 1: Testing Today in Context: History, Impact, and Alternatives* (Chicago: CReATE, 2012), 4, accessed January 10, 2014, http://www.createchicago.org/; Pasi Sahlberg, *Finnish Lessons: What Can the World Learn from Educational Change in Finland?* (New York, NY: Teachers College Press, 2011); Richard Thorndike, *Measurement and Evaluation in Psychology and Education* (8th ed.) (Upper Saddle River, NJ: Prentice Hall, 2011); Howard Wainer, *Uneducated Guesses: Using Evidence to Uncover Misguided education Policies* (Princeton, NJ: Princeton University Press, 2011); James Popham, *Classroom Assessment: What Teachers Need to Know* (Boston, MA: Pearson. 2011); James Popham, "Instructional Insensitivity of Tests: Accountability's Dire Drawback," *Phi Delta Kappan* 89 (2007):146–155; James Popham, *The Truth About Testing: An Educator's Call to Action* (Alexandria, VA: ASCD, 2001); Linda Darling-Hammond, *The Flat World and Education: How America's Commitment to Equity will Determine our Future* (New York, NY: Teachers College Press, 2010); Alfie Kohn, *What Does it Mean to be Well Educated?* (Boston, MA: Beacon Press, 2004); Alfie Kohn, "Standardized Testing Separating Wheat Children from Chaff Children," AlfieKohn.Org, 2002, accessed May, 3, 2013, http://www.alfiekohn.org/article/standardized-testing; Peter Sacks, *Standardized Minds: The High Price of America's Testing Culture and What we can do to Change it* (Cambridge, MA: Perseus, 1999); and others.
38. Chicagoland Researchers and Advocates for Transformative Education. *Research Brief 1: Testing Today in Context: History, Impact, and Alternatives* (Chicago: CReATE, 2012), 4, accessed January 10, 2014, http://www.createchicago.org/.
39. James Popham, *Classroom Assessment: What Teachers Need to Know* (Boston, MA: Pearson, 2011), 83.

40. Alfie Kohn, "Fighting the Tests: A practical guide to Rescuing our Schools," *Phi Delta Kappan* 82, no. 5 (2001): 349–357.
41. See: James Popham, *Classroom Assessment: What Teachers Need to Know* (Boston, MA: Pearson, 2011); James Popham, *The Truth about Testing: An Educator's Call to Action* (Alexandria, VA: ASCD, 2001); Richard Murnane and John P. Papay, "Teachers' Views on No Child Left Behind: Support for the Principles, Concerns about the Practices," *Journal of Economic Perspectives* 24, no. 3 (2010): 151–66; Wayne Au, *Unequal by Design: High-Stakes Testing and the Standardization of Inequality* (New York: Routledge, 2007); Linda Darling-Hammond, "Race, Inequality and Educational Accountability: The Irony of 'No Child Left Behind,'" *Race Ethnicity and Education* 10 (2007): 245–260; David Hursh, "Exacerbating Inequality: The Failed Promise of the No Child Left Behind Act. *Race Ethnicity and Education* 10, no. 3 (2007): 295–308; Kate Menken, "Teaching to the Test: How No Child Left Behind Impacts Language Policy, Curriculum, and Instruction for English Language Learners," *Bilingual Research Journal* 30, no. 2 (2006): 521–546; Rod Paige, "No Child Left Behind: The Ongoing Movement for Public Education Reform. *Harvard Educational Review* 76, no. 4 (2006): 461–473; John Rogers, "Forces of Accountability? The Power of Poor Parents in No Child Left Behind," *Harvard Educational Review* 76 (2006): 611–641; Jennifer Booher-Jennings, "Below the Bubble: 'Educational Triage' and the Texas Accountability System," *American Educational Research Journal* 42 (2005): 231–268; Frances Contreras, "Access, Achievement, and Social Capital: Standardized Exams and the Latino College-Bound Population" *Journal of Hispanic Higher Education* 4 (2005): 197–214; Jo Boaler, "When Learning no Longer Matters—Standardized Testing and the Creation of Inequality," *Phi Delta Kappan* 84 (2003): 502–506; Mary Barksdale-Ladd, and Karen Thomas, "What's at Stake in High-Stakes Testing: Teachers and Parents Speak Out," *Journal of Teacher Education* 51 (2000): 384–397; and others.
42. Provasnik, Stephen et al., "Highlights From TIMSS 2011: Mathematics and Science Achievement of U.S. Fourth- and Eighth-Grade Students in an International Context," National Center for Education Statistics, 2012, accessed May 2, 2014, www.nces.ed.gov/TIMSS.
43. National Center for Education Statistics (2012), *The Nation's Report Card: Trends in Academic Progress 2012*, accessed October 21, 2014, http://nces.ed.gov/pubsearch/pubsinfo.asp.
44. National Center for Education Statistics (2012), *The Nation's Report Card: Trends in Academic Progress 2012*, accessed October 21, 2014, http://nces.ed.gov/pubsearch/pubsinfo.asp.
45. Meredith Broussard," Why Poor Schools Can't Win at Standardized Testing" *The Atlantic,* July 15, 2014, accessed September 30, 2014, http://www.theatlantic.com/features/archive/2014/07/why-poor-schools-cant-win-at-standardized-testing/374287/.

46. Doug Hart, "The 18th OISE Survey of Educational Issues: Public Attitudes Toward Education in Ontario 2012" (Toronto: The Ontario Institute for Studies in Education of the University of Toronto, 2012), 8.
47. Pasi Sahlberg, "Global Educational Reform Movement is Here!" (PasiSahlberg.com, N.D.), accessed September 6, 2014, http://pasisahlberg.com/global-educational-reform-movement-is-here/.
48. Pasi Sahlberg, "What Canada can Learn from Finland" (2014 R.W. Jackson Lecture, Toronto, Ontario, April 17, 2014). Webcast available at https://webcasts.welcome2theshow.com/OISE/2230.
49. Pasi Sahlberg, "What Canada can Learn from Finland" (2014 R.W. Jackson Lecture, Toronto, Ontario, April 17, 2014). Webcast available at https://webcasts.welcome2theshow.com/OISE/2230.
50. Organization for Economic Cooperation and Development, *PISA 2012 Results: Excellence through Equity Giving Every Student the Chance to Succeed, Volume II*. PISA, OECD Publishing, 57–60, accessed August 10, 2014, http://www.oecd.org/pisa/keyfindings/pisa-2012-results-volume-II.pdf. Richard Wilkinson and Kate Pickett. *The Spirit Level: Why More Equal Societies Almost Always Do Better* (London: Allen Lane, 2009).
51. Richard Wilkinson and Kate Pickett, *The Spirit Level: Why Equality is Better for Everyone* (London: Penguin, 2010).
52. Pasi Sahlberg, "What Canada can Learn from Finland" (2014 R.W. Jackson Lecture, Toronto, Ontario, April 17, 2014). Webcast available at https://webcasts.welcome2theshow.com/OISE/2230.
53. Andy Hargreaves and Dennis Shirley, *The Fourth Way: The Inspiring Future for Educational Change* (Thousand Oaks, CA: Corwin Press, 2009), 62.
54. Marshall McLuhan, *Understanding Media: The Extensions of Man* (Boston: MIT Press, 2013), xxi.

2 The History, Logic, and Push for Standardized Testing

1. Karl Marx, *The 18th Brumaire of Louis Bonaparte* (New York: Wildside Press, 2008), 15.
2. Stephen Harper. 39th PARLIAMENT, 2nd SESSION. *House of Commons Debates*. Volume 142, Number 110. June 11, 2008.
3. Osman Özturgut, "Standardized Testing in the Case of China and the Lessons to be Learned for the U.S.," *Journal of International Education Research* 7, no. 2 (2011).
4. Osman Özturgut, "Standardized Testing in the Case of China and the Lessons to be Learned for the U.S.," *Journal of International Education Research* 7, no. 2 (2011). And, Ann Paludan, *Chronicle of the Chinese Emperors: The Reign-by-Reign Record of the Rulers of Imperial China* (New York, New York: Thames and Hudson, 1998).

5. Robert Siegler, "The Other Alfred Binet," *Developmental Psychology* 28, no. 2 (1992).
6. Alfred Binet, "New Methods for the Diagnosis of the Intellectual Level of Subnormals," *L'Année Psychologique* 12 (1905): 192.
7. United States Congress, *Testing in American Schools: Asking the Right Questions* (Washington, DC: Congress of the U.S., Office of Technology Assessment, 1992).
8. United States Congress, *Historical Statistics of the United States* (Washington, DC: Department of Commerce, Bureau of the Census, 1975), 105–111, accessed December 12, 2014, http://www2.census.gov/prod2/statcomp/documents/HistoricalStatisticsoftheUnitedStates1789-1945.pdf.
9. United States Congress, *Historical Statistics of the United States* (Washington, DC: Department of Commerce, Bureau of the Census, 1975), 104, accessed December 12, 2014, http://www2.census.gov/prod2/statcomp/documents/HistoricalStatisticsoftheUnitedStates1789-1945.pdf.
10. Carl Kaestle, "Testing Policy in the United States: A Historical Perspective," Gordon Commission on the Future of Assessment in Education (2012), accessed September 2, 2014, www.gordoncommission.org/publicagtions_reports/assessment_education.html.
11. Carl Kaestle, "Testing Policy in the United States: A Historical Perspective," Gordon Commission on the Future of Assessment in Education (2012): 20, accessed September 2, 2014, www.gordoncommission.org/publicagtions_reports/assessment_education.html.
12. The Mental Measurements Yearbooks have been published by the Buros Institute since 1938.
13. Carl Kaestle, "Testing Policy in the United States: A Historical Perspective," Gordon Commission on the Future of Assessment in Education (2012): 22, accessed September 2, 2014, www.gordoncommission.org/publicagtions_reports/assessment_education.html.
14. Carl Kaestle, "Testing Policy in the United States: A Historical Perspective," Gordon Commission on the Future of Assessment in Education (2012): 40, accessed September 2, 2014, www.gordoncommission.org/publicagtions_reports/assessment_education.html.
15. Sandro Contenta, *Rituals of Failure: What Schools Really Teach* (Toronto: Between The Lines, 1993).
16. Don Klinger et al., "The Evolving Culture of Large-Scale Assessments in Canadian Education," *Canadian Journal of Educational Administration and Policy* 76 (2008): 1–34.
17. Ontario, Royal Commission on Learning, *For the Love of Learning: Report of the Royal Commission on Learning* 4 vols, Toronto: Queen's Printer for Ontario, 1994: 235–245.
18. Council of Ministers of Education, Canada, "Assessment," Council of Ministers of Education, Canada, accessed January 2, 2015, www.cmec.ca/131/Programs-and-Initiatives/Assessment/Overview/index.html.

19. See Don Klinger et al., "The Evolving Culture of Large-Scale Assessments in Canadian Education," *Canadian Journal of Educational Administration and Policy* 76 (2008): 1–34. And, William J. Reese, *Testing Wars in the Public Schools: A Forgotten History* (Cambridge, MA: Harvard UP, 2013).
20. William J. Reese, *Testing Wars in the Public Schools: A Forgotten History* (Cambridge, MA: Harvard UP, 2013), 4.
21. United States, *Historical Statistics of the United States* (Washington, DC: Department of Commerce, Bureau of the Census, 1975), 4, accessed December 12, 2014, http://www2.census.gov/prod2/statcomp/documents/HistoricalStatisticsoftheUnitedStates1789-1945.pdf.
22. Quoted in William J. Reese, *Testing Wars in the Public Schools: A Forgotten History* (Cambridge, MA: Harvard UP, 2013), 4.
23. Carl Kaestle, "Testing Policy in the United States: A Historical Perspective," Gordon Commission on the Future of Assessment in Education (2012): 5, accessed September 2, 2014, www.gordoncommission.org/publicagtions_reports/assessment_education.html.
24. Ken Robinson, "How Schools Kill Creativity," filmed February 2006, TED video, 19:24, posted February 2006, http://www.ted.com/talks/ken_robinson_says_schools_kill_creativity?language=en.
25. United States Congress, *Testing in American Schools: Asking the Right Questions* (Washington, DC: Congress of the U.S., Office of Technology Assessment, 1992), 104.
26. Wayne Au, *Unequal by Design: High-Stakes Testing and the Standardization of Inequality* (New York: Routledge, 2007).
27. Carl Kaestle, "Testing Policy in the United States: A Historical Perspective," Gordon Commission on the Future of Assessment in Education (2012), accessed September 2, 2014, www.gordoncommission.org/publicagtions_reports/assessment_education.html. And, United States, *Testing in American Schools: Asking the Right Questions* (Washington, DC: Congress of the U.S., Office of Technology Assessment, 1992), 103–4.
28. Linda Darling Hammond and Beverly Falk, "Supporting Teacher Learning Through Performance Assessments," in *Beyond the Bubble Test: How Performance Assessment Supports 21st Century Learning*, edited by Linda Darling-Hammond and Frank Adamson, 207–235. (San Francisco: Jossey-Bass, 2014), 207.
29. See: Linda Darling-Hammond, *The Flat World and Education: How America's Commitment to Equity will Determine our Future* (New York, NY: Teachers College Press, 2010); Linda Darling-Hammond, "Race, Inequality and Educational Accountability: The Irony of 'No Child Left Behind,'" *Race Ethnicity and Education* 10 (2007): 245–260; John Rogers, "Forces of Accountability? The Power of Poor Parents in No Child Left Behind," *Harvard Educational Review* 76 (2006): 611–641; Kate Menken, "Teaching to the Test: How No Child Left Behind Impacts Language Policy, Curriculum, and Instruction for English Language Learners," *Bilingual Research Journal* 30, no. 2 (2006): 521–546; Frances Contreras, "Access, Achievement, and Social Capital: Standardized Exams and the Latino College-Bound Population"

Journal of Hispanic Higher Education 4 (2005): 197–214; George Wood, "A View from the field: NCLB's Effects on Classrooms and Schools," in *Many Children Left Behind: How the No Child Left Behind Act Is Damaging our Children and our Schools*, edited by Deborah Meier, 33–52 (Boston, MA: Beacon Press, 2004); James Popham, *The Truth about Testing: An Educator's Call to Action* (Alexandria, VA: ASCD, 2001); and Larry Hedges and Amy Nowell, "Black-White test score convergence since 1965" In *The Black-White Test Score Gap*, ed. Christopher Jencks, Meredith Phillips, 149–181 (Washington, DC: Brookings Institution, 1998).

30. See Darling-Hammond, Linda, and Frank Adamson, *Beyond the Bubble Test: How Performance Assessments Support 21st Century Learning* (San Francisco: Jossey-Bass, 2014). And, Linda Darling-Hammond and Randi Weingarten, "It's Time for a New Accountability in American Education," *Huffington Post*, May 19, 2014, accessed January 3, 2015, http://www.huffingtonpost.com/linda-darlinghammond/its-time-for-a-new-accoun_b_5351475.html.

31. Carl Kaestle, "Testing Policy in the United States: A Historical Perspective," Gordon Commission on the Future of Assessment in Education (2012), accessed September 2, 2014, www.gordoncommission.org/publicagtions_reports/assessment_education.html. And, William J. Reese, *Testing Wars in the Public Schools: A Forgotten History* (Cambridge, MA: Harvard UP, 2013).

32. United States Congress, *Testing in American Schools: Asking the Right Questions* (Washington, DC: Congress of the U.S., Office of Technology Assessment, 1992), 110.

33. Wayne Au, *Unequal by Design: High-Stakes Testing and the Standardization of Inequality* (New York: Routledge, 2007), 36.

34. Alfred Binet, "New Methods for the Diagnosis of the Intellectual Level of Subnormals," *L'Année Psychologique* 12 (1905): 191.

35. Jay MacLeod, *Ain't no makin' it: Aspirations and Attainment in a Low-Income Neighborhood* (Boulder, CO: Westview Press, 2008), 11–24.

36. Margaret Dagenais. "An Effective and Critical History of Canada's National Standardized Testing Program" (PhD diss., University of Regina, 2011).

37. "US Chamber of Commerce Foundation," United States Chamber of Commerce, accessed January 13, 2015, http://www.uschamberfoundation.org/.

38. Alan Singer, "Protest Builds against Pearson, Testing, and Common Core," *Huffington Post*, June 13, 2012, accessed January 13, 2015, http://www.huffingtonpost.com/alan-singer/protest-builds-against-pe_b_1586573.html.

39. John Oliver, "Standardized Testing," Last Week with John Oliver, May 2, 2015, HBO, accessed May 4, 2015, https://www.youtube.com/watch?v=J6lyURyVz7k.

40. Pearson Education,"Pearson Joins President and Mrs. Obama, Education Secretary Duncan for White House Higher Education Summit January 16, 2014," Pearson, accessed January 19, 2015, www.pearsoned.com/pearson-joins-president-and-mrs-obama-education-secretary-duncan-for-white-house-higher-education-summit/#.UtoWTLQo4dU.

41. Influence Explorer, "Pearson Education," Influence Explorer, accessed January 30, 2015, http://influenceexplorer.com/organization/pearson-education/2ec6 7ad263c448739699876db162f88f.
42. Valerie Strauss, "Eighth grader: What Bothered Me Most about New Common Core Test," *Washington Post*, May 8, 2013, accessed January 25, 2015, http:// www.washingtonpost.com/blogs/answer-sheet/wp/2013/05/08/eighth-grader -what-bothered-me-most-about-new-common-core-test/.
43. Lindsay Layton, "How Bill Gates pulled off the Swift Common Core Revolution," *Washington Post*, June 7, 2014, accessed January 19, 2015, www .washingtonpost.com/politics/how-bill-gates-pulled-off-the-swift-common-core -revolution/2014/06/07/a830e32e-ec34-11e3-9f5c-9075d5508f0a_story.html.
44. Jonas Persson, "New Documents Show How Taxpayer Money Is Wasted by Charter Schools —Stringent Controls Urgently Needed as Charter Funding Faces Huge Increase A CMD Reporters' Guide" (Center for Media and Democracy, May 8, 2015) accessed May 9, 2015, http://www.prwatch.org /files/5-8-15_final_cmd_reporters_guide_on_charter_waste_and_lack_of _accountability.pdf.
45. Center for Popular Democracy and Integrity in Education, "Charter School Vulnerabilities for Waste, Fraud, and Abuse" (Center for Popular Democracy, May, 2014), accessed May 2, 2015, http://populardemocracy.org/sites/default /files/FraudandMismgmt5-3-14%28FINALx3.0%29REV.pdf.
46. Diane Ravitch, "What the Best and Wisest Parent Wants for his Child," *Diane Ravitch's Blog*, February 22, 2013, accessed January 21, 2015, dianeravitch. net/2013/02/22/what-the-best-and-wisest-parent-wants-for-his-child-2/.
47. Paulo Freire, *Pedagogy of the Oppressed* (New York: Continuum, 1997), 1–67.
48. Linda Darling-Hammond, "Reaching Out: International Benchmarks for Performance Assessment," in *Beyond the Bubble Test: How Performance Assessment Supports 21st Century Learning*, edited by Linda Darling-Hammond and Frank Adamson, 93–129 (San Francisco: Jossey-Bass, 2014), 93.

3   Testing at the Tipping Point: HSST as a Governing Education Principle In and Out of the Classroom

1. See: Maria Veronica Santelices and Mark Wilson, "Unfair Treatment? The Case of Freedle, the SAT, and the Standardization Approach to Differential Item Functioning," *Harvard Educational* Review 1 no. 7 (2010); Abigail Thernstrom and Stephan Thernstrom, *No Excuses: Closing the Racial Gap in Learning* (New York: Simon and Schuster, 2004); Rebecca Zwick, *Rethinking the SAT: The Future of Standardized Testing in University Admissions* (New York: Routledge Falmer, 2004), 203–204; and Richard Herrnstein and Charles Murray, *The Bell Curve: Intelligence and Class Structure in American Life* (New York: Free Press, 1994), 281–282.
2. Arnold Dodge and Ruth Powers Silverberg, "Dominant Discourse, Educational Research, and the Hegemony of Test Scores," *Critical Education*

6, no. 1 (2015): 1, accessed February 21, 2015, http://ojs.library.ubc.ca/index.php/criticaled/article/view/184561.
3. Arnold Dodge and Ruth Powers Silverberg, "Dominant Discourse, Educational Research, and the Hegemony of Test Scores," *Critical Education* 6, no. 1 (2015): 2, accessed February 21, 2015, http://ojs.library.ubc.ca/index.php/criticaled/article/view/184561.
4. Arnold Dodge and Ruth Powers Silverberg, "Dominant Discourse, Educational Research, and the Hegemony of Test Scores," *Critical Education* 6, no. 1 (2015): 7–8, accessed February 21, 2015, http://ojs.library.ubc.ca/index.php/criticaled/article/view/184561.
5. Arnold Dodge and Ruth Powers Silverberg, "Dominant Discourse, Educational Research, and the Hegemony of Test Scores," *Critical Education* 6, no. 1 (2015): 9, accessed February 21, 2015, http://ojs.library.ubc.ca/index.php/criticaled/article/view/184561.
6. Arnold Dodge and Ruth Powers Silverberg, "Dominant Discourse, Educational Research, and the Hegemony of Test Scores," *Critical Education* 6, no. 1 (2015): 11, accessed February 21, 2015, http://ojs.library.ubc.ca/index.php/criticaled/article/view/184561.
7. Arnold Dodge and Ruth Powers Silverberg, "Dominant Discourse, Educational Research, and the Hegemony of Test Scores," *Critical Education* 6, no. 1 (2015): 11, accessed February 21, 2015, http://ojs.library.ubc.ca/index.php/criticaled/article/view/184561.
8. Janet Ecker, "Statement from Education Minister Janet Ecker About the Grade 10 Literacy Test," *News By Ministry, Ministry of Education*, October 15, 2001, accessed February 13, 2015, http://newsarchive.ontario.ca/getorg_ef167.html?okey=68451&lang=eng&y=2001&m=10&d=18.
9. Generally, a learning accommodation refers to supports that help a learner reach the same curriculum and/or learning goals as her peers, while a modification indicates a change to the overall learning and/or curriculum goals.
10. See: Vicki E. Alger, "Teacher Incentive Pay that Works: A Global Survey of Programs Improving Student Achievement," Fraser Institute, accessed February 15, 2015, http://www.fraserinstitute.org/uploadedFiles/fraser-ca/Content/research-news/research/publications/teacher-incentive-pay-that-works.pdf.
11. Audrey Amrein and David Berliner, "High-Stakes Testing, Uncertainty, and Student Learning," *Education Policy Analysis Archives* 10 no. 18 (2002): 1–74, accessed February 1, 2014, http://epaa.asu.edu/epaa/v10n18/.
12. James Popham, The Truth About Testing: An Educator's Call to Action (Alexandria, VA: ASCD, 2001).
13. Michael Fullan and Andy Hargreaves, *Professional Capital: Transforming Teaching in Every School* (New York, Teachers College Press, 2012).
14. Richard D. Kahlenberg and Halley Potter, "What Charter Schools Can Teach Us About Teacher Voice," *Teachers College Record* March 09, 2015, accessed March 16, 2015, http://www.tcrecord.org/Content.asp?ContentID=17890.

15. Valerie Strauss, "Netflix's Reed Hastings Has a Big Idea: Kill Elected School Boards Update)," *Washington Post*, March 14, 2014, accessed June 12, 2014, http://www.washingtonpost.com/blogs/answer-sheet/wp/2014/03/14/netflixs-reed-hastings-has-a-big-idea-kill-elected-school-boards/.
16. Dexter Mullins, "New Orleans to be Home to Nation's First All-Charter School District," *Aljazeera America*, April 4, 2014, accessed June 7, 2014, http://america.aljazeera.com/articles/2014/4/4/new-orleans-charterschoolseducationreformracesegregation.html.
17. United Stated Department of Education, "Laws & Guidance Elementary & Secondary Education," accessed November 21, 2014, http://www2.ed.gov/programs/titleiparta/index.html.
18. United Stated Department of Education, "Laws & Guidance Elementary & Secondary Education," accessed November 21, 2014, http://www2.ed.gov/programs/titleiparta/index.html.
19. Valerie Strauss, "The New School Reform Model: 'Dumping the Losers,' *Washington Post*, April 11, 2014, accessed May 12, 2014, http://www.washingtonpost.com/blogs/answer-sheet/wp/2014/04/11/the-new-school-reform-model-dumping-the-losers/.
20. Jesse H. Rhodes, "Learning Citizenship? How State Education Reforms Affect Parents' Political Attitudes and Behavior," *Political Behavior,* March (2014).
21. Arne Duncan, "Secretary Arne Duncan's Remarks at OECD's Release of the Program for International Student Assessment (PISA) 2009 Results," *United States Department of Education*, December 7, 2010, accessed February 7, 2014, http://www.ed.gov/news/speeches/secretary-arne-duncans-remarks-oecds-release-program-international-student-assessment-pisa-2009-results.
22. Arne Duncan, "Secretary Arne Duncan's Remarks at OECD's Release of the Program for International Student Assessment (PISA) 2009 Results," *United States Department of Education*, December 7, 2010, accessed February 7, 2014, http://www.ed.gov/news/speeches/secretary-arne-duncans-remarks-oecds-release-program-international-student-assessment-pisa-2009-results.
23. Caroline Alphonso, "Canada's Fall in Math-Education Ranking Sets off Alarm Bells," *Globe & Mail,* December 3, 2014, accessed September 3, 2014, http://www.theglobeandmail.com/news/national/education/canadas-fall-in-math-education-ranking-sets-off-red-flags/article15730663/.
24. Linda Darling-Hammond, "Reaching Out: International Benchmarks for Performance Assessment," in *Beyond the Bubble Test: How Performance Assessment Supports 21st Century Learning*, edited by Linda Darling-Hammond and Frank Adamson, 93–129. (San Francisco: Jossey-Bass, 2014), 94.
25. Nina Bascia, "Teacher Unions and Teacher Quality. In *Routledge International Handbook of Teacher Quality and Policy,* edited by Gerald Motoba and Sakiko Ikomo, n.p. (New York: Routledge, in press).
26. Kristin Rushowy, "Math: Number One Problem for Ontario School Boards," *Toronto Star,* August 27, 2014, accessed January 3, 2015, http://www.thestar.com/yourtoronto/education/2014/08/27/math_number_one_problem_for_ontario_school_boards.html.

4 Revising the Pedagogical Form: Test-Oriented Teaching and Learning

1. Pseudonyms have been used for all participants and all schools.
2. Marguerite Jackson, "In the Know with EQAO: A Practical Recipe for Math Success Students do Better on the EQAO Grade 9 Assessment of Mathematics When They Know the Test will Affect their Final Course Mark," *www.eqao.com*, May 2012, accessed January 12, 2015, http://www.eqao.com/pdf_e/12/EQAO_Intheknow_RecipeMathSuccess.pdf.
3. Center for Education Policy, "Choices, Changes, and Challenges Curriculum and Instruction in the NCLB Era," December, 2007: abstract, accessed March 3, 2015, http://www.cep-dc.org/displayDocument.cfm?DocumentID=312.
4. David Wilson, "Developmentally Appropriate Practice in the Age of Testing: New Reports Outline Key Principles for PreK–3rd Grade," *Harvard Education Letter* 25, no. 3 (2009).
5. Brian Stecher, "Looking Back: Performance Assessments in an Era of Standards-Based Educational Accountability," in *Beyond the Bubble Test: How Performance Assessment Supports 21st Century Learning*, edited by Linda Darling-Hammond and Frank Adamson, 17–52 (San Francisco: Jossey-Bass, 2014), 27.
6. See George Wood, Linda Darling-Hammond, Monty Neill, and Pat Roschewski, "Refocusing Accountability: Using Local Performance Assessments to Enhance Teaching and Learning for Higher Order Skills." Briefing Paper Prepared for Members of The Congress of The United States, accessed January 5, 2015, http://www.fairtest.org/sites/default/files/PerformanceAssessments.pdf; Laurie Shepard, "The Hazards of High Stakes Testing," *Issues in Science and Technology* 19, no. 2 (2002); and National Research Council, *Education for Life and Work: Developing Transferable Knowledge and Skills in the 21st Century* (Washington, DC: The National Academies Press, 2012).
7. Brian Stecher, "Looking Back: Performance Assessments in an Era of Standards-Based Educational Accountability," in *Beyond the Bubble Test: How Performance Assessment Supports 21st Century Learning*, edited by Linda Darling-Hammond and Frank Adamson, 17–52 (San Francisco: Jossey-Bass, 2014) 40–41.
8. Linda Darling-Hammond, and Frank Adamson, *Beyond the Bubble Test: How Performance Assessments Support 21st Century Learning* (San Francisco: Jossey-Bass, 2014), 6.
9. PLCs, refer to professional learning communities, an approach used in many schools whereby teachers are intentionally grouped, usually during school time, to learn and collaborate with regard to a specific approach, initiative, or curriculum item; often with an overall focus on student learning.
10. Despite the hurdles to inclusive and differentiated practice posed by standardization, student-centered teaching and learning enjoy widespread support among many educators, scholars, researchers, and education leaders. However, important work by the late Jeanne S. Chall (specifically her book

The Academic Achievement Challenge: What Really Works in the Classroom) argues content-centered pedagogy results in greater student achievement than student-centered pedagogy. While these are important concerns, they are ultimately beyond the scope of this work. There is no evidence that Chall's vision of content-centered teaching is akin to test-oriented teaching and learning. This is to say, there may be as much tension between standardization and Chall's content-centered pedagogy as there is with standardization and the student-centered approaches described here.

11. See Carol Ann Tomlinson, "Mapping a Route Toward a Differentiated Instruction," *Educational Leadership* 57 no. 1 (1999). And Carol Ann Tomlinson, *The Differentiated Classroom: Responding to the Needs of All Learners* (New Jersey: Pearson Education, 1999).
12. Kun Yuan and Vi-Nhuan Le, "Estimating the Percentages of Students who were Tested on Cognitively Demanding Items Through the State Achievement Tests," Santa Monica, CA: Rand Corporation, November 2012, accessed January 3, 2014, http://www.rand.org/content/dam/rand/pubs/working_papers/2012/RAND_WR967.pdf.
13. Brian Stecher, "Looking Back: Performance Assessments in an Era of Standards-Based Educational Accountability," in *Beyond the Bubble Test: How Performance Assessment Supports 21st Century Learning*, edited by Linda Darling-Hammond and Frank Adamson, 17–52 (San Francisco: Jossey-Bass, 2014), 19.
14. Open Court was a reading program used in all Los Angeles schools.
15. Topanga Canyon is wealthy community in the northwest of Los Angeles.

5 Not What I Signed up for: The Changing Meaning of Being a Teacher

1. American psychologist Abraham Maslow theorized a dependent hierarchy of human needs as follows: Physiological needs including food, water, and shelter; safety and security needs; social acceptance needs; esteem needs including confidence in self and work; and self-actualization needs, including knowing what one's purpose is and how to fulfill it.
2. National Association of Secondary School Principals, "Value-Added Measures in Teacher Evaluation," 2015, accessed April 13, 2015, http://www.nassp.org/Content.aspx?topic=Value_Added_Measures_in_Teacher_Evaluation.
3. For an example of The Institute's work on this, see: Vicki Alger, "Teacher Incentive Pay that Works: A Global Survey of Programs that Improve Student Achievement," September, 2014, Barbara Mitchell Centre for Improvement in Education, Frasier Institute, accessed January 3, 2015, https://www.fraserinstitute.org/uploadedFiles/fraser-ca/Content/research-news/research/publications/teacher-incentive-pay-that-works.pdf.
4. See: Morgan S. Polikoff and Andrew C. Porter, "Instructional Alignment as a Measure of Teaching Quality," *Educational Evaluation and Policy Analysis* 20,

no. 10 (2013); Marcus Winters and Joshua Cowen, "Who Would Stay, Who Would be Dismissed? An Empirical Consideration of Value-Added Teacher Retention Policies," *Educational Researcher* 42 (2013); John Papay, "Different Tests, Different Answers: The Stability of Teacher Value-Added Estimates across Outcome Measures," *American Educational Research Journal* 48 (2012); and James Popham, "Instructional Insensitivity of Tests: Accountability's Dire Drawback," *Phi Delta Kappan* 89 (2007).
5. Alfie Kohn, "Standardized Testing Separating Wheat Children from Chaff Children," alfiekohn.org, 2002, accessed May, 3, 2013, http://www.alfiekohn.org/article/standardized-testing.
6. Alfie Kohn, "Standardized Testing Separating Wheat Children from Chaff Children," alfiekohn.org, 2002, accessed May 3, 2013, http://www.alfiekohn.org/article/standardized-testing.
7. See: Richard J. Murnane and John P. Papay, "Teachers' Views on No Child Left Behind: Support for the Principles, Concerns about the Practices," *Journal of Economic Perspectives* 24, no. 3 (2010). And, Lisa Abrams, *Teachers' Views on High-Stakes Testing: Implications for the Classroom, Policy Brief* (Education Policy Studies Laboratory, Arizona State University College of Education, 2004).
8. James Popham, *The Truth about Testing: An Educator's Call to Action* (Alexandria, VA: ASCD, 2001).
9. Ian Lovett, "Teacher's Death Exposes Tensions in Los Angeles," *New York Times*, November 9, 2010, accessed June 3, 2014, http://www.nytimes.com/2010/11/10/education/10teacher.html?_r=0.
10. Alexandra Zavis and Tony Barboza, "Teacher's Suicide Shocks School," *Los Angeles Times*, September 28, 2010, accessed March 1, 2015, http://articles.latimes.com/2010/sep/28/local/la-me-south-gate-teacher-20100928.
11. Doris Santoro, "Good Teaching in Difficult Times: Demoralization in the Pursuit of Good Work," *American Journal of Education* 118, no. 1 (2011): 3.
12. Sandra Acker, *The Realities of Teacher's Work: Never a Dull Moment* (New York: Cassell, 1999).
13. Doris Santoro, "Good Teaching in Difficult Times: Demoralization in the Pursuit of Good Work," *American Journal of Education* 118, no. 1 (2011): 3.
14. The Toronto Distract School Board's Model Schools Program provides a range of special supports (from eyeglasses, to extra instruction, to extra training for students and teachers) in the 150 schools ranked as having the lowest levels of learning opportunity of the Board's 600 plus schools.
15. See: Susan Embertson, *Test Design: Developments in Psychology and Psychometrics* (New York: Academic Press, 1985); Robert Glaser, Alan Lesgold and Susanne Lajoie, *"Toward a Cognitive Theory for the Measurement of Achievement,"* in *The Influence of Cognitive Psychology on Testing*, ed. Royce R. Ronning, John A. Glover, Jane C. Conoley, and Joseph C. Witt, 41–85. (Hillsdale, NJ: Lawrence Erlbaum Associates, 1987); and, National Research Council, "Knowing What Students Know: The Science and Design of Educational Assessment" (Washington, DC: National Academies Press, 2001).

16. David Wilson, "Developmentally Appropriate Practice in the Age of Testing: New Reports Outline Key Principles for PreK–3rd Grade," *Harvard Education Letter* 25, no. 3 (2009): 1–3, accessed March 2, 2015, http://hepg.org/hel-home/issues/25_3/helarticle/developmentally-appropriate-practice-in-the-age-of#home.
17. Sue Bredekamp and Lorrie Shepard, "How Best to Protect Children from Inappropriate School Expectations, Practices, and Policies," *Young Children* 44, no. 3 (1989): 22–23.
18. Suzanne Lane, "Performance Assessment: The State of the Art," in *Beyond the Bubble Test: How Performance Assessment Supports 21st Century Learning*, ed. Linda Darling-Hammond and Frank Adamson, 133–184. (San Francisco: Jossey-Bass, 2014) 137–138.
19. Constructivism has its critics (see: Paul Kirschner, John Sweller, and Richard Clark, "Why Minimal Guidance During Instruction Does Not Work: An Analysis of the Failure of Constructivist, Discovery, Problem-Based, Experiential, and Inquiry-Based teaching," *Educational Psychologist* 41 no. 2 (2006): 75–86; and Charlotte Hua Liu and Robert Matthews, "Vygotsky's Philosophy: Constructivism and its Criticisms," *Examined International Education Journal*" 6, no. 3 (2005): 386–399). However, the testing-oriented teaching and learning outlined in Chapters 3, 4, and 5 by no means provides a solution to the problems raised by those opposed to constructivist pedagogy.
20. See: Lev Vygotsky, *Mind in society: The Development of Higher Mental Processes* (Cambridge, MA: Harvard University Press 1978); John Dewey, *The Quest for Certainty: A Study of the Relation of Knowledge and Action* (New York: Putnam, 1960/1929); and Jean Piaget, *The Psychology of Intelligence* (New York: Routledge, 1950).
21. Kelly Maxwell, Sharon Ritchie, Sue Bredekamp, and Tracy Zimmerman, *Issues in PreK–3rd Education: Using Developmental Science to Transform Children's Early School Experiences (#4)* (Chapel Hill: University of North Carolina, FPG Child Development Institute, First School, 2009): 2–4, accessed September 11, 2014, http://files.eric.ed.gov/fulltext/ED507444.pdf.

6 A Lack of Accountability: Teacher Perspectives on Equity, Accuracy, and Standardized Testing

1. On the United States, see, for example: Arlo Kempf and Ruth Powers Silverberg, "Academic Disobedience: Engaging Michael Apple's Nine Tasks of the Critical Scholar in an Age of Standardization," in *School against Neoliberal Rule: Educational Fronts for Local and Global Justice: A Reader,* ed. Mark Abendroth and Brad Porfilio, 187–206 (Charlotte, NC: Information Age Publishing, 2015); James Popham, *Classroom Assessment: What Teachers Need to Know* (Boston, MA: Pearson, 2011); James Popham, *The Truth about Testing: An Educator's Call to Action* (Alexandria, VA: ASCD, 2001); Richard Murnane and John P. Papay, "Teachers' Views on No Child Left Behind: Support for

the Principles, Concerns about the Practices," *Journal of Economic Perspectives* 24, no. 3 (2010): 151–166; Wayne Au, *Unequal by Design: High-Stakes Testing and the Standardization of Inequality* (New York: Routledge, 2007); Linda Darling-Hammond, "Race, Inequality and Educational Accountability: The Irony of 'No Child Left Behind,'" *Race Ethnicity and Education* 10 (2007): 245–260; David Hursh, "Exacerbating Inequality: The Failed Promise of the No Child Left Behind Act. *Race Ethnicity and Education* 10, no. 3 (2007): 295–308; Kate Menken, "Teaching to the Test: How No Child Left Behind Impacts Language Policy, Curriculum, and Instruction for English Language Learners," *Bilingual Research Journal* 30, no. 2 (2006): 521–546; Paige (2006), John Rogers, "Forces of Accountability? The Power of Poor Parents in No Child Left Behind," *Harvard Educational Review* 76 (2006): 611–664; Jennifer Booher-Jennings, "Below the Bubble: 'Educational Triage' and the Texas Accountability System," *American Educational Research Journal* 42 (2005): 231–268; Frances Contreras, "Access, Achievement, and Social Capital: Standardized Exams and the Latino College-Bound Population," *Journal of Hispanic Higher Education* 4 (2005): 197–214; George Wood, "A View from the field: NCLB's Effects on Classrooms and Schools," in *Many Children Left Behind: How the No Child Left Behind Act Is Damaging our Children and our Schools*, ed. Deborah Meier, 33–52 (Boston: Beacon Press, 2004); Jo Boaler, "When Learning no Longer Matters – Standardized Testing and the Creation of Inequality," *Phi Delta Kappan* 84 (2003): 502–506; Zeus Leonardo, "The War on Schools: NCLB, Nation Creation and the Educational Construction of Whiteness," *Race Ethnicity and Education* 10 (2007): 261–278; and Mary Barksdale-Ladd, and Karen Thomas, "What's at Stake in High-Stakes Testing: Teachers and Parents Speak Out," *Journal of Teacher Education* 51 (2000): 384–397. On Canada, see, for example: Laura-Lee Kearns, "High-stakes Standardized Testing and Marginalized Youth: An Examination of the Impact on Those Who Fail," *Canadian Journal of Education* 34, no. 2 (2011): 112–130; Joel Westheimer, "No Child Left Thinking: Democracy at Risk in Canada's Schools," *Education Canada* 50, no. 2 (2010): 5–8; Laura-Lee Kearns, *Equity, Literacy Testing and Marginalized Youth: The Social Construction of 'Illiterate' Identities* (PhD diss., University of Toronto, Toronto, ON, Canada, 2008); Don Klinger and Rebecca Luce-Kapler, "Walking in their Shoes: Students' Perceptions of Large-Scale High-Stakes Testing," *Canadian Journal of Program Evaluation* 22, no. 3 (2008): 29–52; Frank Nezavdal, "The Standardized Testing Movement: Equitable or Excessive?," *McGill Journal of Education* 38, no. 1 (2003): 65–77; and Bernie Froese-Germain, "Standardized Testing: Undermining Equity in Education," Report prepared for the National Issues in Education Initiative (Ottawa: Canadian Teachers' Federation, 1999).

2. Brian Stecher, "Looking Back: Performance Assessments in an Era of Standards-Based Educational Accountability," in *Beyond the Bubble Test: How Performance Assessment Supports 21st Century Learning*, ed. Linda Darling-Hammond and Frank Adamson, 17–52 (San Francisco: Jossey-Bass, 2014), 39.

3. See also: Michael Kane, "Validation," in *Educational Measurement*, ed. L Robert Brennan, 17–64 (Westport: Praeger Publishers Wiley, 2006); Samuel Messick, "Validity," in *Educational Measurement*, ed. Robert Lynn, 53–91. (New York: American Council on Education, 1989); and Madhabi Chatterji, "Bad Tests or Bad Test Use? A Case of SAT Use to Examine Why We Need Stakeholder Conversations on Validity," *Teachers College Record*, 115 no. 9 (2013): 1–10.
4. Brian Stecher, "Looking Back: Performance Assessments in an Era of Standards-Based Educational Accountability," in *Beyond the Bubble Test: How Performance Assessment Supports 21st Century Learning*, ed. Linda Darling-Hammond and Frank Adamson, 17–52 (San Francisco: Jossey-Bass, 2014), 39.
5. Valerie Strauss, "The New School Reform Model: 'Dumping the Losers,'" *Washington Post*, April 11, 2014, accessed May 12, 2014, http://www.washingtonpost.com/blogs/answer-sheet/wp/2014/04/11/the-new-school-reform-model-dumping-the-losers/.
6. Reliability and validity are complex issues in testing and I provide here only a basic explanation to guide the presentation of these results. Two major concerns raised by researchers but which fall, for the most part beyond the scope of this study because they were not raised repeatedly by teachers, are concerns about the relationship between the content taught and the content tested, and the grading of the tests themselves. Such concerns may raise further questions about validity and reliability.
7. CAT4 refers to the Canadian Achievement Test, a diagnostic standardized test administered in some Ontario schools.
8. Nathaniel Von Der Embse, Justin Barterian, and Natasha Segool, "Test Anxiety Interventions for Children and Adolescents: A Systematic Review of Treatment Studies From 2000–2010," *Psychology in the Schools* 50 (2013): 57–71.
9. Astrid Gregor, "Examination Anxiety: Live with It, Control It or Make It Work for You? *School Psychology International* 26 (2005): 617–635.
10. David Putwain, "Deconstructing Test Anxiety," *Emotional & Behavioural Difficulties* 13 (2008): 141–155; Pedro Rosario et al., "Test Anxiety: Associations with Personal and Family Variables" *Psicothema* 20, no. 4 (2008): 563–570; Jolyn Sena, Patricia Lowe, and Steven Lee, "Significant Predictors of Test Anxiety Among Students with and without Learning Disabilities," *Journal of Learning Disabilities* 40 (2007): 360–376; and Moshe Zeidner, "Does Test Anxiety Bias Scholastic Aptitude Test Performance by Gender and Sociocultural Group?" *Journal of Personality Assessment* 55, no. 145 (1990).
11. Here LD refers to students with one or more learning disabilities, DL refers to students who have learning delays, and MID refers to students with mild intellectual disabilities.
12. Linda Darling-Hammond, "Is the Invisible Hand a Magic Wand? Privatization versus Public Investments in National Educational Systems," Remarks presented at the American Educational Research Association, Chicago, April 19, 2015.

13. Huffington Post, "Public School Funding Unequal: State and Local School Finance Systems Perpetuate Per-Student Spending Disparities," *Huffington Post*, September 9, 2012, accessed November 3, 2013, http://www.huffingtonpost.com/2012/09/20/state-and-local-school-fi_n_1898225.html.
14. Patty Winsa, "As Fundraising Gap Grows, Toronto's Wealthy Schools Leaving Poor Schools Behind," *Toronto Star*, April 11, 2015, accessed April12, 2015, http://www.thestar.com/yourtoronto/education/2015/04/11/as-fundraising-gap-grows-torontos-wealthy-schools-leaving-poor-schools-behind.html.
15. John Ibbitson and Gloria Galloway, "Ottawa Hinges Funds for Native Schools on Chiefs' Support for Education Act," *The Globe and Mail*, December 10, 2013, accessed June 3, 2014, http://www.theglobeandmail.com/news/politics/ottawa-hinges-funds-for-native-schools-on-chiefs-support-for-education-act/article15836201/.
16. See Kenneth Tyler et al., "Linking Home-School Dissonance to School Based Outcomes for African American High School Students," *Journal of Black Psychology* 36, no. 4 (2010): 410–425; Gwendolyn Webb-Johnson, "Are Schools Ready for Joshua? African American Culture among Students Identified as Having Behavioral/Emotional Disorders," *Qualitative Studies in Education* 15 (2002): 653–671; Gloria Ladson-Billings, "The Evolving Role of Critical Race Theory in Educational Scholarship," *Race Ethnicity and Education* 8, no. 1 (1995): 115–120; and Arlo Kempf, "Cuban Teacher Perspectives on Race and Racism: The Pedagogy of Home-School Relations," *Teachers College Record* 116 no. 6 (2014): 1–38.
17. Raymond Pacheone and Stuart Kahl, "Where Are We Now: Lessons Learned and Emerging Directions," in *Beyond the Bubble Test: How Performance Assessment Supports 21st Century Learning*, ed. Linda Darling-Hammond and Frank Adamson, 53–91 (San Francisco: Jossey-Bass, 2014) 53.
18. See: Jamal Abedi, "Adapting Performance Assessments for English Language Learners," in *Beyond the Bubble Test: How Performance Assessment Supports 21st Century Learning*, ed. Linda Darling-Hammond and Frank Adamson, 185–205 (San Francisco: Jossey-Bass, 2014); Guillermo Solano-Flores, "Who Is Given Tests in What Language by Whom, When, and Where? The Need for Probabilistic Views of Language in the Testing of English Language Learners," *Educational Researcher* 37, no. 4 (2008): 189–199; and Kate Menken, "Teaching to the Test: How No Child Left Behind Impacts Language Policy, Curriculum, and Instruction for English Language Learners," *Bilingual Research Journal* 30, no. 2 (2006): 521–546.
19. See: Paulo Freire and Donaldo Macedo, *Literacy: The Word and the World* (New York: Praeger, 1987).
20. CASI refers to Comprehension, Attitudes, Strategies, and Interests; a standardized test commonly administered in elementary Model Schools and other contexts.
21. MART refers to Methods and Resources Teacher. Among other things, MARTs are responsible for providing additional support for teachers in supporting students with exceptionalities around EQAO standardized testing.

22. Kate Menken, "Teaching to the Test: How No Child Left Behind Impacts Language Policy, Curriculum, and Instruction for English Language Learners," *Bilingual Research Journal* 30, no. 2 (2006): 521–546.
23. Diane Ravitch, "Must Watch: VAM Outrage in Florida," Diane Ravitch's Blog, March 29, 2015, accessed April 2, 2015, http://dianeravitch.net/2015/03/29/must-watch-vam-outrage-in-florida/.
24. Linda Darling-Hammond, "Is the Invisible Hand a Magic Wand? Privatization Versus Public Investments in National Educational Systems," Remarks presented at the American Educational Research Association, Chicago, April 19, 2015.
25. For example: Claude Goldenberg et al., "Cause or Effect? A Longitudinal Study of Immigrant Latino Parents' Aspirations and Expectations, and Their Children's School Performance," *American Educational Research Journal* 38 (2001): 547–582; Fred Ramirez, "Dismay and Disappointment: Parental Involvement of Latino Immigrant Parents," *Urban Review* 35, no. 2 (2003): 93–110; and Maria Estela Zarate, "Understanding Latino Parental Involvement in Education: Perceptions, Expectations, and Recommendations," *The Tomás Rivera Policy Institute* (Los Angeles: University of Southern California, 2007), accessed January 5, 2015, http://files.eric.ed.gov/fulltext/ED502065.pdf.
26. Quoted in Valerie Strauss, "How and Why Convicted Atlanta Teachers Cheated on Standardized Tests" (April 1, 2015), accessed April 2, 2015, http://www.washingtonpost.com/blogs/answer-sheet/wp/2015/04/01/how-and-why-convicted-atlanta-teachers-cheated-on-standardized-tests/.
27. CNN, "Cheating Scandal Hits Atlanta Schools: CNN's Suzanne Malveaux talks with Michael Bowers, Former Georgia Attorney General, About the Charges 35 teachers Face," CNN.com, April 2, 2015, accessed April 10, 2015, http://www.cnn.com/videos/bestoftv/2013/04/02/exp-nr-atlanta-schools-cheating-scandal.cnn/video/playlists/atlanta-school-cheating-scandal/.

7 Implications: Synthesis of Findings, Resistance, and Alternatives

1. Discussed in Chapter 3, parent trigger policies can allow for low-performing schools to be retooled with all staff replaced, to be closed and reopened after what amounts to an auctioning of the school, to be privatized outright, or to be closed entirely. In this highly political process, these changes can be "triggered" by a parent petition.
2. Parent Revolution, "About Us," n.d., accessed January 4, 2015, http://parentrevolution.org/who-we-are/.
3. Diane Ravitch, "The Big Money Behind Parent Revolution," *Diane Ravitch's Blog,* April 11, 2013, accessed June 2, 2014, http://dianeravitch.net/2013/04/11/the-big-money-behind-parent-revolution/.
4. Muskogee Phoenix, "McDonald's to Provide Free Breakfasts for Test Season," *Muskogee Phoenix,* April 12, 2015, accessed April 24, 2015, http://www.musko

geephoenix.com/news/mcdonald-s-to-provide-free-breakfasts-for-test-season/article_545c5b3c-8d42-5dbe-aabb-24b450e763a3.html. Frank Adamson, "Is the Invisible Hand a Magic Wand? Privatization Versus Public Investments in National Educational Systems," Remarks presented at the American Educational Research Association, Chicago, April 19, 2015.

5. Amanda Marcotte, "Education Reformer Praises Standardized Tests for Boosting Home Prices in Wealthy Suburbs," *Slate Magazine*, April 20, 2015, accessed April 21, 2015, http://www.slate.com/blogs/xx_factor/2015/04/20/one_standardized_testing_supporter_in_new_york_lets_it_slip_it_s_all_about.html.

6. Frank Adamson, "Is the Invisible Hand a Magic Wand? Privatization Versus Public Investments in National Educational Systems," Remarks presented at the American Educational Research Association, Chicago, April 19, 2015.

7. Valerie Strauss, "Pearson Criticized for Finding Test Essay Scorers on Craigslist," *Washington Post*, January 16, 2013, accessed March 5, 2015, http://www.washingtonpost.com/blogs/answer-sheet/wp/2013/01/16/pearson-criticized-for-finding-test-essay-scorers-on-craigslist/.

8. Nicky Wolf, "Pearson Admits to Monitoring Students' Social Media use During its Online Tests," *The Guardian*, March 18, 2015, accessed April 2, 2015, http://www.theguardian.com/education/2015/mar/18/pearson-monitoring-students-social-media-tests.

9. Linda Darling-Hammond, "Reaching Out: International Benchmarks for Performance Assessment," in *Beyond the Bubble Test: How Performance Assessment Supports 21st Century Learning*, edited by Linda Darling-Hammond and Frank Adamson, 93–129 (San Francisco: Jossey-Bass, 2014), 100.

10. See for example: Alan Stoskopf, "An Untold Story of Resistance: African-American Educators and I.Q. Testing in the 1920's and '30's" *Rethinking Schools* 14, no. 1 (1999), accessed February 2, 2015, http://www.rethinkingschools.org//cmshandler.asp?archive/14_01/iq141.shtml; Wayne Au, *Unequal by Design: High-Stakes Testing and the Standardization of Inequality* (New York: Routledge, 2007); Dana Goldstein, *The Teacher Wars: A History of America's Most Embattled Profession* (New York: Doubleday, 2014); William J. Reese, *Testing Wars in the Public Schools: A Forgotten History* (Cambridge: Harvard UP, 2013); and Jesse Hagopian (Ed.), *More Than a Score: The New Uprising Against High Stakes Testing*, San Francisco: Haymarket, 2014).

11. Swapna Venygopal Ramaswamy, "155,000 New York Kids Boycott Standardized Tests," *USA Today*, April 16, 2015, accessed April 17, 2015, http://www.usatoday.com/story/news/nation/2015/04/16/parents-optout-standardized-tests/25896607/.

12. Laura McKenna, "What Happens When Students Boycott a Standardized Test?," *The Atlantic*, April 9, 2015, accessed April 02, 2015, http://www.theatlantic.com/education/archive/2015/04/what-happens-when-students-boycott-a-standardized-test/390087/.

13. Ontario Ministry of Education, *Growing Success: Assessment, Evaluation, and Reporting in Ontario Schools* (Toronto: Queen's Printer for Ontario, 2010).

14. Andy Hargreaves and Michael Fullan, "The Power of Professional Capital: With an Investment in Collaboration, Teachers Become Nation Builders," *JSD The Learning Forward Journal* 34, no. 3 (2013): 36.
15. Andy Hargreaves and Michael Fullan, "The Power of Professional Capital: With an Investment in Collaboration, Teachers Become Nation Builders," *JSD The Learning Forward Journal*, 34, no. 3 (2013): 36.
16. Linda Darling-Hammond, "Standards, Accountability and School Reform," *Teachers College Record* 106, no. 6 (2004).
17. Linda Darling-Hammond and Elle Rustique-Forrester, "The Consequences of Student Testing for Teaching and Teacher Quality," *Yearbook of the National Society for the Study of Education* 104, no. 2 (2005).
18. Linda Darling-Hammond, and Frank Adamson, *Beyond the Bubble Test: How Performance Assessments Support 21st Century Learning* (New York: Jossey-Bass, 2014), 11.
19. Raymond Pecheone and Stuart Kahl, "Where We are Now: Lessons Learned and Emerging Directions," in *Beyond the Bubble Test: How Performance Assessment Supports 21st Century Learning*, ed. Linda Darling-Hammond and Frank Adamson, 53–91 (San Francisco: Jossey-Bass, 2014).
20. Brian Stecher, "Looking Back: Performance Assessments in an Era of Standards-Based Educational Accountability," in *Beyond the Bubble Test: How Performance Assessment Supports 21st Century Learning*, edited by Linda Darling-Hammond and Frank Adamson, 17–52 (San Francisco: Jossey-Bass, 2014), 35.
21. Brian Stecher, "Looking Back: Performance Assessments in an Era of Standards-Based Educational Accountability," in *Beyond the Bubble Test: How Performance Assessment Supports 21st Century Learning*, ed. Linda Darling-Hammond and Frank Adamson, 17–52 (San Francisco: Jossey-Bass, 2014), 39.
22. Gloria Ladson-Billings, *The Dream Keepers: Successful Teachers of African-American Children* (San Francisco: Joss-Bass, 1994).

Bibliography

Abedi, Jamal. "Adapting Performance Assessments for English Language Learners." In *Beyond the Bubble Test: How Performance Assessment Supports 21st Century Learning*, edited by Linda Darling-Hammond and Frank Adamson, 185–205. San Francisco: Jossey-Bass, 2014.

Abrams, Lisa. *Teachers' Views on High-Stakes Testing: Implications for the Classroom, Policy Brief.* Education Policy Studies Laboratory, Arizona State University College of Education, 2004.

Acker, Sandra. *The Realities of Teacher's Work: Never a Dull Moment.* New York: Cassell, 1999.

Adamson, Frank. "Is the Invisible Hand a Magic Wand? Privatization Versus Public Investments in National Educational Systems." Remarks presented at the American Educational Research Association, Chicago, Illinois, April 19, 2015.

Alberta Education. "Breakdown of Alberta Student Population." n.d. Accessed November 3, 2014. http://education.alberta.ca/department/stats/students/student population.aspx.

Algers, Vicki. "Teacher Incentive Pay that Works: A Global Survey of Programs that Improve Student Achievement." September, 2014. Barbara Mitchell Centre for Improvement in Education, Frasier Institute. Accessed January 3, 2015. https://www.fraserinstitute.org/uploadedFiles/fraser-ca/Content/research-news /research/publications/teacher-incentive-pay-that-works.pdf.

Alphonso, Caroline. "Canada's Fall in Math-Education Ranking Sets off Alarm Bells." *Globe & Mail,* December 3, 2014. Accessed September 3, 2014. http:// www.theglobeandmail.com/news/national/education/canadas-fall-in-math -education-ranking-sets-off-red-flags/article15730663/.

Alvarez, Lizette. "States Listen as Parents Give Rampant Testing an F." *New York Times,* November 9, 2014. Accessed November 10, 2014. http://www.nytimes .com/2014/11/10/us/states-listen-as-parents-give-rampant-testing-an-f.html? _r=0 2014.

Amrein, Audrey, and David Berliner. "High-Stakes Testing, Uncertainty, and Student Learning." *Education Policy Analysis Archives* 10, no. 18 (2002): 1–74.

Au, Wayne. *Unequal by Design: High-Stakes Testing and the Standardization of Inequality.* New York: Routledge, 2007.

Barksdale-Ladd, Mary Thomas, and Karen Thomas. "What's at Stake in High-Stakes Testing: Teachers and Parents Speak Out." *Journal of Teacher Education* 51 (2000): 384–397.

Bascia, Nina. "Teacher Unions and Teacher Quality. In *Routledge International Handbook of Teacher Quality and Policy*, edited by Gerald Motoba and Sakiko Ikomo, n.p. New York: Routledge, in press.

Binet, Alfred. "New Methods for the Diagnosis of the Intellectual Level of Subnormals." *L'Année Psychologique* 12 (1992): 191–244.

Boaler, Jo. "When Learning no Longer Matters—Standardized Testing and the Creation of Inequality." *Phi Delta Kappan* 84 (2003): 502–506.

Booher-Jennings, Jennifer. "Below the Bubble: 'Educational Triage' and the Texas Accountability System." *American Educational Research Journal* 42 (2005): 231–268.

Bredekamp, Sue, ed. *Developmentally Appropriate Practice in Early Childhood Programs Serving Children from Birth Through Age 8*, Expanded Edition. Washington, DC: National Association for the Education of Young Children, 1990.

Bredekamp, Sue, and Lorrie Shepard. "How Best to Protect Children from Inappropriate School Expectations, Practices, and Policies." *Young Children* 44, no. 3 (1989): 14–24.

Brennan, Robert. "Revolutions and Evolutions in Current Educational Testing: CASMA Research Report Number 6." *Center for Advanced Studies in Measurement and Assessment*. 2004. Accessed May 7, 2014. http://www.uiowa.edu/~casma/wallace.casma.rpt.pdf.

British Columbia Ministry of Education. "Getting the Facts on FSA." n.d. Accessed October 1, 2014. https://www.bced.gov.bc.ca/assessment/fsa/info/facts.htm#tdD.

Broussard, Meredith. "Why Poor Schools Can't Win at Standardized Testing." *The Atlantic,* July 15, 2014. Accessed September 30, 2014. http://www.theatlantic.com/features/archive/2014/07/why-poor-schools-cant-win-at-standardized-testing/374287.

Chall, Jeanne S. *The Academic Achievement Challenge: What Really Works in the Classroom?* New York: Guilford Press, 2000.

Center for Advanced Studies in Measurement and Assessment. "About Us." University of Iowa, College of Education, 2014. Accessed July 24, 2014, from: http://www.education.uiowa.edu/centers/casma/home.

Center for Education Policy. "Choices, Changes, and Challenges Curriculum and Instruction in the NCLB Era." Center for Education Policy, December, 2007. Accessed March 3, 2015. http://www.cep-dc.org/displayDocument.cfm?DocumentID=312.

Center for International Education Benchmarking. *South Korea Overview.* Washington, DC: Center for International Education Benchmarking, 2012. Accessed October 3, 2014. http://www.ncee.org/programs-affiliates/center-on-international-education-benchmarking/top-performing-countries/south-korea-overview/.

Center for Popular Democracy and Integrity in Education. "Charter School Vulnerabilities for Waste, Fraud, and Abuse." Center for Popular Democracy, May 2014. Accessed May 2, 2015. http://populardemocracy.org/sites/default/files/FraudandMismgmt5-3-14%28FINALx3.0%29REV.pdf.

Chatterji, Madhabi. "Bad Tests or Bad Test Use? A Case of SAT Use to Examine Why We Need Stakeholder Conversations on Validity." *Teachers College Record* 115 no. 9 (2013): 1–10.

Chicagoland Researchers and Advocates for Transformative Education. *Research Brief 1: Testing Today in Context: History, Impact, and Alternatives.* Chicago: CReATE, 2012. Accessed January 10, 2014. http://www.createchicago.org/.

Chingos, Matthew. *Strength in Numbers: State Spending on K-12 Assessment Systems.* Washington, DC: Brown Center on Education Policy at Brookings, 2012. Accessed June 2014. http://www.brookings.edu/~/media/research/files/reports/2012/11/29%20cost%20of%20assessment%20chingos/11_assessment_chingos_final_new.

Clarke, Marguerite; Arnold Shore; Kathleen Rhoades; Lisa Abrams; Jing Miao; and Jie Li. "Perceived Effects of State-Mandated Testing Programs on Teaching and Learning: Findings from Interviews with Educators in Low-, Medium-, and High-Stakes States." Boston: Lynch School of Education, Boston College, National Board on Educational Testing and Public Policy Boston, 2003.

CNN. "Cheating Scandal Hits Atlanta Schools: CNN's Suzanne Malveaux talks with Michael Bowers, Former Georgia Attorney General, About the Charges 35 teachers Face." CNN.com, April 2, 2015. Accessed April 10, 2015. http://www.cnn.com/videos/bestoftv/2013/04/02/exp-nr-atlanta-schools-cheating-scandal.cnn/video/playlists/atlanta-school-cheating-scandal/.

Contenta, Sandro. *Rituals of Failure: What Schools Really Teach.* Toronto: Between The Lines, 1993.

Contreras, Frances. "Access, Achievement, and Social Capital: Standardized Exams and the Latino College-Bound Population." *Journal of Hispanic Higher Education* 4 (2005): 197–214.

Copple, Carol, and Sue Bredekamp, eds. *Developmentally Appropriate Practice in Early Childhood Programs Serving Children from Birth Through Age 8.* Washington, DC: National Association for the Education of Young Children, 2009.

Council of Ministers of Education, Canada. "Assessment." CMEC, n.d. Accessed January 2, 2015. www.cmec.ca/131/Programs-and-Initiatives/Assessment/Overview/index.html.

Dagenais, Margaret. "An Effective and Critical History of Canada's National Standardized Testing Program." PhD diss., University of Regina, 2011.

Darling-Hammond, Linda. "Is the Invisible Hand a Magic Wand? Privatization Versus Public Investments in National Educational Systems." Remarks presented at the American Educational Research Association, Chicago, Illinois, April 19, 2015.

Darling-Hammond, Linda. *The Flat World and Education: How America's Commitment to Equity will Determine our Future.* New York, NY: Teachers College Press, 2010.

Darling-Hammond, Linda. "Race, Inequality and Educational Accountability: The Irony of 'No Child Left Behind.'" *Race Ethnicity and Education* 10 (2007): 245–260.

Darling-Hammond, Linda. "Standards, Accountability and School Reform." *Teachers College Record* 106, no. 6 (2004): 1047–1085.

Darling-Hammond, Linda. "Reaching Out: International Benchmarks for Performance Assessment." In *Beyond the Bubble Test: How Performance Assessment Supports 21st Century Learning*, edited by Linda Darling-Hammond and Frank Adamson, 93–129. San Francisco: Jossey-Bass, 2014.

Darling-Hammond, Linda, and Frank Adamson. "Developing Assessments of Deeper Learning: The Costs and Benefits of Using Tests that Help Students Learn," Stanford, CA: Stanford Center for Opportunity Policy in Education, 2013.

Darling-Hammond, Linda, and Frank Adamson, eds. *Beyond the Bubble Test: How Performance Assessments Support 21st Century Learning.* New York: Wiley, 2014.

Darling Hammond, Linda, and Beverly Falk. "Supporting Teacher Learning Through Performance Assessments." In *Beyond the Bubble Test: How Performance Assessment Supports 21st Century Learning*, edited by Linda Darling-Hammond and Frank Adamson, 207–235. San Francisco: Jossey-Bass, 2014.

Darling-Hammond, Linda, and Elle Rustique-forrester. "The Consequences of Student Testing for Teaching and Teacher Quality." *Yearbook of the National Society for the Study of Education* 104, no. 2 (2005): 289–319.

Darling-Hammond, Linda, and Randi Weingarten. "It's Time for a New Accountability in American Education." *Huffington Post*, May 19, 2014. Accessed January 3, 2015. www.huffingtonpost.com/linda-darlinghammond/its-time-for-a-new-accoun_b_5351475.html

Després, Sébastien; Steven Kuhn; Pauline Ngirumpatse; and Marie-Josée Parent. *Accountability or Illusion of Success? A Call to Review Standardized Testing in Ontario.* Ottawa: Action Canada Task Force Report, 2013. Accessed June 2014. http://testingillusion.ca/wp-content/uploads/2013/01/illusion_of_success_EN.pdf.

Dewey, John. *The Quest for Certainty: A Study of the Relation of Knowledge and Action.* New York: Putnam, 1960/1929.

Dodge, Arnold, and Ruth Powers Silverberg. "Dominant Discourse, Educational Research, and the Hegemony of Test Scores." *Critical Education* 6, no. 1 (2015): 1–22. Accessed February 21, 2015. http://ojs.library.ubc.ca/index.php/criticaled/article/view/184561.

Duncan, Arne. "Secretary Arne Duncan's Remarks at OECD's Release of the Program for International Student Assessment (PISA) 2009 Results." *United States Department of Education*, December 7, 2010. Accessed February 7, 2014. http://www.ed.gov/news/speeches/secretary-arne-duncans-remarks-oecds-release-program-international-student-assessment-pisa-2009-results.

Ecker, Janet. "Statement from Education Minister Janet Ecker About the Grade 10 Literacy Test." *News By Ministry, Ministry of Education*. October 15, 2001. Accessed February 13, 2015. http://newsarchive.ontario.ca/getorg_ef167.html?okey=68451&lang=eng&y=2001&m=10&d=18

Education Quality and Accountability Office. *A Parent's Guide to EQAO Tests.* Toronto: Education Quality and Accountability Office, n.d.). Accessed May 3, 2014. http://www.eqao.com/pdf_e/07/07P086e.pdf.

Education Quality and Accountability Office. *2011–2012 Annual Report.* Toronto: Queen's Printer for Ontario, 2012. Accessed September 15, 2014. http://www.eqao.com/pdf_e/12/AnnualReport2011_2012_en.pdf.

Embertson, Susan. *Test Design: Developments in Psychology and Psychometrics.* New York: Academic Press, 1985.

Engel, Brenda. "An Approach to Assessment in Early Literacy." In *Achievement Testing in Early Childhood Education: The Games Grown-ups Play*, edited by Constance Kamii, 119–134. Washington, DC: National Association for the Education of Young Children, 1990.

Feenberg, Andrew. *Critical Theory of Technology.* New York: Oxford, 1991.

Freire, Paulo. *Pedagogy of the Oppressed.* New York: Continuum, 1997.

Freire, Paulo, and Donaldo Macedo. *Literacy: The Word and the World*, New York: Praeger, 1987.

Froese-Germain, Bernie. "Standardized Testing: Undermining Equity in Education." Report prepared for the National Issues in Education Initiative, Ottawa: Canadian Teachers' Federation, 1999.

Glaser, Robert; Alan Lesgold; and Susanne Lajoie. "Toward a Cognitive Theory for the Measurement of Achievement." In *The Influence of Cognitive Psychology on Testing,* edited by Royce Ronning, John A. Glover, Jane C. Conoley, and Joseph C. Witt, 41–85. Hillsdale, NJ: Lawrence Erlbaum Associates, 1987.

Goering, Chris. "Opt Out? Why Parents Should Opt-In to Standardized Testing." *Huffington Post,* May 21, 2014. Accessed February 17, 2015. http://www.huffingtonpost.com/chris-goering/standardized-test-opt-out-movement_b_5347225.html.

Goldenberg, Claude; Ronald Gallimore; Leslie Reese; and Helen Garnier. "Cause or Effect? A Longitudinal Study of Immigrant Latino Parents' Aspirations and Expectations, and Their Children's School Performance." *American Educational Research Journal* 38 (2001): 547–582.

Goldstein, Dana. *The Teacher Wars: A History of America's Most Embattled Profession.* New York: Doubleday, 2014.

Gregor, Astrid. "Examination Anxiety: Live with it, Control it or Make it Work for you? *School Psychology International* 26 (2005): 617–635.

Hagopian, Jesse, ed. *More Than a Score: The New Uprising against High Stakes Testing.* San Francisco: Haymarket, 2014.

Hargreaves, Andy, and Michael Fullan. *Professional Capital: Transforming Teaching in Every School.* New York: Teachers College Press, 2012.

Hargreaves, Andy, and Michael Fullan. "The Power of Professional Capital: With an Investment in Collaboration, Teachers Become Nation Builders." *JSD The Learning Forward Journal* 34, no. 3 (2013): 36–39.

Hargreaves, Andy, and Dennis Shirley. *The Fourth Way: The Inspiring Future for Educational Change.* Thousand Oaks, CA: Corwin Press, 2009.

Harper, Stephen. 39th Parliament, 2nd Session (no. 110). *House of Commons Debate.* June 11, 2008.

Hart, Doug. "The 18th OISE Survey of Educational Issues: Public Attitudes Toward Education in Ontario 2012." Toronto: The Ontario Institute for Studies in Education of the University of Toronto, 2012. Accessed August 5, 2014. http://www.oise.utoronto.ca/oise/UserFiles/File/OISE%20Survey/18th_OISE_Survey/OISE%20SURVEY%2018.pdf.

Hedges, Larry and Amy Nowell. "Black-White test score convergence since 1965." In *The Black-White Test Score Gap,* edited by Christopher Jencks, Meredith Phillips, 149–181. Washington, DC: Brookings Institution, 1998.

Herrnstein, Richard, and Charles Murray. *The Bell Curve: Intelligence and Class Structure in American Life.* New York: Free Press, 1994.

Huffington Post. "Public School Funding Unequal: State and Local School Finance Systems Perpetuate Per-Student Spending Disparities." *Huffington Post,* September 9, 2012. Accessed November 3, 2013. http://www.huffingtonpost.com/2012/09/20/state-and-local-school-fi_n_1898225.html.

Hursh, David. "Exacerbating Inequality: The Failed Promise of the No Child Left Behind Act. *Race Ethnicity and Education* 10, no. 3 (2007): 295–308.

Ibbitson, John, and Gloria Galloway. "Ottawa Hinges Funds for Native Schools on Chiefs' Support for Education Act." *The Globe and Mail,* December 10, 2013. Accessed June 3, 2014. http://www.theglobeandmail.com/news/politics/ottawa-hinges-funds-for-native-schools-on-chiefs-support-for-education-act/article15836201/.

Influence Explorer. "Pearson Education." InfluenceExplorer.com, N.d. Accessed January 30, 2015. http://influenceexplorer.com/organization/pearson-education/2ec67ad263c448739699876db162f88f.

Jackson, Marguerite. "In the Know With EQAO: A Practical Recipe for Math Success Students do Better on the EQAO Grade 9 Assessment of Mathematics When They Know the Test will Affect their Final Course Mark." www.eqao.com, May 2012. Accessed January 12, 2015. www.eqao.com/pdf_e/12/EQAO_Intheknow_RecipeMathSuccess.pdf.

Kahlenberg, Richard, and Halley Potter. "What Charter Schools Can Teach Us about Teacher Voice." *Teachers College Record,* March 09, 2015. Accessed March 16, 2015. http://www.tcrecord.org/Content.asp?ContentID=17890.

Kane, Michael. "Validation." In *Educational Measurement,* edited by L Robert Brennan, 17–64. Westport: Praeger Publishers, 2006.

Kearns, Laura-Lee. "High-stakes Standardized Testing and Marginalized Youth: An Examination of the Impact on Those Who Fail." *Canadian Journal of Education* 34, no. 2 (2011): 112–130.

Kearns, Laura-Lee. "Equity, Literacy Testing and Marginalized Youth: The social Construction of 'Illiterate' Identities." PhD diss., University of Toronto, Toronto, 2008.

Kempf, Arlo. "Cuban Teacher Perspectives on Race and Racism: The Pedagogy of Home-School Relations." *Teachers College Record* 116, no. 6 (2014): 1–38.

Kempf, Arlo, and Ruth Powers Silverberg, R. "Academic Disobedience: Engaging Michael Apple's Nine Tasks of the Critical Scholar in an Age of Standardization." In *School against Neoliberal Rule: Educational Fronts for Local and Global Justice: A Reader*, edited by Mark Abendroth and Brad Porfilio, 187–206. Charlotte, NC: Information Age Publishing, in 2015.

Klinger, Don, Christopher Deluca, and Tess Miller. "The Evolving Culture of Large-Scale Assessments in Canadian Education." *Canadian Journal of Educational Administration and Policy* 76 (2008): 1–34. Accessed July 5, 2014. www.umanitoba.ca/publications/cjeap/articles/klinger.html.

Klinger, Don, and Rebecca Luce-Kapler. "Walking in their Shoes: Students' Perceptions of Large-Scale High-Stakes Testing." *Canadian Journal of Program Evaluation* 22, no. 3 (2008): 29–52.

Klinger, Don, Todd Rogers, John O. Anderson, Cheryl Poth, and Ruth Calman. "Contextual and School Factors Associated with Achievement on a High-Stakes Examination." *Canadian Journal of Education* 29, no. 3 (2006): 771–797.

Kirschner, Paul, John Sweller, and Richard Clark. "Why Minimal Guidance During Instruction Does Not Work: An Analysis of the Failure of Constructivist, Discovery, Problem-Based, Experiential, and Inquiry-Based teaching." *Educational Psychologist* 41, no. 2 (2006): 75–86.

Kohn, Alfie. Getting Hit on the Head Lessons: Justifying Bad Educational Practices as Preparation for More of the Same. *Education Week*, September 7, 2005. Accessed February 12, 2015. http://www.alfiekohn.org/article/getting-hit-head-lessons/.

Kohn, Alfie. *What Does It Mean to be Well Educated?* Boston, MA: Beacon Press, 2004.

Kohn, Alfie. "Standardized Testing Separating Wheat Children from Chaff Children." AlfieKohn.Org, 2002. Accessed May, 3, 2013. http://www.alfiekohn.org/article/standardized-testing.

Kohn, Alfie. "Fighting the Tests: A Practical Guide to Rescuing our Schools." *Phi Delta Kappan* 82, no. 5 (2001): 349–357. http://www.alfiekohn.org/teaching/ftt.htm.

Kohn, Alfie. "Standardized Testing and Its Victims." *Education Week*, September 27, 2000. Accessed October 1, 2014. http://www.alfiekohn.org/teaching/edweek/staiv.htm.

Kohn, Alfie. *The Case Against Standardized Testing: Raising the Scores, Ruining the Schools.* Boston, MA: Beacon, 2000.

Ladson-Billings, Gloria. "The Evolving Role of Critical Race Theory in Educational Scholarship. *Race, Ethnicity and Education* 8, no. 1 (1995): 115–120.

Ladson-Billings, Gloria. *The Dream Keepers: Successful Teachers of African-American Children.* San Francisco: Joss-Bass, 1994.

Layton, Lindsay. "How Bill Gates pulled off the Swift Common Core Revolution." *Washington Post*, June 7, 2014. Accessed January 19, 2015. www.washingtonpost.com/politics/how-bill-gates-pulled-off-the-swift-common-core-revolution/2014/06/07/a830e32e-ec34-11e3-9f5c-9075d5508f0a_story.html.

Lazarín, Melissa. *Testing Overload in America's Schools*. Washington, DC: Center for American Progress, 2014.

Leonardo, Zeus. "The War on Schools: NCLB, Nation Creation and the Educational Construction of Whiteness." *Race Ethnicity and Education* 10 (2007): 261–278.

Lovett, Ian. "Teacher's Death Exposes Tensions in Los Angeles." *New York Times*, November 9, 2010. Accessed June 3, 2014. http://www.nytimes.com/2010/11/10/education/10teacher.html?_r=0.

Liu, Charlotte Hua, and Robert Matthews. "Vygotsky's Philosophy: Constructivism and its Criticisms." *Examined International Education Journal* 6, no. 3 (2005): 386–399.

Lynch, Matthew. "Education Officials to Re-examine Standardized Testing." *Education Week*, October 22, 2014. Accessed October 23, 2014. http://blogs.edweek.org/edweek/education_futures/2014/10/education_officials_to_re-examine_standardized_testing.html?qs=standardized+testing.

MacLeod, Jay. *Ain't no Makin' it: Aspirations and Attainment in a Low-Income Neighborhood*. Boulder, CO: Westview Press, 2008.

Marcotte, Amanda. "Education Reformer Praises Standardized Tests for Boosting Home Prices in Wealthy Suburbs." *Slate Magazine*, April 20, 2015. Accessed April 21, 2015. http://www.slate.com/blogs/xx_factor/2015/04/20/one_standardized_testing_supporter_in_new_york_lets_it_slip_it_s_all_about.html.

Marx, Karl. *The 18th Brumaire of Louis Bonaparte*. New York: Wildside Press, 2008.

Maxwell, Kelly, Sharon Ritchie, Sue Bredekamp, and Tracy Zimmerman. *Issues in PreK–3rd Education: Using Developmental Science to Transform Children's Early School Experiences (#4)*. Chapel Hill: University of North Carolina, FPG Child Development Institute, FirstSchool, 2009. Accessed September 11, 2014. http://files.eric.ed.gov/fulltext/ED507444.pdf.

McKenna, Laura. "What Happens When Students Boycott a Standardized Test?" *The Atlantic*, April 9, 2015. Accessed April 02, 2015, http://www.theatlantic.com/education/archive/2015/04/what-happens-when-students-boycott-a-standardized-test/390087/.

McLuhan, Marshall. *Understanding Media: The Extensions of Man*. Boston, MA: MIT Press, 2013.

Menken, Kate. "Teaching to the Test: How No Child Left Behind Impacts Language Policy, Curriculum, and Instruction for English Language Learners." *Bilingual Research Journal* 30, no. 2 (2006): 521–546.

Messick, Samuel. "Validity." In *Educational Measurement*, edited by Robert Lynn, 53–91. New York: American Council on Education, 1989.

Mullins, Dexter. "New Orleans to be Home to Nation's First All-Charter School District." *Aljazeera America*, April 4, 2014. Accessed June 7, 2014. http://america.aljazeera.com/articles/2014/4/4/new-orleans-charterschoolseducationreformracesegregation.html.

Murnane, Richard J., and John P. Papay. "Teachers' Views on No Child Left Behind: Support for the Principles, Concerns about the Practices." *Journal of Economic Perspectives* 24, no. 3 (2010): 151–166.

Muskogee Phoenix. "McDonald's to Provide Free Breakfasts for Test Season." *Muskogee Phoenix*, April 12, 2015. Accessed April 24, 2015. http://www.muskogeephoenix.com/news/mcdonald-s-to-provide-free-breakfasts-for-test-season/article_545c5b3c-8d42-5dbe-aabb-24b450e763a3.html.

National Association of Secondary School Principals. "Value-Added Measures in Teacher Evaluation." Reston VG: National Association of Secondary School Principals, 2015. Accessed April 13, 2015. http://www.nassp.org/Content.aspx?topic=Value_Added_Measures_in_Teacher_Evaluation.

National Association of State Boards of Education. *Caring Communities: Supporting Young Children and Families*. Alexandria, VA: NASBE, 1991.

National Center for Education Statistics. *The Nation's Report Card: Trends in Academic Progress 2012*. US Department of Education, Institute of Education Sciences, 2012. Accessed October 21, 2014. http://nces.ed.gov/pubsearch/pubsinfo.asp?

National Research Council. *Education for Life and Work: Developing Transferable Knowledge and Skills in the 21st Century*. Washington, DC: The National Academies Press, 2012.

National Research Council. *Knowing What Students Know: The Science and Design of Educational Assessment*. Washington, DC: National Academies Press, 2001.

National Research Council. *High Stakes: Testing for Tracking, Promotion, and Graduation*. Washington, DC: The National Academies Press, 1999.

Nelson, Howard. *Testing More, Teaching Less, What America's Obsession with Student Testing Costs in Money and Lost Instructional Time*. Washington, DC: American Federation of Teachers, 2013.

Nezavdal, Frank. "The Standardized Testing Movement: Equitable or Excessive?" *McGill Journal of Education* 38, no. 1 (2003): 65–77.

Norden, Eric. "A Candid Conversation with the High Priest of Popcult and Metaphysician of Media." *Playboy*, March 1969.

Ohanian, Susan. "Let's Turn the Tables." *SusanOhanian.Org*, April 18, 2003. Accessed October 3, 2014. http://susanohanian.org/show_commentary.php?id=61.

Ohio Department of Education. "Ohio Achievement Assessments 2014, Grades 5–8 Reading & Mathematics Grades 5 & 8 Science, Directions for Administration Manual." Columbus: Ohio Department of Education Office of Curriculum and Assessment, 2014. Accessed January 15, 2015. https://education.ohio.gov/getattachment/Topics/Testing/Ohio-Achievement-Assessments/G5-8-DFA-Spring-2014.pdf.aspx.

Oliver, John. "Standardized Testing." *Last Week With John Oliver*, HBO, May 2, 2015. Accessed May 4, 2015. https://www.youtube.com/watch?v=J6lyURyVz7k.

Ontario. Royal Commission on Learning. *For the Love of Learning: Report of the Royal Commission on Learning*. 4 vols. Toronto: Queen's Printer for Ontario, 1994.

Ontario Ministry of Education. *Growing Success: Assessment, Evaluation, and Reporting in Ontario Schools*. Toronto: Queen's Printer for Ontario, 2010.

Organization for Economic Cooperation and Development. *PISA 2012 Results: What Makes Schools Successful? Resources, Policies and Practices Volume 4*. Paris: OECD Publishing, 2013.

Organization for Economic Cooperation and Development. *PISA 2012 Results: Excellence through Equity Giving Every Student the Chance to Succeed, Volume II*. Paris: OECD Publishing, 2013. Accessed August 10, 2014. http://www.oecd.org/pisa/keyfindings/pisa-2012-results-volume-II.pdf.

Organization for Economic Cooperation and Development. *Reviews of National Policies for Education: Improving Lower Secondary Schools in Norway*. Paris: OECD Publishing, 2011.

Özturgut, Osman. "Standardized Testing in the Case of China and the Lessons to be Learned for the U.S." *Journal of International Education Research* 7, no. 2 (2011): 1–6.

Paige, Rod. "No Child Left Behind: The Ongoing Movement for Public Education Reform. *Harvard Educational Review* 76, no. 4 (2006): 461–473.

Paludan, Ann. *Chronicle of the Chinese Emperors: The Reign-by-Reign Record of the Rulers of Imperial China*. New York, New York: Thames and Hudson, 1998.

Papay, John. "Different Tests, Different Answers: The Stability of Teacher Value-Added Estimates across Outcome Measures. *American Educational Research Journal* 48 (2012): 163–193.

Parent Revolution. "About Us." ParentRevolution.Org, N.d. Accessed January 4, 2015. http://parentrevolution.org/who-we-are/.

Pearson. "Pearson Joins President and Mrs. Obama, Education Secretary Duncan for White House Higher Education Summit January 16, 2014. PearsonEd.com, n.d. Accessed January 19, 2015. www.pearsoned.com/pearson-joins-president-and-mrs-obama-education-secretary-duncan-for-white-house-higher-education-summit/#.UtoWTLQo4dU.

Pecheone, Raymond, and Stuart Kahl. "Where We Are Now: Lessons Learned and Emerging Directions." In *Beyond the Bubble Test: How Performance Assessment Supports 21st Century Learning*, edited by Linda Darling-Hammond and Frank Adamson, 53–91 (San Francisco: Jossey-Bass, 2014).

Persson, Jonas. "New Documents Show How Taxpayer Money Is Wasted by Charter Schools—Stringent Controls Urgently Needed as Charter Funding Faces Huge Increase A CMD Reporters' Guide." Center for Media and Democracy, May 8, 2015. Accessed May 9, 2015. http://www.prwatch.org/files/5-8-15_final_cmd_reporters_guide_on_charter_waste_and_lack_of_accountability.pdf.

Philip, Thomas. "Articulating the Purpose of a Social Foundations of Education Course through Instructor Self-Interviews." *Studying Teacher Education* 9 (2013): 203–218.

Piaget, Jean. *The Psychology of Intelligence*. New York: Routledge, 1950.

Polikoff, Morgan, and Andrew Porter. "Instructional Alignment as a Measure of Teaching Quality." *Educational Evaluation and Policy Analysis* 20, No. 10 (2013): 1–18.

Pollan, Michael. "How Schools Kill Creativity," Filmed February 2006. TED Video, 19:24. Posted February 2006. http://www.ted.com/index.php/talks/michael_pollan_gives_a_plant_s_eye_view.html.

Popham, James. *Classroom Assessment: What Teachers Need to Know.* Boston, MA: Pearson, 2011.

Popham, James. "Instructional Insensitivity of Tests: Accountability's Dire Drawback." *Phi Delta Kappan* 89 (2007): 146–155.

Popham, James. *The Truth About Testing: An Educator's Call to Action.* Alexandria, VA: ASCD, 2001.

Powell, Douglas, and Irving Sigel. "Searches for Validity in Evaluating Young Children and Early Childhood Programs. In *Issues in Early Childhood Education. Yearbook in Early Childhood Education,* edited by Bernard Spodek and Olivia Saracho, 190–212. New York: Teachers College Press, 1991.

Provasnik, Stephen, David Kastberg, David Ferraro, Nita Lemanski, Stephen Roey, and Frank Jenkins. "Highlights From TIMSS 2011: Mathematics and Science Achievement of U.S. Fourth- and Eighth-Grade Students in an International Context." US Department of Education, Institute of Education Sciences 2012. Accessed May 2, 2014. www.nces.ed.gov/TIMSS.

Putwain, David. "Deconstructing Test Anxiety." *Emotional & Behavioural Difficulties* 13 (2008): 141–155.

Ramaswamy, Swapna Venygopal. "155,000 New York Kids Boycott Standardized Tests." *USA Today,* April 16, 2015. Accessed April 17, 2015. http://www.usatoday.com/story/news/nation/2015/04/16/parents-opt-out-standardized-tests/25896607/.

Ramirez, Fred. "Dismay and Disappointment: Parental Involvement of Latino Immigrant Parents." *The Urban Review* 35, no. 2 (2003): 93–110.

Ravitch, Diane."Must Watch: VAM Outrage in Florida." *Diane Ravitch's Blog,* March 29, 2015. Accessed April 2, 2015. http://dianeravitch.net/2015/03/29/must-watch-vam-outrage-in-florida/.

Ravitch, Diane. "The Big Money behind Parent Revolution." *Diane Ravitch's Blog,* April 11, 2013. Accessed June 2, 2014. http://dianeravitch.net/2013/04/11/the-big-money-behind-parent-revolution/.

Ravitch, Diane. *Reign of Error: The Hoax of the Privatization Movement and the Danger to America's Public Schools.* New York: Knopf, 2013.

Ravitch, Diane. "What the Best and Wisest Parent Wants for His Child." *Diane Ravitch's Blog,* February 22, 2013. Accessed January 21, 2015. dianeravitch.net/2013/02/22/what-the-best-and-wisest-parent-wants-for-his-child-2/.

Reese, William J. *Testing Wars in the Public Schools: A Forgotten History.* Cambridge, MA: Harvard UP, 2013.

Rhodes, Jesse H. "Learning Citizenship? How State Education Reforms Affect Parents' Political Attitudes and Behavior." *Political Behavior* March (2014). Accessed February 1, 2015. http://link.springer.com/article/10.1007/s11109-014-9270-8/fulltext.html.

Robinson, Ken. "How Schools Kill Creativity," filmed February 2006, TED video, 19:24, posted February 2006, http://www.ted.com/talks/ken_robinson_says_schools_kill_creativity?language=en.

Rogers, John. "Forces of Accountability? The Power of Poor Parents in No Child Left Behind." *Harvard Educational Review* 76 (2006): 611–641.

Rosário, Pedro, José Carlos Núñez, Ana Salgado, Julio Antonio González-Pienda, Antonio Valle, Cristina Joly, and Ana Bernardo. "Test Anxiety: Associations with Personal and Family Variables." *Psicothema* 20, no. 4 (2008): 563–570.

Rotberg, Iris, C. "Assessment Around the World." *Educational Measurement* 54 (2006): 1–7.

Rushowy, Kristin. "Math: Number One Problem for Ontario School Boards," *Toronto Star*, August 27, 2014. Accessed January 3, 2015. http://www.thestar.com/yourtoronto/education/2014/08/27/math_number_one_problem_for_ontario_school_boards.html.

Sacks, Peter. *Standardized Minds: The High Price of America's Testing Culture and What We can Do to Change it*. Cambridge, MA: Perseus, 1999.

Sahlberg, Pasi. "What Canada can Learn from Finland." 2014 R.W. Jackson Lecture, Toronto, Ontario, April 17, 2014. Accessed September 6, 2014. https://webcasts.welcome2theshow.com/OISE/2230.

Sahlberg, Pasi. *Finnish Lessons: What Can the World Learn from Educational Change in Finland?* New York, NY: Teachers College Press, 2011.

Sahlberg, Pasi. "Global Educational Reform Movement Is Here!" *PasiSahlberg.com*, n.d. Accessed September 6, 2014. http://pasisahlberg.com/global-educational-reform-movement-is-here/.

Santoro, Doris. "Good Teaching in Difficult Times: Demoralization in the Pursuit of Good Work." *American Journal of Education* 118, no. 1 (2011): 1–23.

Santelices, Maria Veronica, and Mark Wilson. "Unfair Treatment? The Case of Freedle, the SAT, and the Standardization Approach to Differential Item Functioning." *Harvard Educational Review* 1, no. 7 (2010): 106–134. Accessed January 30, 2015. http//hepg.metapress.com/content/J94675W001329270.

Sena, Jolyn, Patricia Lowe, and Steven Lee. "Significant Predictors of Test Anxiety Among Students with and without Learning Disabilities." *Journal of Learning Disabilities* 40 (2007): 360–376.

Shepard, Laurie. "The Hazards of High Stakes Testing." *Issues in Science and Technology* 19, no. 2 (2002).

Siegler, Robert. "The Other Alfred Binet." *Developmental Psychology* 28 (1992): 179–190.

Singer, Alan. "Protest Builds against Pearson, Testing, and Common Core." *Huffington Post*, June 13, 2012. Accessed January 13, 2015. www.huffingtonpost.com/alan-singer/protest-builds-against-pe_b_1586573.html.

Solano-Flores, Guillermo. "Who Is Given Tests in What Language by Whom, When, and Where? The Need for Probabilistic Views of Language in the Testing of English Language Learners." *Educational Researcher* 37, no. 4 (2008): 189–199.

Stecher, Brian. "Looking Back: Performance Assessments in an Era of Standards-Based Educational Accountability." In *Beyond the Bubble Test: How Performance Assessment Supports 21st Century Learning*, edited by Linda Darling-Hammond and Frank Adamson, 17–52. San Francisco: Jossey Bass, 2014.

Stoskopf, Alan. "An Untold Story of Resistance: African-American Educators and I.Q. Testing in the 1920's and '30's." *Rethinking Schools* 14, no. 1 (1999).

Accessed February 2, 2015. http://www.rethinkingschools.org//cmshandler.asp?archive/14_01/iq141.shtml.

Strauss, Valerie. "How and Why Convicted Atlanta Teachers Cheated on Standardized Tests." *Washington Post*, April 1, 2015. Accessed April 2, 2015. http://www.washingtonpost.com/blogs/answer-sheet/wp/2015/04/01/how-and-why-convicted-atlanta-teachers-cheated-on-standardized-tests/.

Strauss, Valerie. "Netflix's Reed Hastings Has a Big Idea: Kill Elected School Boards (Update)." *Washington Post*, March 14, 2014. Accessed June 12, 2014. http://www.washingtonpost.com/blogs/answer-sheet/wp/2014/03/14/netflixs-reed-hastings-has-a-big-idea-kill-elected-school-boards/.

Strauss, Valerie. "The New School Reform Model: 'Dumping the Losers.'" *Washington Post*, April 11, 2014. Accessed May 12, 2014. http://www.washingtonpost.com/blogs/answer-sheet/wp/2014/04/11/the-new-school-reform-model-dumping-the-losers/.

Strauss, Valerie. "Eighth Grader: What Bothered me Most about New Common Core Test." *Washington Post*, May 8, 2013. Accessed January 25, 2015. www.washingtonpost.com/blogs/answer-sheet/wp/2013/05/08/eighth-grader-what-bothered-me-most-about-new-common-core-test/.

Strauss, Valerie. "Pearson Criticized for Finding Test Essay Scorers on Craigslist." *Washington Post*, January 16, 2013. Accessed March 5, 2015. http://www.washingtonpost.com/blogs/answer-sheet/wp/2013/01/16/pearson-criticized-for-finding-test-essay-scorers-on-craigslist/.

Thernstrom, Abigail, and Stephan Thernstrom. *No Excuses: Closing the Racial Gap in Learning*. New York: Simon and Schuster, 2004.

Thorndike, Richard. *Measurement and Evaluation in Psychology and Education* (8th ed.). Upper Saddle River, NJ: Prentice Hall, 2011.

Topol, Barry, John Olson, and Ed Roeber. *The Cost of New Higher Quality Assessments: A Comprehensive Analysis of the Potential Costs for Future State Assessments*. Stanford, CA: Stanford Center for Opportunity Policy in Education, 2010. Accessed October 2, 2014. https://edpolicy.stanford.edu/sites/default/files/publications/getting-higher-quality-assessments-evaluating-costs-benefits-and-investment-strategies.pdf.

Turner, Cory. "U.S. Tests Teens A Lot, but Worldwide, Exam Stakes Are Higher." *National Public Radio*, April 30, 2014. Accessed October 3, 2014. http://www.npr.org/2014/04/30/308057862/u-s-tests-teens-a-lot-but-worldwide-exam-stakes-are-higher.

Tyler, Kenneth, Lynda Brown-Wright, Danelle Stevens-Watkins, Deneia Thomas, Ruby Stevens, Clarissa Roan-Belle, Nadia Gadson, and La Toya Smith. "Linking Home-School Dissonance to School Based Outcomes for African American High School Students." *Journal of Black Psychology* 36, no. 4 (2010): 410–425.

United States. *Testing in American Schools: Asking the Right Questions*. Washington, DC: Congress of the U.S., Office of Technology Assessment, 1992.

United States. *Historical Statistics of the United States*. Washington, DC: Department of Commerce, Bureau of the Census, 1975: 105–111. Accessed

December 12, 2014. http://www2.census.gov/prod2/statcomp/documents/HistoricalStatisticsoftheUnitedStates1789-1945.pdf.
United States Chamber of Commerce. "US Chamber of Commerce Foundation." USchamberfoundation.org, n.d. Accessed January 13, 2015. http://www.uschamberfoundation.org/.
United Stated Department of Education. "Laws & Guidance Elementary & Secondary Education." US Department of Education, n.d. Accessed November 21, 2014. http://www2.ed.gov/programs/titleiparta/index.html.
Von Der Embse, Nathaniel, Justin Barterian, and Natasha Segool. "Test Anxiety Interventions for Children and Adolescents: A Systematic Review of Treatment Studies From 2000–2010." *Psychology in the Schools* 50, no. 1 (2013): 57–71.
Vygotsky, Lev. *Mind in Society: The Development of Higher Mental Processes.* Cambridge, MA: Harvard University Press, 1978.
Wainer, Howard. *Uneducated Guesses: Using Evidence to Uncover Misguided Education Policies.* Princeton, NJ: Princeton University Press, 2011.
Webb-Johnson, Gwendolyn. "Are Schools Ready for Joshua? African American Culture Among Students Identified as Having Behavioral/Emotional Disorders. *Qualitative Studies in Education* 15 (2002): 653–671.
Westheimer, Joel. "No Child Left Thinking: Democracy at Risk in Canada's Schools." *Education Canada* 50, no. 2 (2010): 5–8.
Wilkinson, Richard, and Kate Pickett. *The Spirit Level: Why Equality Is Better for Everyone.* London: Penguin, 2010.
Wilson, David. "Developmentally Appropriate Practice in the Age of Testing: New Reports Outline Key Principles for PreK–3rd Grade." *Harvard Education Letter* 25, no. 3 (2009): 1–3. Accessed March 2, 2015, http://hepg.org/hel-home/issues/25_3/helarticle/developmentally-appropriate-practice-in-the-age-of#home.
Winsa, Patty. "As Fundraising Gap Grows, Toronto's Wealthy Schools Leaving Poor Schools Behind." *Toronto Star*, April 11, 2015. Accessed April12, 2015. http://www.thestar.com/yourtoronto/education/2015/04/11/as-fundraising-gap-grows-torontos-wealthy-schools-leaving-poor-schools-behind.html.
Winters, Marcus and Joshua Cowen. "Who Would Stay, Who Would be Dismissed? An Empirical Consideration of Value-Added Teacher Retention Policies. *Educational Researcher* 42 (2013): 330–337.
Wolf, Nicky. "Pearson Admits to Monitoring Students' Social Media use During Its Online Tests." *The Guardian*, March 18, 2015. Accessed April 2, 2015. http://www.theguardian.com/education/2015/mar/18/pearson-monitoring-students-social-media-tests.
Wood, George. "A View from the field: NCLB's Effects on Classrooms and Schools." In *Many Children Left Behind: How the No Child Left Behind Act Is Damaging our Children and Our Schools*, edited by Deborah Meier, 33–52. Boston, MA: Beacon Press, 2004.
Wood, George, Linda Darling-Hammond, Monty Neill, and Pat Roschewski. "Refocusing Accountability: Using Local Performance Assessments to Enhance

Teaching and Learning for Higher Order Skills." Briefing Paper Prepared for Members of The Congress of The United States, 2007. Accessed January 5, 2015. http://www.fairtest.org/sites/default/files/PerformanceAssessments.pdf.

Yuan, Kun and Vi-Nhuan Le. "Estimating the Percentages of Students who were Tested on Cognitively Demanding Items Through the State Achievement Tests." Santa Monica, CA: Rand Corporation, 2012. Accessed January 3, 2014. http://www.rand.org/content/dam/rand/pubs/working_papers/2012/RAND_WR967.pdf.

Zarate, Maria Estela. "Understanding Latino Parental Involvement in Education: Perceptions, Expectations, and Recommendations." *The Tomás Rivera Policy Institute*, Los Angeles: University of Southern California, 2007. Accessed January 5, 2015. http://files.eric.ed.gov/fulltext/ED502065.pdf.

Zavis, Alexandra, and Tony Barboza. "Teacher's Suicide Shocks School," *Los Angeles Times*, September 28, 2010. Accessed March 1, 2015. http://articles.latimes.com/2010/sep/28/local/la-me-south-gate-teacher-20100928.

Zeidner, Moshe. "Does Test Anxiety Bias Scholastic Aptitude Test Performance by Gender and Sociocultural Group?." *Journal of Personality Assessment* 55, no. 145 (1990).

Zinn, Howard. *You Can't be Neutral on a Moving Train: A Personal History of Our Times*. Boston, MA: Beacon Press, 2002.

Zwaagstra, Michael. "Is NSTU Digging in against Standardized Testing?" *Chronicle Herald*, October 8, 2014. Accessed October 9, 2014. http://thechronicleherald.ca/opinion/1242308-is-nstu-digging-in-against-standardized-tests.

Zwick, Rebecca. *Rethinking the SAT: The Future of Standardized Testing in University Admissions*. New York: Routledge Falmer, 2004.

Index

Academic Performance Index (API), 59, 74
accountability, 19, 25–7, 42–4, 46–8, 114, 124, 159, 191
　rhetoric of, 14, 22, 52–5, 66, 102–3
　teacher vision of, 105, 109–10, 126, 165–7
achievement gap, 9, 24
　facing English Language Learners, 129
　facing low income students, 9, 24, 140
　facing racially minoritized students, 9, 24
Airbnb, 64
Alberta, Canada, 16, 18, 35–6, 123
alienation, teacher feelings of, 100, 107
ambivalence of technology, 14
American Center for Progress, 15
American Federation of Teachers, 15, 17
American Legislative Exchange Council (ALEC), 5, 46
Annual Yearly Progress (AYP), 59, 75
anti-discriminatory education, 84
antiracist pedagogy, 10, 100, 144–8
anxiety. *See* standardized testing
aptitude assessment. *See* intelligence quotient
arts-informed teaching, 125
assessment of, for, and as learning, 121, 183
Atlanta Public Schools scandal, 157–9
Au, Wayne, 40, 199, 202, 203, 211, 215, 217

banking model of education, 1, 48
behaviorism. *See* behaviorist
behaviorist, 8, 43, 47–8
Bill and Melinda Gates Foundation, 46, 110
Binet, Alfred, 32, 40–1
blank slate, 48
Bowers, Mike, 158
Brown Center on Education Policy, 17
Brown v. Board of Education, 2
bubble test, 39, 60, 90, 186
bureaucratization of public schooling, 38–9
Business Roundtable group, 5

California Standards Test (CST), 73, 88
Center for International Education Benchmarking, 20
Center for Media and Democracy, 47
Center for Popular Democracy, 47
Change the Stakes, 175
charter school industry.
　See charter schools
charter schools, 34, 47, 64, 110, 162
Chase Manhattan Bank, 5
cheating, 22, 55, 62, 131, 150, 156–9
China, 21, 31, 43, 68
cognitive development, 124, 127
Common Core State Standards Initiative (CCSSI), 3, 5, 8, 10, 15, 17, 30, 34–6, 39–40, 45–6, 67, 123, 161, 154, 166–7, 176, 179–80
　future of, 184–7

community-oriented teaching, 120, 145
competition and education, 27–8, 44, 57, 68, 105, 129–30
　Cold War, 43–4
constructivist theories of teaching and learning, 2, 8, 27, 31, 47, 101, 117, 123, 125, 127, 165
Council of Ministers of Education, Canada (CMEC), 36
creativity, 42, 44, 47
critical consciousness-raising, 47, 60, 191
critical education approaches, 144, 147, 171
critical inquiry, 76, 79
critical pedagogy, 9–10, 48, 84–5, 121, 144
cultural assimilation, 30
culturally relevant and responsive pedagogy (CRRP), 125, 144
culturally relevant and responsive teaching (CRRT), 125, 144
curriculum-driven teaching and content, 74
curriculum-embedded performance components, 185

daily life in schools, 19, 63, 71, 139
data driven accountability. *See* accountability
Data Recognition Corporation, 18
　see also testing companies
demoralization of teachers, 100, 109–15, 145
deprofessionalization, 27, 100, 105, 165, 184
　see also teacher-proof teaching and curricula
Dewey, John, 1–2, 125
diagnostic assessment, 15, 41, 84, 133, 182
differences between the US and Canada, 12, 69, 96, 101, 108, 121, 141, 164, 167, 177–80

differentiated instruction, 9–10, 85–9, 120, 125, 144, 165, 170, 184
disposable rubber gloves, 3
Dodge, Arnold, 52–6, 66
drill and kill, 11, 56, 155
Duncan, Arne, 46–7, 68, 177

early schooling in Canada and the US, 29–30
economic inequality, 140
　booster funding, 156–7
　per student funding, 140–1, 157
education and private companies, 5, 18, 44–7, 64, 118, 162–3, 192
Education Quality and Accountability Office (EQAO), 10–11, 28
　cancellation of the 2015 tests, 189
　future of, 187–90
　literacy test, 51, 55–6, 94, 173
　(*see also* standardized testing)
educational change, 2, 37, 187, 191
educational standardization, 2–3, 5, 9, 25, 28, 37, 40, 43–4, 47, 49, 56, 63, 66–7, 115, 117, 144, 175, 186, 191
edupreneurs, 64
efficiency as a rationale for standardized testing, 38–9
Einstein, Albert, 40
Eisenhower, Dwight, 33
Elementary and Secondary Education Act (ESEA), 33–4, 36
Elementary Teachers' Federation of Ontario (ETFO), 4
England, testing in, 9, 21, 26
English as a Second Language (ESL), 65
　students, 154
　teaching ESL students, 146, 148–9
EQAO. *See* Education Quality and Accountability Office
equality and inequality, 24–5, 27, 39, 55, 129, 134–58
　see also under standardized testing

equality of access in education, 39
equality of treatment in education, 39
equity, 24–5, 27, 39, 55, 129, 134–58
  see also under standardized testing
equity-centered pedagogy, 130, 143–4, 150, 159, 186
eugenics, 40, 42
Evil Questions Asked of (or Attacking) Ontarians, 11, 95, 170
exit examinations, 35
extra-curricular activities, 9, 43, 96
  the arts, physical education, and social sciences as, 96
extrinsic motivation, 48

fairness as a rationale for standardized testing, 38–9
Feenberg's Critical Theory of Technology, 13–14
feminist education, 9, 84, 144
Finland, 68
  testing in, 19, 21, 165, 180
Florida, testing in, 17, 151
Flower Elementary, 74–6, 80, 94, 108, 141, 155–6
Flynt, Luke, 151
Frasier Institute, 102
Freire, Paulo, 1–3, 48
Fullan, Michael, 184
functionalism, 47

Garfield High School, 4, 169
Gates, Bill, 44, 46, 110
  see also Bill and Melinda Gates Foundation
Gleason, Mark, 65
Global Educational Reform Movement (GERM), 26
graduation rates, 25, 181
Green Dot Charter Schools, 162
Growing Success, 121, 183

Hargreaves, Andy, 184
Hastings, Reed, 64

high pressure teaching environments, 9–10, 59, 96, 118, 126, 130, 151, 153, 156, 159
high-stakes standardized testing (HSST)
  architecture of, 52–6
  and conflation, 54–6
  and normalization, 53
  at the regional, national, and international levels, 66–8
  for schools and boards of education, 63–6
  and simplification, 53–4
  for students, 56–9
  for teachers, 59–63 (*see also* standardized testing)
holistic education, 1, 125, 191
home culture, 63, 75, 77, 102–3, 111, 127, 136–43, 155–6
Human Capital Theory of Education (HCTE), 31, 42–4
  as a rational for standardized testing, 42–4

IBM, 5, 46
  see also product placement *under* standardized testing
Imperial Examination (China), 31
inclusive education, 130, 143–50
Independent Education Plan (IEP), 132, 136
Indigenous children, 29, 140
industrial model of production in education, 38, 87
Industrial Revolution, 38
inequality. *See* equality
inquiry-based learning, 9, 76, 79, 85–6, 106, 120–1, 185, 187, 190
instrumental interpretation of technology, 14
Intel, 5
intelligence quotient (IQ), 32–8, 140
intelligence testing, 31–40

international competiveness, 53
intrinsic motivation, 48
IQ test. *See* intelligence quotient

Japan, testing in, 10, 20–1, 161
Johnson, Lyndon, 33

Kaestle, Carl, 33–4, 45, 201–3
Kennedy, Bobby, 34
Keppel, Francis, 34
Kohn, Alfie, 22, 24, 103, 169
Kress, Sandy, 47

labor market readiness, 53
Ladson Billings, Gloria, 187, 213, 216, 223
large-scale assessment, 18, 35–6, 57, 83, 127, 164, 178–9, 181–2, 185, 187–8, 190–1
Law School Admission Test (LSAT), 15, 51
least effective. *See* teacher rating
Lego, 30, 46
Los Angeles Times, 75, 88, 99, 112–14, 153, 169
low pressure teaching environments, 9, 59, 94, 96, 118, 126, 151, 157, 159, 168, 174, 178
low-income students, 9, 25, 35, 39, 62, 65, 85, 96, 103, 105, 108, 125, 129, 139, 141–3, 146–7, 150–2, 155, 157–8, 174, 176

mandatory attendance and schooling age, 49, 60
market logic, 31, 38, 44–7
 as a rationale for standardized testing, 44–7
Maslow's hierarchy of needs, 100, 105, 208
mathematics learning outcomes and scores, 26, 69
McGraw Hill, 18, 46
 see also testing companies

Measures of Academic Progress (MAP), 4, 169
media representation of teachers, 88, 109–11
Medical College Application Test (MCAT), 15, 51
mental age, 32
Michigan, standardized testing in, 34
Miramonte Elementary School, 114
mission schools, 29
Model Schools, 120, 147
moral rewards of teaching, 9, 115–17, 127, 145, 152, 165
Mug root beer, 30, 46
multiple choice tests, 11, 33, 60, 78–9, 85, 89–90, 152, 173, 186
multiple intelligences, 85
myth of a level playing field, 23

National Assessment of Educational Progress (NAEP), 25, 34
National Defense Education Act (NDEA), 33
neoliberalism, 5, 43, 172, 177, 191
New Orleans, 64
New York Democrats for Education Reform, 163
norm-referenced standardized testing, 23, 31, 34–5, 37, 41, 53–4, 60, 69, 103, 130, 137
North Hollywood, 57, 74–5

Obama, Barack, 34, 40, 46–7, 68
Occupy the Department of Education, 175
Office of Economic Opportunity, 33
opt-out, 3–4, 91, 176, 178
Organization for Economic Cooperation and Development (OECD), 20, 26–8, 44, 68

Pan-Canadian Assessment Program (PCAP), 36
Parent Revolution, 162

parent trigger, 64, 162, 214
parents'
  expectations surrounding homework, 102
  expectations surrounding involvement, 156
  pushback against standardized testing, 11, 14, 67, 72, 91, 161, 175–7
  understandings of standardized tests, 2–4, 11, 14, 58–9, 63, 66, 83, 86, 95, 102, 106, 112, 148, 153, 155, 162–3
Pearson Education, 18, 35, 45–7, 49, 133, 166–7
performance assessment, 44, 189
performance standards for teachers, 34
Philadelphia Schools Partnership, 65
Physical Health Education (PHE), 6, 20, 56, 72, 74, 77, 96, 124, 165
Piaget, Jean, 2, 125
Popham, James, 23, 63, 109, 198–9, 203, 205, 209–10, 227
Powers Silverberg, Ruth, 52–6, 66
pre-service teacher training, 1, 13, 44, 60, 67, 99, 117, 121–2, 127, 165, 184, 186
problem-posing education, 48
  see also critical pedagogy
professional capital, 184
professional development (PD), 2, 6, 45, 60–2, 117, 120–2, 127, 143, 150, 159, 165, 183
professional judgement, 106, 123, 168, 183
professional learning community (PLC), 84, 120, 122, 133, 207
Program for International Student Assessment (PISA), 20, 28, 37, 43–4, 68–9, 167
  Canadian reactions and results, 26, 44, 68–9
  and Ontario teacher training, 69
  US reaction and results, 26, 44, 68–9
Program Improvement (PI), 74, 92, 105
Progress in International Reading Literacy Study (PIRLS), 37
project-based learning, 9, 56, 76, 79, 85–6, 120
Prudential, 5
public discourse on education, 67
public education, 2, 35, 39, 42, 45, 49, 53, 100, 109, 116, 162
public mass education, 30–40
public opinion of teachers, 95, 109–17
public satisfaction with education, 7, 27
public support for teachers.
  See public opinion of teachers

race and education, 132–7, 144
  racially isolated schools, 140
  (see also racially minoritized students)
  per student funding, 140–1
Race to the Top (RTTT), 8, 24, 30, 34, 67, 162
racially minoritized students, 5, 25, 59, 62, 125, 127, 129, 136, 139–40, 142–3, 145–7, 150, 152, 155, 158, 166, 176, 178
racism and racial bias, 22, 24, 40, 42, 100, 105, 137, 144, 175
Racketeering Influenced Corrupt Organizations (RICO), 157
Ravitch, Diane, 10, 17, 166, 196, 204, 214
Reese, William, 37, 202–3, 215
reflexive teaching, 125
reliability of standardized testing.
  See standardized testing
religious education, 30, 43
repeatability, 131
residential schools, 29
Rueles, Rigoberto, 113, 153

safe harbor, 105
Sahlberg, Pasi, 26
Santoro, Doris, 115–16

SAT Optional Movement, 51
Save Our Schools, 175
School Achievement Indicators Program (SAIP), 36
school attendance laws. *See* mandatory attendance and schooling age
school choice, 26–7, 54, 134, 162
school fundraising, 141, 156–7
school privatization, 24, 64, 105, 162–3
schools as sites of mass production, 38, 87
Singapore, testing in, 20–1
social hierarchy as a rationale for standardized testing, 39–42
social justice and education, 84, 146, 172
   see also equity-centered pedagogy; inclusive education
social nature of teaching and learning, 8
   see also constructivist theories of teaching and learning
Socratic method, 48
sorting as a rationale for standardized testing, 39–42
South Korea, testing in, 20, 167
South Los Angeles (South LA), 5, 57, 90, 99–100, 105–6, 108, 114, 141, 176–7
South Side of Chicago, 151, 177
standard test taker, 28, 31
standard-aligned curriculum, 149
standardization movement, 5, 34, 45, 53, 60, 191
standardized testing
   academic resistance to, 175–8
   age appropriateness of, 8, 78, 91, 101, 123–5, 127, 168, 179
   alternatives to, 179–90
   to assess teachers, 19, 53, 102, 104, 124, 126
   and classroom time, 16–18, 73–7, 101
   and cultural bias, 9–10, 51, 137–40, 146–7
   diminishing the work of teaching, 102, 114–15, 117, 126, 165
   as a disincentive to teaching disadvantaged students, 10, 61, 113, 116–17, 154, 159
   and English Language Learners, 87, 99, 129–30, 136, 145, 148–50, 156, 166, 190
   and environmental/home factors, 23–43, 63, 75, 102–3, 111–22, 127, 130, 136, 141–3, 149, 155–6, 166
   and federal funding (US), 15, 33–7, 49, 64–5, 67, 140, 154, 156
   financial costs associated with, 17–19
   and high income schools, 137–40
   and impacts on instruction, 69, 83–90
   and inequality, 4, 7, 9, 22–4, 40–1, 54–5, 102–3, 136–8, 140–50
   in international perspective, 19–22
   and learners with exceptionalities, 4, 58, 91, 130, 134–7, 142, 148–50, 156, 166
   and narrowing/contracting of the curriculum, 8, 53, 60, 72, 77–83, 90, 96, 165
   and physical activity, 6, 20, 24, 56, 72, 74, 77, 96, 124, 165
   and politicians resisting, 175–8
   and population growth, 32–6, 38
   and product placement, 30, 46
   publishing results of, 63, 75, 88, 99, 103, 108–14, 132, 153, 163, 169
   quantity of, 15–16
   and real estate prices, 27, 54, 89, 163
   and as a reflection of student academic ability, 22–5, 54, 131–3, 183–4
   and reliability, 23, 28, 104, 124, 131, 134, 137, 149, 177
   and school culture, 6, 37, 56–66
   and stigma, 91–3

and stress, 4, 28, 86, 91, 93–4, 97, 114, 119, 135–6, 149, 165, 180, 185
and student anxiety and mental health, 3, 9, 29, 61, 90–1, 95–7, 133–7, 159, 165–6
and student experiences of, 90–6, 123–5, 130, 133–7, 152–3
and student motivation, 48, 152–3
and teacher buy-in, 96, 108, 191
and teacher professional development, 45, 60–2, 117, 120–2, 127, 143–5, 150, 159, 165, 183
as technology, 13–14, 28
and tutoring, 18, 49, 140–1, 143, 155, 159
and validity, 9, 22–3, 28, 41, 54–5, 124, 130–2, 134, 137, 142, 149, 151–2, 157–8, 166, 177
and value-added measures (VAM), 101–2, 104, 108–9, 113–14, 116, 126–7, 173, 177, 184–5
Stanford Center for Opportunity Policy in Education, 18
Stone, Cliff, 33
student achievement in comparative perspective, 36–7
student safety, 125
student self-regulation, 125
student-centered teaching and learning, 1, 85–6, 144, 165, 172, 192, 208
substantive interpretation of technology, 14
suicide, 20, 113, 151

teach to the test. *See* teaching to the test
teacher
  autonomy, 9, 100, 118–21, 123
  burnout, 115
  driven assessments (*see* teacher: generated assessment)
  evaluation of (*see under* standardized testing)
  feelings of frustration, 91, 100, 106, 108, 115, 118, 153
  generated assessment, 35, 179–91
  helping students on standardized tests, 156–8 (*see also* cheating)
  professional judgment, 9, 62, 64, 101, 113–15
  professional latitude/freedom, 9, 27, 76, 79
  relationships with the public, 108–14, 117, 127, 165, 168 (*see also under* standardized testing)
  resistance to standardized testing, 4, 10, 118, 169–75, 178
  tenure, 65, 101, 108–10, 127, 163, 168, 172–4, 177
  voice, 4, 10, 49, 62, 69, 116, 164, 187, 190–1
teacher rating, 99, 113–14
teacher-proof teaching and curricula, 3, 25, 48, 109, 117–18, 145, 179, 184
see also deprofessionalization
Teachers and Testing Study, 2, 7, 8–9, 15–16, 24, 56, 69, 73, 93, 96, 109, 178, 212
teachers' work, 2, 4–6, 16, 60, 63, 72, 77–83, 90, 96, 108–9, 152–8, 165
  changing nature of, 3, 6, 27, 69, 83–91, 100, 106, 108–9, 115, 118, 152–8, 165
  intensification of, 3, 7, 26
teaching to the test, 2, 6, 47–8, 52, 62, 72, 86, 89, 96, 104, 107, 144, 151–2, 161, 169, 188–9
technology and education, 2, 13–14, 18, 28, 33, 42, 61, 183
test anxiety. *See* standardized testing
test oriented teaching and learning (TOTL), 6, 8, 48, 56, 59, 71, 81, 82, 85, 97, 102, 110, 115, 117, 119–20, 125–6, 152, 159, 165–6, 182–3

test preparation, 16–17, 19, 28, 45, 48, 56, 59–62, 65, 73–6, 78, 87–8, 91, 93–4, 101, 103–4, 106–7, 139–40, 152, 155, 159
testing companies, 18, 35, 45–7, 49, 166–7
testing industry, 44–7
see also testing companies
The New York Times, 17
The Washington Post, 46
Title One School Funding, 33–4, 64–5, 67, 154–6
transient students, 99, 153
Trends in International Mathematics and Science Study (TIMSS), 24, 37
Turkey, testing in, 20–1
twenty-first-century education, 1–2, 47, 161, 185
twenty-first-century learners, 19, 40, 109
twenty-first-century skills, 68

Uber, 64
United States Department of Education (DOE), 18, 65, 175
 annual budget, 18
UnitedOpt, 175
universal education, 30–5

validity of standardized testing.
 See under standardized testing
value-added measures (VAM).
 See under standardized testing
Vygotsky, Lev, 2, 125–6, 210

Walton Foundation, 162
War on Poverty, 33
Word Bank education project funding, 68
World War I, 33

Zinn, Howard, 14
zone of proximal development (ZDP), 126